Budapest 1900

Budapest 1900

A Historical Portrait of a City and Its Culture

John Lukacs

Grove Press
New York

Grove Press
841 Broadway
New York, NY 10003

Published in Canada by General Publishing Company, Ltd.

Library of Congress Cataloging-in-Publication Data

Lukacs, John, 1924–
Budapest 1900 / by John Lukacs. — 1st ed.
p.   cm.
Bibliography: p.
Includes index.
ISBN 1-55584-060-4
ISBN 0-8021-3250-2 (pbk.)
1. Budapest (Hungary)—Civilization.   I. Title.
DB988.L84   1988
943.9'1—dc19   88-15290
CIP

Manufactured in the United States of America
Designed by Ronnie Ann Herman
Map by Arnold Bombay
First Edition 1988
First Evergreen Edition 1990

DEDICATED TO
MONSIGNOR BÉLA VARGA,
A GOD-GIVEN INCARNATION
OF WHAT IS NOBLE AND BEST
IN MAGYAR HUMANISM

AJÁNLOM
FŐTISZTELENDŐ VARGA BÉLÁNAK,
AZ ISTENADTA NEMES
MAGYAR EMBERSZERETET
MEGTESTESITŐJÉNEK

Table of Contents

List of Illustrations

Introduction

In 1900 Budapest was the youngest of the great metropolises of Europe (perhaps, except for Chicago, of the world). In twenty-five years its population had trebled and its buildings had doubled, and the city was pulsing with physical and mental vigor. Among other things, this provides a certain contrast to its then twin capital of the Austro-Hungarian Dual Monarchy, to Vienna in 1900, about which so many books have been published in English during the last twenty-five years. Most of these have concentrated on certain themes; they are, therefore, fairly selective portraits of a city. Most of these, too, have been liberal not only in their selection of themes but also in their chronological treatment. I have been more rigorous: except for the last chapter, which is a kind of coda for English-speaking readers who may wish to know what happened "Since Then" (the title of that chapter), this book is centered on 1900—at the most, on the ten years 1896 to 1906. This was not difficult, because by a historically unusual coincidence the year 1900 was a zenith and a turning point in the history of Budapest in more than one way, and on more than one level (and so was that year of crisis,

1905–06). Perhaps more difficult was my attempt to compose the portrait of a city on many levels, including its physical description together with the description of the lives of its various classes of people.

In doing this I followed the practice of previous books of mine, in accord with my historical philosophy, proceeding along a hierarchy: in this case, from a description of the physical city and its material conditions (Chapter 2) to its people (Chapter 3) and their politics (Chapter 4), to the conditions and manifestations of their intellectual lives and art (Chapter 5), and to some of their less tangible but nonetheless evident mental and spiritual inclinations (Chapter 6). The detailed Table of Contents should illustrate this further.

There is considerable interest and respect due Budapest in 1900, but *Budapest 1900* was not inspired by nostalgia. There was a duality in the life of the city then (as there is now). One—in retrospect, pungent and attractive—element in its character was the coexistence of a virile, and sometimes coarse, provinciality together with an urbane sensitivity, an authentic sophistication that was unusual because it was Magyar as well as cosmopolitan. Nearly a century, full of terrible tragedies in the history of Budapest, has passed since; and during these ninety years Hungarians themselves have had great difficulties in coming to terms with the merits and demerits of Budapest in 1900. One sentence, written fifty-one years ago, by Lóránt Hegedüs, a highly cultured Hungarian liberal and principled conservative, may illustrate that duality: "How many barren stony layers *at such a fortunate time, unequalled in the history of a small nation!* . . . rare precious metals among the mass of useless debris!" The italics are mine.

Pickering Close
near Phoenixville, Pennsylvania
1986–88

Budapest 1900

Colors, Words, Sounds

On the night of the first of May in 1900 Mihály Munkácsy, the Hungarian painter, died in a private sanatorium in Germany. He was buried in Budapest nine days later. His funeral—like that of Victor Hugo in Paris fifteen years before, on another day in May—"was not to be the obsequies of a dead man. It was to be the celebration of an immortal. The nineteenth century was to enter into history with the man who had echoed its enthusiasms and its passions."*

The catafalque rose on Heroes' Square in Budapest (Victor Hugo's body had lain in state under the Arc de Triomphe), before the six Corinthian columns and the neoclassical peristyle of the Hall of Arts. The sarcophagus of Munkácsy rested on top of a catafalque, forty-five feet high. The sarcophagus was designed, and completed in haste, by a well-known Hungarian sculptor, assisted by his students; the catafalque by a famous Hungarian architect, an apostle

*The sources of quotations, citations, passages and all other references will be found in the References and Bibliography, pp. 227–236.

3

of Magyar modernism. This was odd because, except for a large bas-relief of a prancing stag in front, there was nothing either very Magyar or very modern in these designs. The sarcophagus was white, the catafalque velvet-black. Two enormous masts, draped with black flags, were crowned by white-painted laurel wreaths. There was a double row of topiary standards, with their black-green leaves. Amid these cascades of blackness another large white bas-relief in the lower center of the bier stood out, with Munkácsy's profile in a gilded frame. Four bronze torches flamed and smoked around the catafalque. It was a cool, windy day in May.

There was one element of an asymmetrical and Hungarian panache above this monumental funereal *mise-en-scène:* a huge black veil, draped on one side from the attic peak of the Hall of Arts, sweeping down in a half-circle. It suggested something like a great national actress in the act of mourning.

There was the national government and the municipality of Budapest: ministers, the mayor, black-coated, top-hatted. There were bishops, hussars, four heralds in costumes copied from one of Dürer's funeral paintings, three riders holding tall silver staves with black lanterns affixed to them. Incense and myrrh wafted away in the breeze. At half past three the funeral procession began to move: the hearse (decorated, too, in medieval style, by Hungarian painters) drawn by six black-blanketed, silver-caparisoned horses, and eight carriages packed high with wreaths.

The noise of the city died down. On the Pest side of the Danube the trolley cars had stopped. Black flags flew. The procession wended westward, on to the broad expanse of Andrássy Avenue. At that moment the sounds of the loud clip-clopping of the horses were softened, because Andrássy Avenue was paved with hardwood blocks. The Minister of Culture and Religion had ordered the schools closed for the day; the students were commanded to line the streets along the funeral route. The great procession flowed down that avenue, the pride of Pest, past the villas and the wrought-iron railings of the new rich, the consulates of the Great Powers, the May greenery and the young horse chestnuts.

At Octagon Square, a mile down Andrássy Avenue, a trumpeter halted the march, to direct the procession to turn leftward to the Ring. The bishops and the ministers stepped into their carriages. In front of the terraces of the coffeehouses gypsy bands played Munkácsy's favorite Hungarian songs. Stiff in black stood the Carpenters' and the Housepainters' Guild, and the choral society of a factory sent the bass of their threnody up the afternoon sky. There was a moment of disturbance: the chorus of the School of Blind Children was told to step forward to sing, but the mounted policeman in front had not been alerted, he rode into their frightened ranks to push them back. But there was no other commotion, save for the fear of some people that the narrow ornamental balconies of the newly built monumental apartment houses might crumble under the weight of the assembled spectators. On the second-story balcony of No. 44 Elizabeth Ring stood a small white-bearded figure, the grand old man of Hungarian literature, Mór Jókai. He lifted his hat as the procession passed under him. Women curtsied; there were women who knelt. A mile down the Ring, then another turn, on to Rákóczi Avenue, toward the city cemetery. By that time the crowd was dispersing in the violet twilight.

The lights were coming on along the boulevards of Budapest. In their shadows the vinous nocturnal energy of the city sprang to life, with its raucous, vinegary sounds filling the gaps of the night air. There was the sense of an odd holiday just past, of a mourning after. Again there was a curious parallel with that day in Paris fifteen years before, when the British Ambassador wrote to Queen Victoria that "there was nothing striking, splendid or appropriate either in the monstrous catafalque erected under the Arc de Triomphe, or in the trappings of the funeral. There was nothing mournful or solemn in the demeanour of the people. . . ."

T his was the second time in six years that such a giant funeral took place in Budapest. In March 1894 the body of the great exile, the national leader Lajos Kossuth, had been brought home. Kossuth and Munkácsy had been the two most famous Hungarians known abroad. Hungarians knew that. It was one of the reasons, perhaps the main reason, for Munkácsy's apotheosis: the honor Hungary gained through his reputation in the world.

His path was the path of a comet. He was born in 1844, of German-Hungarian parents, in a dusty, backward town in north-eastern Hungary: Munkács. Like many other people in his time, he would Magyarize his name—in his case, with an aristocratic flourish, appending the nobilitarian *y* at the end—from Lieb to Munkácsy. His early life was sad. His parents died. The orphan became a carpenter's apprentice in the home of a relative. He was a poor, thin wisp of a boy, racked by illnesses. During his adolescence he showed a talent for drawing. A sympathetic painter took him as a companion to the provincial town of Arad. From there he went up to Pest, and then to Vienna (where he failed to enroll in the Academy of Fine Arts—whether because of lack of tuition money or want of accomplishment we do not know) and back to Pest and then to Munich and Düsseldorf, where he made some kind of living from sketching but failed to make an impression either on his Hungarian painter companions or on his occasional German teachers. Then came the turning point. In 1868 he painted a large canvas, *Siralomház* ("The Last Night of a Condemned Prisoner"). It is a dark and exotic painting, exotic in its theme rather than in its execution: a Hungarian brigand, in peasant dress, sits and leans against a table, surrounded by shadowy figures in anxious grief. The background is dark, the brushstrokes strong, naturalistic, showing considerable talent in composition and in the art of contrast; the style is reminiscent of Courbet. It was an instant success. One of the earliest American private collectors, the Philadelphia merchant William P. Wilstach, bought it for 2,000 gold thalers. Munkácsy was not yet twenty-six years old.

In 1870 this painting was shown in the Paris Salon. It earned the Gold Medal and celebrity for its painter. Munkácsy moved to Paris. He married the widow of a baron. Mme. Munkácsy had social ambitions. They had a palace built on the Avenue Villiers. Cabinet ministers, artists, ambassadors, Russian dukes and the King of Sweden attended their dinners. Munkácsy was handsome. He had dark eyes, a beautifully kept beard, there was a suggestion of an elegant bohemian in the lavallière cravat that he habitually wore. *"Dieu, qu'il est beau,"* a Parisian woman said. He chose a mistress, the wife of a Parisian painter. A powerful art dealer from Munich, Sedlmayer, became his agent—more, his factotum. He kept telling Munkácsy what to paint. Munkácsy's paintings were sold for very large sums, more than sixty of them to rich Americans who had begun to collect art. They included Cornelius and William Vanderbilt, Jay Gould, William Astor, August Belmont, the financial genius Edward T. Stotesbury of Philadelphia, General Russell Alger the Governor of Michigan, Joseph Pulitzer the newspaper magnate (who was born in Hungary), Delmonico the New York restaurateur. His most successful enterprise was the large painting "Christ Before Pilate," a subject that Sedlmayer had suggested. It was bought by the "Merchant Prince," the rising department store magnate John Wanamaker from Philadelphia, for $150,000, the equivalent of nearly $2 million one hundred years later. It is still exhibited every Easter in Wanamaker's department store.* Before it was shipped to Philadelphia Sedlmayer showed "Christ Before Pilate" on a European tour, for three years. At the time (1881–84) there were people, including critics, who wrote that Munkácsy was the greatest living artist, the creator of the greatest modern work of art in the world, the peer of Michelangelo and Rembrandt. We know this from a folio volume that Sedlmayer had printed and that included reviews of Munkácsy, who had become so famous that a letter by an American admirer, addressed to "Munkácsy, Europe," was delivered to him in Paris. In 1886 Sedlmayer arranged for a triumphal tour in the United States. More of Munkácsy's paintings were sold (including a sequel to "Christ Before Pilate" to Wanamaker). President Cleveland received Munkácsy in the White House, the Secretary of the Navy gave a dinner in Washington and Delmonico a festive banquet in New York. A "Hungarian" gypsy band played a "Munkácsy March" on the New York pier when he boarded the liner *La Champagne* for France.†

His success reverberated in his native country, to which he remained loyal throughout his life. He funded a modest purse for young Hungarian painters for their study in Paris. When "Christ Before Pilate" was shown in Pest there were 80,000 paying visitors; the chairman of the committee was Bishop Arnold Ipolyi, the most learned Hungarian prince of the church at the time. Around 1890 the Hungarian government commissioned Munkácsy to paint a monumental canvas for the new Parliament building, *Honfoglalás* ("The Conquest of Hungary"). Árpád, the founder, prime prince of the Hungarian tribes, sits erect on his white stallion, receiving the homage of the inhabitants of the Hungarian hills and plain. It is well beneath the standards of Munkácsy's best work. But he was already a sick man. A disease, latent from his youth, probably syphilis, had affected his body and his brain. Few people in Hun-

---

*No longer. It was sold for $60,000 in 1988, after Wanamaker's had been bought by a conglomerate.

†Two generations later a Hungarian biographer of Munkácsy (Géza Perneczky) compared the launching of "Christ Before Pilate" to a Hollywood superproduction. An American art historian (John Maass) wrote about Munkácsy's American tour that Sedlmayer "anticipated . . . publicity methods of the American film industry, including the 'personal appearance tour' of the star. . . . Scenes in biblical films like 'The Robe' (1953) and 'Barabbas' (1962) are strikingly similar to 'Christ Before Pilate.'"

gary knew that. He was a national hero; a national treasure; the most famous son of Hungary in the world.

A comet: or, rather, a meteor. People speak of a meteoric rise when, in reality, a meteor is marked by its fall. That was the case with poor Munkácsy. He was a self-made painter, an artist of remarkable gifts, with a considerable talent for depth and contrast; but perhaps his best paintings are those surviving ones that are the least known—a few summer landscapes and a few portraits. There was a duality in his talent and, perhaps, in his entire personality. He could be profound, yet he was habitually superficial. He was obsessed with technique, yet he worked very fast. His masters, besides Rembrandt, were the late-Renaissance painters; yet he seldom visited Italy, and never traveled beyond Florence. He was a Francophile who never learned to speak or write French well. We may now see that his canvases—their subjects as well as their execution —are period pieces. At his best he could approximate the standards of Courbet, perhaps of Millet. But the Munkácsy meteor lit up the Parisian sky only briefly, and at the very time—in the 1870s—when the new generation of the Impressionists left the Salon well behind. Munkácsy execrated them. Before his death he wrote his wife that what he would really like was to start an academy "to do away with the exaggerations of the Impressionists." Long before that the French critics turned away from Munkácsy. Dumas *fils,* who liked him personally, said to his Hungarian friend Zsigmond Justh: "Munkácsy is an inflated reputation who has both profited from his wife and been damaged by her."* Huysmans looked at "Christ Before Pilate" and wrote that Munkácsy had a taste for nothing but décor: *"le rastaquouère de la peinture,"* a dubious adventurer. Others called his house a *"palais de poncif,"* a palace of a hack. Two years before Munkácsy's death the contents of the house on the Avenue Villiers were auctioned off: the gobelins, china, Persian rugs, antique guns, and some of his paintings went for almost nothing. A later generation was to find that the very material of his paintings was deteriorating. Munkácsy habitually used a black bitumen ground for his large canvases. This tended to fade his colors with the passing of time.

---

*Sedlmayer may have damaged his reputation worse. Not only malicious critics but all kinds of people found it distasteful when Sedlmayer showed "The Dying Mozart" against a musical accompaniment, or when he sold tickets for the showings of the "Christ Before Pilate" tour, a new practice at the time.

The pomp and the circumstance of Munkácsy's state funeral obscured all of this;* and in the grandiloquence of the Budapest newspapers in May 1900 there was no trace of a reflective tone. But it must not be thought that the recognition of Munkácsy's limitations was the particular reaction of Parisian critics, of a culture five hundred miles to the west and many years ahead of Budapest. As so often in the history of Magyar intellect and art, worldwide fame was one thing, true merit another; and the two would rarely correspond. At the very time, 1873, when the Munkácsy comet reached its apogee in the salons of Paris, a Magyar painter, Pál Szinyei-Merse, painted a canvas, "May Picnic" *(Majális),* that eventually came to be regarded as the finest Hungarian painting of the nineteenth century. I write "eventually," because its initial reception in Budapest was so inadequate that Szinyei-Merse turned away from painting for many years to come. Yet it is significant that both the composition and execution of "May Picnic" corresponds exactly with the time and the emergence of the vision of the great French Impressionists, the early Monet or Renoir. In Paris Munkácsy had a young Hungarian friend, László Paál, who died tragically young, but whose canvases, as we now know, represent superb individual variants of the Barbizon school. (Millet regarded him as the most promising of the younger painters.) In the Budapest of 1900, of every thousand people to whom Munkácsy's name was a household word, perhaps one knew the name of Paál. Yet years before Munkácsy passed away painters in Hungary had already rejected the pictorial tradition that he represented. That tradition—despite Munkácsy's Francophilia and his Paris residence and his Paris success—was essentially a German, a Munich one; but by the 1890s the best Hungarian painters had broken away from that. They withdrew, not into bohemian conventicles, but to serious workshops in the country, in Nagybánya, Gödöllő, Szolnok, to open their windows, to go ahead with a Hungarian school of plein-air painting, built up with colors that would not fade. The first exhibition of the Nagybánya painters took place in 1897; and by 1900 modern

---

*Perneczky, p. 51: "This funeral was the last Munkácsy super-production, with all of the grotesque exaggerations of eclecticism, produced for a public avid for entertainment, festivities and impressive theatrics. . . . An honest and detached study should show us Munkácsy's great pictorial talents—and also that his faults and mistaken directions corresponded with the errors and mistaken ways of his nation."

painting in Hungary had not only begun, it was in full development.

These painters were criticized, indeed, excoriated by some of the conservatives whose bastion was that Hall of Arts from where Munkácsy's body was sent forth on his last journey, but no matter: these painters knew not only what they were doing but also where they stood—and sat. In 1900 in Budapest the painters', sculptors' and architects' habitual coffeehouse was the Japan on Andrássy Avenue, with its tables that sometimes bore their penciled drawings on their raspberry-color marble surfaces (on one occasion a respectful art collector cajoled the owner of the coffeehouse into selling him one of these tables, which he then had carted home). The Japan was only a few steps away from the grandiose apartment houses of the Ring. That Elizabeth Ring—not only its buildings but its atmosphere, colors, sounds, and the language along its pavements—was typical of Budapest in 1900; but so, too, were the minds and the talk of the people in the Japan.

This city," wrote Gyula Krúdy about Budapest, "smells of violets in the spring, as do mesdames along the promenade above the river on the Pest side. In the fall, it is Buda that suggests the tone: the odd thud of chestnuts dropping on the Castle walk; fragments of the music of the military band from the kiosk on the other side wafting over in the forlorn silence. Autumn and Buda were born of the same mother." In Budapest the contrast of the seasons, and of their colors, is sharper than in Vienna. It was surely sharper in 1900, before the age of the omnipresent automobile exhausts and diesel fumes. Violet in Budapest was, as Krúdy wrote, a spring color; it was the custom to present tiny bouquets of the first violets to women as early as March. They came from the market gardens south and west of the city, sold along the Corso and in the streets by peasant women. In March, too, came the sound and the smell of the rising river. The Danube runs swifter and higher in Budapest than in Vienna. It would often flood the lower quays, and the sound and sight of that swirling mass of water would be awesome. By the end of April a pearly haze would bathe the bend of the river and the bridges and quays, rising to Castle Hill. That light would endure through the long summer mornings, lasting until the mature clarities of late September.

At night the shadows retreated, and a new, dark-green atmosphere grew over the city like a canopy of promise. This was not the acid green springtime of Western Europe: May and June in Hungary, even in Budapest, have something near-Mediterranean about them. The smoke from the myriads of chimneys retreated with the shadows (except, of course, the highblown smoke of the mills and factories in the outer districts). The chairs and tables were put out before the cafés and in the open-air restaurants. It was then that the nocturnal life of Budapest blossomed, a life with singular habits and flavors that began early in the evening and lasted into the dawn, in which so many people partook. There were avenues in Budapest which were more crowded at ten at night than at ten in the morning, but not because they were concentrations of nightlife, such as Montmartre or Piccadilly. The freshness of the dustless air, especially after the May showers, brought the presence of the Hungarian countryside into the city. Somewhat like parts of London in the eighteenth century (or Philadelphia in the nineteenth), this smoky, swollen, crowded and metropolitan Budapest was still a city with a country heart, with a sense that a provincial Arcadia was but an arm's length away. By May the violets were gone but there was a mixture of acacias and lilacs and of the apricots, the best ones of which in Hungary were grown within the municipal confines of Budapest. There was the sense of erotic promises, earthy and tangible as well as transcendent. It penetrated the hearts of the people, and not only of the young; and it was not only a matter of espying the sinuous movements of women, movements more visible now under their light summery frocks. It was a matter of aspirations.

Summer was hot, hotter than in Vienna, sultry at times, broken by tremendous thunderstorms, but almost never damp. When the dark thunderheads convened high over the dry, dusty streets, they carried the promise of relief and the return of the long pleasant summer evenings, for the evenings were almost always cool. There is not much difference between a May and an August night in Budapest, except of course in the vegetation. Even on the hottest of days the trees were green, never sere. Summer was the recurrent feeling, the promise of pleasure in *le bel, le frais, le vivace aujourd'hui;* and a Budapest bourgeoise or a young gentry wife threw open the double-leaved windows and leaned over her geraniums with the same movement—and perhaps, too, with the same movement of the heart—as a Frenchwoman on the Côte d'Azur at summertime circa 1900, a little out of season but *fraîche, belle, vivace,* nonetheless. Surrounded by the yellow, powdery Hungarian countryside, Budapest then spread along the banks of the Danube like a green bower; or, perhaps (for those who prefer vegetables to flowers), rather like a super-large green cabbage whose outer leaves were edged, here and there, with the black rime of smoke from the factory chimneys. The crowded town, packed with people and rows of apartment houses, gave the impression—and the feeling—of a summer resort, perhaps even that of a spa. Few people complained of the summer in Budapest, except for those who employed it as the pretext to proclaim their departure to vacation places well-known. A profusion of fruit, greenery and fish spilled out from the markets to the sidewalks. Young people stayed up late, into the dawn. Older people, daydreaming on hot afternoons, turned their thoughts to the winter season to come, thinking of new circumstances, new quarrels, new flirtations.

Autumn can be a short season in Budapest; in any event, its beauties are unpredictable, like those of rapidly maturing women —or, perhaps, unpredictable like the melancholy of Hungarian men. It is not only that the owl of Minerva flies at dusk; it is also that the best writers of Hungary, living in Budapest around 1900, had autumn in their hearts. The instruments of their internal music were not springtime violins, or the summery bravura of the gypsy bands whose music in the summer mixed with the crunch of the gravel and with the clanging of the dishes in the open-air taverns and restaurants. The deepest, the truest sound of Magyar prose is not that of a canting and chanting violin; it is that of a cello.

March, not April, is the cruelest month in Budapest; and November the saddest. A century ago it was the only month when that great bell of clear air over the Hungarian plains became striated with damp fog. That fog swirled around the broad pillars of the Danube bridges, it rose to cloud the high hills of Buda. On All Souls' Day thousands of people streamed toward the cemeteries of Budapest, with flowers in their hands, on that holy day which is perhaps taken more seriously in Hungary than elsewhere because of the national temperament. *Temetni tudunk*—a terse Magyar phrase whose translation requires as many as ten English words to give its proper (and even then, not wholly exact) sense: "How to bury people—that is one thing we know." The greatest tragedies in the history of modern Hungary—the execution of thirteen martyred Hungarian generals after the collapse of the War of Independence in 1849, the collapse of the ancient monarchy in the defeat of the First World War in 1918, the collapse of the deeply torn and divided effort to free Hungary from its deadly alliance with Hitler's Reich in 1944, the collapse of the great national rising in 1956, centered in Budapest—all happened in October or early November. For Budapest in 1900 the last three of these great tragedies were still unknown.

And then, one morning—it would come as early as in the third week of November, and surely before the middle of December—one of two new things was happening. A clear sky had risen over Budapest again, with the paler gold of a winter sun refracted by the crystalline cold. Or the sky was gray but rich, great flakes of snow were coming down all over Budapest: a celestial filling, like the goose down in the comforters of its bedrooms. In 1900 in Budapest winters came earlier than they come now. They were colder and snowier. There were still years (though not in the calendar year 1900) when the entire stretch of the Danube was frozen, and adventurous men could walk across the ridges of ice from Pest to Buda. There was a sense of feasting and of innocence in the air. Unlike in the snow-laden country, winter in Budapest was something else than a season of long rest and sleep; it was another season full of promise and excitement. The streets of the Inner City were filled before noon, with women and girls parading in their winter finery, and with promenading gentlemen in their fur-collared great-coats. Girls without furs were equipped at least with a furry muff. They were stepping in and out of the confectioneries and the flower shops and the glove-makers with tiny packages wrapped in rosy, crinkly papers, hanging daintily from the tips of their little fingers. Among the horse-drawn carriages on the avenues in 1900 there still slid in and out a few sleighs—black-lacquered, drawn by black horses, and with silvered tackle, with the laps of their passengers wrapped in ancient fur-lined blankets. What the city offered was this agreeable and satisfying contrast of exterior ice and interior fire: of the diamantine, light blue, crackling cold climate of the streets only a few steps away from the inner atmosphere of the houses with the cozy warmth of their cosseted bourgeois interiors, with deep-red carpets underfoot and perhaps with crimson tongues of fire not only in the grates of the tile stoves but in many hearts. Even in the dark, grimy streets, with their forbidding doorways and freezing entrances, the white snow thick around provided not only a contrast in color but in atmosphere: gazing inside to sense the hot interior fug, or looking outside from their cramped interiors into the snowy streets was equally good. The crunch of the snow, its odd chemical smell, the roofs and the windowsills and the shop signs and the monuments of Budapest picked out in white gave the city a compound of secure feeling. Behind those windowsills the house-wives patted the long square insulating bolsters between the double windows into place; and the few walkers along the quays or up along the deserted streets and parapet walks on Castle Hill must surely have been lovers.

It was the season of long dinners, of heavily laden tables with the roasts, sausages, bacons, fowl and game sent up to the families from the country; of the smells of wet wool and leather and pastry cream and perfume in the shops of the Inner City; of the anticipations of Christmas, of dancing assemblies and balls; and for the young, the chance of meeting on the skating rink of the Budapest Skating Club, on the frozen lake in City Park, under electric lights on weekday evenings. When the little blue flag of the club was up at Octagon Square it meant that the ice was sufficiently hard for the skaters—and for their flirtations, while the girls' chaperones would gossip behind the windows of the clubhouse that was warm as an oven, aglow in the dark like the redness behind the isinglass of a stove, reeking of oiled leather, coal-smoke and the melted ice on the rough floors of that waiting room. It was a city of distinct anticipation and of distinct seasons, more distinct than now.

The year 1900 was the noon hour of Budapest, even in winter. Summer was galloping in its skies and in its heart. Foreign visitors arriving in that unknown portion of Europe, east of Vienna, were astounded to find a modern city with first-class hotels, plate-glass windows, electric tramcars, elegant men and women, the larg-est Parliament building in the world about to be completed. Yet the city was not wholly cosmopolitan. There was the presence of the Hungarian provinces within its streets and within its people, so many of whom had come to Budapest from the provinces where they were born. In another sense, too, it was less cosmopolitan than the backward, unkempt town of a century before, whose inhabi-tants had been a mixture of Magyars, Germans, Swabians, Greeks, and Serbs. Now everyone, including the considerable number of Jews, spoke and sang, ate and drank, thought and dreamed in Hungarian. This was a very class-conscious society: there was as great a difference between the National Casino of the feudal aris-tocracy and the Café New-York of the writers, artists and artistes as there was between the elegant clubhouse and the plebeian grand-stand at the racetrack. These worlds were separate, yet they were not entirely unbridgeable. Certain aristocrats respected the writers and painters; in turn, most of the writers and painters admired the aristocrats, especially when these were to the manner born. They read the same papers, sometimes the same books, saw the same plays, knew the same purveyors. They dined in different places, their tables were set differently; but their national dishes, their favorite musicians, their physicians, and their actresses were often the same. In Budapest there was no particular *vie de bohème* restricted to writers and artists; indeed, the city did not have an artists' quarter—no Bloomsbury or Soho, no Montmartre or Montparnasse, no Munich Schwabing.

It was a grand place for literature. The ancient Magyar language, the vocabulary of which was reconstructed and enriched with great care, sometimes haltingly, by the patriot writers and classicists of the early nineteenth century, had become rich, muscular, flexible and declarative, lyrical and telling. But the Magyar language is an orphan among the languages of Europe. It does not belong to the great Latin, Germanic or Slavic language families. Mostly because of this, Hungarian literature had no echoes, no reverberations, no reputation beyond Hungary. During the entire nineteenth century only one Hungarian writer, Mór Jókai, was frequently translated abroad; and by 1900 Jókai—as well as the style and scope of his novels—had grown very old. But in 1900 Budapest rang with the reverberations of literature. Every Hungarian writer knew that. During the literary, cultural and political revival of the nation in the nineteenth century none of the great poets and writers had been born in Budapest. In 1900 this was still largely true, but they all had gravitated there. They lived in Budapest not only because of the evident advantages of living close to the newspapers and publishers who would purchase their words. They needed the atmosphere of the city. This was true even of such fine writers as Géza Gárdonyi or Kálmán Mikszáth,* who were truly provincial in the best sense of that adjective: country writers, saturated with the colors, odors and music of the countryside and with the speech of its people. But for the first time in the history of Hungarian literature, in 1900

---

*When Theodore Roosevelt came to Budapest in 1910 he said that his desire to see Hungary had been kindled by his reading of Mikszáth's novel *Szent Péter esernyője* ("Saint Peter's Umbrella"), translated into English in 1901.

there were writers who chose not only to write in, but *of* Budapest. They were not necessarily the greatest writers of that period, though some of them were. In 1900 Budapest, and Hungarian literature, had become inescapably intertwined.

So I am compelled to describe three writers who wrote about Budapest in 1900—in the ascending order of their talents. They were Tamás Kóbor, Ferenc Körmendi and Gyula Krúdy. The very title of Kóbor's book and the very date of its publication fit our theme exactly. The title of his novel was, simply and squarely, *Budapest,* written in the year 1900 and published in 1901. Portions of it actually appeared, seriatim, in 1900 in the literary periodical *A Hét,* which was the principal literary periodical at the time; Kóbor was one of its principal contributors. He was the very first Hungarian novelist who was actually born in Budapest.* Kóbor's *Budapest* is a period piece, largely forgotten now, but not without some merit, and of considerable interest for our purposes. What Kóbor attempted in *Budapest* was a Budapest version of Arthur Schnitzler's *La Ronde,* the famous book published in Vienna as *Reigen* four years before.† It is surely possible, and almost probable, that Kóbor was influenced by Schnitzler. The theme of both books is a chain (in *Budapest* a sequence rather than a circular chain) of sexual liaisons, of love affairs. There is, however, a great difference between the two books. Schnitzler was a very talented craftsman; Kóbor's writing is more uneven, cruder. Schnitzler's main interest was sexuality; Kóbor's the social portrait of a city. Schnitzler is a sometimes brilliant journalist, an exponent of that bourgeois neurosis within a culture that agitated and inspired the theories of Freud; but his portraiture of a place is definitely secondary to his main theme. Kóbor's book is deeply pessimistic, whereas Schnitzler's pessimism is implied: in almost all of Schnitzler's writing one senses a cynical smile on his lips, whereas there is no smile on Kóbor's face at all. In Kóbor's *Budapest* the conditions of the sexual lives of kept girls and married women and their husbands are meant to illustrate his main concern, which is the immorality—immorality, rather than neurosis—of a city where misery and riches, servility and haughti-

---

*The only other writer of considerable stature born in Budapest was the brilliant literary critic Jenő Péterfy, who was also a musicologist and thoroughly bilingual (his occasional German essays were masterpieces of style). A nervous and profound man, inclined to depressions, he killed himself in 1899.

†Kóbor's *title* may have been influenced by Zola's *Paris,* also published in 1896.

ness, abjectness and power, the still strong presence of a feudal class-consciousness and the ever stronger, ever increasing influence of money live side by side. And it is the abjectness of moneylessness, the poverty-ridden lives of women and their daughters in the dark warrens of apartment houses with which Kóbor was so familiar, which shocks and moves us in his book. His description of the lives and the conditions of the upper class is much less successful. It is a book of miseries rather than of grandeurs, a somber book full of harsh smoke and strong, unrefined flavors. As Kóbor wrote in his Introduction in 1901: "I directed my light to the depths above which Budapest is being built." He did not quite succeed, in part because its depth does not a building make. Yet Kóbor's *Budapest*, with its dark wintry scenes, remains a significant corrective to that no less real climate of summer that in 1900 galloped in the skies of Budapest and in its heart.

Another book that illuminates that place and time, in a very different way, is the monumental novel of a writer who is largely forgotten, even in his native country, despite the fact that his *A boldog emberöltő* ("The Happy Generation") had indifferent and abbreviated translations in Paris and New York. Ferenc Körmendi's writing career in Hungary was very short, a mere seven years in the 1930s, after which he left Hungary for England and then the United States, where he wrote little. Significant of *The Happy Generation* is, again, its chronological condition—in this case, the lynchpin of Körmendi's entire theme. It is the story of a man who is born in Budapest on January 1, 1900, on the first day of the new century. It is a great Budapest *haut-bourgeois* novel, even though, I repeat, it is not (perhaps not yet) so recognized. Körmendi was as much influenced by Thomas Mann as Kóbor had been by Schnitzler's *La Ronde*. * But there is an essential difference between Mann's *Buddenbrooks* and *The Happy Generation*. *Buddenbrooks* is the story of the rise and tragic decline of three generations of a family; *The Happy Generation* is the story of a half-generation, the life and family of a single thirty-year-old man, a descent from a sunlit plateau of prosperity and security to the tragic collapse of his own desire for more life. It is entitled *The Happy Generation* because in 1900, when its protagonist is born on Andrássy Avenue, every-

*One of the weaker portions of *The Happy Generation* consists of its young protagonist's love affair during a year spent in a Swiss tuberculosis sanatorium, amidst men and women from many nations—the obvious influence of *The Magic Mountain*.

thing is suffused with the optimism of security, respectability, cultivation and progress; indeed, on one occasion his father says so.
"The generation," he tells his two sons, "in which you will grow
up will be fortunate* . . . there seems to be no reason why it should
not be so."

Of course this novel, unlike Kóbor's *Budapest,* was written and
inspired by retrospect, by the painful and melancholy retrospect of
the 1930s (it was published in 1934, the year after Hitler had
assumed power), when the world of 1900 seemed so blessed, so far
away, so irretrievably lost. In this, *The Happy Generation* precedes
Stefan Zweig's *The World of Yesterday* by nearly a decade and is a
novel, not a wistful memoir; but the respect for the secure standards
and values of the world of 1900 is as strong in Körmendi's novel
as in Zweig's nobly pathetic reminiscences written in his Brazilian
exile. For our purposes, *The Happy Generation* is important because
it shows the sunny atmosphere of the Andrássy Avenue bourgeoisie
at and after the turn of the century: not only the sureties and the
securities but also the presence of the solid bourgeois virtues of
personal and civilizational probity, perhaps concentrated in the
admirable doctor and father, the head of the Hegedüs family. Their
spacious apartment may be full of bibelots, their curtains may be
heavy, but the sunshine of that summery Budapest of 1900 filters
through. It is a world of protective affinities: of a few old family
portraits, many comfortable armchairs, and the noonday scent of
the forever first course of the Sunday family dinner. With all of this,
The Happy Generation is not really tainted with nostalgia, while it is
a nearly perfect rendition not only of the atmosphere but of the
mental aspirations of a class of people, of a place, of a time. It is the
greatest work of Körmendi (surely in size: 850 pages), who was not
a *very* great writer; yet *The Happy Generation* deserves recognition
not only in the annals of literature but also by historians who wish
to know much about that place and time.

And now we come to the greatest writer of Magyar prose in the
twentieth century, perhaps to the greatest prose writer in all Hungarian literature, and surely one of the great writers of Europe—
even though he is seldom translated and remains largely unknown
outside Hungary. This is Gyula Krúdy, who arrived in Budapest in
1896, when he was not yet eighteen, and whose first contributions

*He actually says "happy" *(boldog)* but somehow that English word is not quite
appropriate here or, indeed, in the book title. Perhaps it should be "blessed."

had been printed by provincial newspapers when he was thirteen. He was one of those writers in the Hungarian provinces for whom Budapest had become a magnet. His father wanted him to be a lawyer. "I shall be a poet in Budapest," the son said. (He never wrote a single poem there.) The father, a member of the old, impoverished gentry of his province and country, disinherited him, for more than one reason. It was a break not only between two generations but between two centuries. Again there is a chronological coincidence. The father died on December 30, 1900, the exact last moment of the old century. By that time his son was a published writer in modern Budapest. The first volume of his stories was printed in 1899, when he was twenty years old. His first long novel appeared in 1901.

Except for short absences, he remained in Budapest for the rest of his life. But for many years he did not write about Budapest. He wrote about melancholy provinces on the great Hungarian plains, about little towns in the shadows of the Carpathian mountains. It was not until later, about 1912, that he began to turn the magical searchlight of his memories on Budapest. Thereafter he would write often about the city, and about the city around 1900, in his own lyrical style, with a depth and with an evocative music, in ways in which no one has written about it either before or since, and perhaps—no, most probably—no one ever will.

For this introductory chapter of this book I must translate a few of his passages about Budapest at some length. This is inevitable, since he is the writer of colors, odors and sounds. His descriptions of Budapest were scattered in hundreds of places in his novels, sketches and feuilletons. Here and there some of them have been put together in small volumes, published decades after his death. In this fantastic profusion of his passages and writings about Budapest there is a duality or, rather, an evolution. Krúdy, who with all of his liberality of spirit and startlingly modern prose style, was a very historically minded writer, a reactionary in the best sense of that much abused word, would flail, on occasion, the loud, commercial, shamelessly eager metropolis of 1900—contrasting its spirit with its slower, calmer, respectable, near-provincial past. At times he wrote that the city lost its virtue around the time—perhaps in 1896, the year of the great Millennium Fair—when cannons boomed and the city glowed, celebrating the greatness of Hungary, the very year when he had arrived in Budapest. He wrote once about Franz Josef's visit to Budapest in 1896, to this once town of "smaller houses and modest citizens, of young, rosy, patriotic girls waving their handkerchiefs, of a quiet and unrebellious antiquity." But now "Pest had thrown off its mask of modesty; each year she put on more and more jewelry; the unassuming had become loud, the thrifty had turned to gambling, the virgins brought up in severe convents had begun to take pride in the fulness of their breasts. . . . Pest had become unfaithful. . . ."

> This *raffinée* courtesan of a city had forgotten the triumphs of the young monarch at whose bosom she had once thrown herself, in the time of her fresh innocence. . . . Her shoulders no longer breathed the odor of holy water. Pest lifted her once downcast eyes; she was no longer satisfied with little presents of honey and gilded walnuts. She had become conscious of her developing charms; she discovered her new side that was both *gamine* and cosmopolitan; this once little wallflower had begun to appreciate herself; and the thrifty old gentleman was disturbed to find that the demanding cocotte that Pest had become no longer loved him. The naïve virgin, who in the 1860s so happily imitated the crown-like hairdo of the thin-waisted Queen Elizabeth whom she had seen at the Merchants' and Artisans' Ball—she had become a wide-hipped, eager, unbridled female. The gentlemen, who at the time of the Coronation had begun to train their sideburns with the help of the Kishíd Street barbers, had become fewer and fewer; and now only old janitors, veteran soldiers and ancient civil servants wore the Franz Josef beard. . . .

The mythical hero of an unfinished Krúdy novel

> . . . saw that in the forest of the town the white-waisted, sentimental, virginal birches trembling in the wind had become fewer and fewer; he saw that those embroideries and needlepoints and laces that had been stitched by busy, light, feminine fingers were disappearing from the drawingrooms in the houses of the old citizenry; that the coiffures and the countenances of women no longer resembled the antique Madonnas in the churches of the Inner City or of Buda, but that the fashions were now dictated by infamous transient female personages, dancers and cocottes. . . . The tone of talk is ever more frivolous, the pursuit of pleasure ever more

shameless as it whispers its selected phrases bending over the uncovered shoulders of the women in the theaters, or on the streets bending at the sides of their veiled hats, or even in the apartments of families where one can still smell the scent of the wax candles from a Christmas Eve hardly past. . . .

He saw, too,

> . . . the blue-white towers and the endlessly rising roofs; the white ships multiplying on the river and the rainbow-hued Danube bridges . . . the coming and going of wrinkles on the faces of those ladies whom one could find out of their houses every time, and who keep a spirit from the Thousand and One Nights in their homes (in the form of a scrubby little maid who does all the work, who sews the torn clothes of the children and cooks the midday meal for the husband). He saw the proud gentlemen forced into higher and higher collars to hide the premature folds of their necks and the premature trembling of their heads; he saw those heart-rending days in spring when the new frocks bedeck the pavements like flowers in the meadows; and the lilting, snowy days in winter when the sun comes out at noon on Andrássy Avenue to encourage the poor office girls to step out with the gait of duchesses. . . .

Sometime during the darkening years of the First World War Krúdy's flagellation of Budapest began to give way to a quieter, lyrical kind of nostalgia, a remembering of what was lovely and good in Budapest at its once noontime. And by 1920 and 1921, when Budapest—surely the spirit of Budapest—was under attack by a nationalist wave of sentiment and by the nationalist regime, "They are reviling Budapest in the Parliament," Krúdy began.

> Well, Pest has never been an agreeable town. But desirable, yes: like a racy, full-blooded young married woman about whose flirtations everyone knows and yet gentlemen are glad to bend down and kiss her hand. . . . No matter how we country people may have been irritated, it was in Budapest that Hungarian culture, about which so many of the old, blessed Magyar people had dreamed, received its hallmark. Here the dancing in the theaters is the best, here everyone in a crowd may think that he is a gentleman even if he had left

jail the day before; the physicians' cures are wonderful, the lawyers are world-famous, even the renter of the smallest rooms has his bath, the shopkeepers are inventive, the policeman guards the public peace, the gentlefolk are agreeable, the streetlights burn till the morning, the janitor will not allow a single ghost inside, the tramcars will carry you to the farthest places within an hour, the city clerks look down on the state employees, the women are well-read from their theater magazines, the porters greet you humbly on the street corners, the innkeeper inquires of your appetite with his hat in hand, the coach drivers wait for you solemnly during an entire day, the salesgirls swear that your wife is the most beautiful of women, other girls in the nightclubs and orpheums hear out your political opinions politely, you find yourself praised in the morning newspaper after you had witnessed an accident, well-known men use the spittoons in the café gardens, you are being helped into your overcoat, and the undertaker shows his thirty-two gold teeth when you take your leave from this city forever.

Yes, in those times:

How much is there to say about those blessed, peacetime years! Of the air of Budapest which, true, was often dust-laden in the wind blowing from the Rákos fields; but that air became that much sweeter in spring when the wind had turned and began to breathe from the direction of the Buda hills; dependable old gentlemen insist that one could then smell the violets from Mount Gellért within the city. . . . And listen again to the talk of these respectable men, because you will learn that in those times it was not at all shocking to wear houndstooth trousers in the spring, and a tiny bouquet in one's lapel, to wait on a certain street corner as if one were the swain of the Swabian flower seller and not of the lady in the blue veil who would approach from Váci Street. . . .

Váci Street—the main shopping street of the Inner City:

The little squares of the Inner City were like confectionery boxes. There the breeze from the Danube was pirouetting with the rays of the sun, there gleamed the hired carriages at their stations from which countesses with their delicate feet had just descended; old pensioners sat on benches in their spotless clothes; the grocer with his wicker baskets and the baker smelling of his fresh kaiser rolls kissed the hands of the chambermaids in their black bombazine when these had rung the bell; the serpentine waists of the vendeuses, the white blouses of the millinery girls . . . and the silvery heads of the booksellers gave the tone to this district. Whoever settles in the Inner City will remain a distinguished person for the rest of his life. It was easy to dress well from its shopwindows, easy to learn how to be fashionable, and every purchaser could have credit. The famous shops that sold the best goods from London, suits, hats, gloves, were memorable like a grand foxhunt in autumn. The merchandise from Paris arrived directly, scented like women before a grand soirée. . . . The waiter in the coffeehouse put the recent *Le Figaro* in your hands. The barber had learned his trade in Paris; virgins embroidered initials on linens; the spiceshop had the odors of a great freighter just arrived from Bombay. Around the hotels shone the footwear of wealthy foreigners, the carriage curtains would seldom veil the adventurous demi-mondaines, the jewels blinded with their shine and the bank tellers paid out brand-new bills. Blessed Inner City years! Like youth—will they ever return?

And in other streets, too:

Women smelled like oranges in Japan. Rákóczi Avenue was full of women of doubtful repute; yet they were pretty and young enough to be princesses in Berlin. Around the Emke coffeehouse stiff lieutenants and fake country gentlemen kept reviewing them. . . . The youngest girls wore silk stockings, and white-haired women found their own brand of connoisseurs. The city was blessed with its cult of women. The eyes of men trembled, the women were so beautiful: black-haired ones, as if they had come from Seville, and in the tresses of the blond ones tales from an Eastern sun were playing hide-and-seek, like fireflies in the summer meadows.

The tone of the cello was deepest when Krúdy saw the duality of Budapest:

They kept on building every day, palaces topped by towers rising toward the sun; and at night it was as if there were endless burials—an everlasting row of tumbrils hauled the old broken matter out of the town, the cadavers of old people and of old houses, of old streets and old customs.

Perhaps from these translated excerpts English-speaking readers may be able to recognize, or at least sense, the particular tone not only of Krúdy's language but of the Magyar literary language—and of the Magyar spirit—which is that extraordinary combination, the constant presence of a minor key within the basic key of a major.

So beneath the noisy boom of Budapest there was that presence of a wistful and melancholy tone; and there was more to it than the echo of nostalgic memories, heard only in solitude and silence in the deep of the night, when the city noise had died down. But that blending of major and minor, of optimism and pessimism, of light and darkness is, after all, the inevitable human condition, and also the condition of any culture that is worthwhile. It is only that some people—and this is true about Hungarians—are more conscious of it than are others. As Pascal said, men are both beasts and angels. Hungarians know that—which is the reason why the fanatic insistence of a Dostoevsky about that duality and about its coexistence in the human soul leaves them, by and large, unmoved: that unkempt Russian tells them nothing that they do not know.

In 1900 not only the colors and tastes and sounds but also the psychic tones of Budapest and Vienna were very different from each other. Budapest was still full of self-confidence. Its building fever, its financial prosperity were the consequences of that condition. This had much to do with the Magyar temperament, in which a deep-rooted (and nonreligious) pessimism is often broken by sudden bursts of appetite for life, of a physical appetite stronger but perhaps less finely woven than what the French phrase *joie de vivre* suggests. The results of this were visible, and palpable, in 1900. Vienna may have been neurotic; Budapest was not. There were plenty of troubles, dissatisfactions, shadows, darknesses in the life of the city; but there was, as yet, no definite desire to break with the past and no self-conscious doubts about the future. Within Magyar pessimism there is the sad music of the futility of human endeavors, but none of that Germanic *Angst:* the tone is often

melancholy, but the appetite for life—including the material pleasures of words, sounds, colors, tastes and touches—abounds. The
Hungarian mind inclines to psychosis rather than to neurosis; but
the German idea of the subconscious (as distinct from the uncon-
scious), the idea that something is truer because it is "deeper," has
had no appeal to the Hungarian mind, especially when it is expressed in intellectual categories whose very language is removed
from the everyday realities of life. The Hungarian mind is very
observant and sensitive to every psychic nuance, but it tends to
recognize these from expressions of the conscious mind. Long after
1900, Freud's influence in Budapest was slight. One of the reasons
for this is the declarative character of the Hungarian language and
of Hungarian habits of speech. There is this odd contradiction of
the Hungarian temperament: a deep masculine reserve, but without the inclination to hide one's prejudices, loves and hates. There
were Hungarian disciples of Freud (Sándor Ferenczi), and there
were Hungarian writers of great talent, Mihály Babits and Géza
Csáth, who wrote profoundly about schizophrenia; but the great
Magyar writers, knowers and alchemists of the human soul such as
Krúdy, obsessed as they were with dreams and with the reality of
dreams, never felt any need to expatiate upon the "subconscious";
and what they did not know about the strange inclinations of the
male and the female, of the child and the mature spirit and mind,
may not have been worth knowing.

Much of this is fairly evident from the literature of the relations
of the sexes at the time, when the erotic life, too, of Budapest was
less neurotic than that of Vienna. It was largely untainted by the late
nineteenth-century despair of the Romantic Agony. At worst,
erotic life was crude and male-dominated. At best, it was late-
aristocratic rather than late-bourgeois, in the sense that the desire
to please had a definite priority over the wish to be loved. Perhaps
this is why foreigners found Hungarian men even more attractive
than they found Hungarian women, whose beauty did have a definite renown at the time; for instance, many Viennese women married Hungarian men in 1900, while the reverse of such alliances
was rarer. Romantic love, the desire to please, is the main theme
of writers such as Krúdy, who otherwise was startlingly and at times
even shockingly knowledgeable of the frailties of the sexes. The
very different, but thoroughly Budapestian writer Ernő Szép, in one
of his best novels: "I was telling myself: I am in love, I love. To
enjoy this woman physically: ah! there's an animal. I *am* an animal,

too, but what I feel is not only that but its very opposite. . . . And, as a man, what I want from a woman I'll take in a way that is a hundred times sweeter for her than it is for me. She will be happy with me between her faintings and tears. Her fever will come, her tremblings will come, and her mouth will smother in the pillow a burning scream that cannot be heard beyond the wallpaper. . . ." And the serious Catholic Mihály Babits in his otherwise dark novel, *Halálfiai*: "That was the age of love in Hungary, of the love learned from the oldest Magyar novelist, a love that had turned to a phraseology: for what else could have been interesting in life?" A great poem by Babits is entitled *Two Sisters.* The two sisters are Desire and Sorrow. The poem is a deep, pessimistic *tour de force* of parallel and paradox (Sorrow becomes Desire, and Desire becomes Sorrow), but there is nothing neurotic or decadent in it. In the Budapest of 1900 desire and sorrow may have been sisters, but desire surely dominated that family scene; and, for once, Desire was the older sister and Sorrow the younger one.

This Hungarian comprehension of human nature (a comprehension that, however, is almost always individual, never collective), together with the reluctance of the Magyar mind at abstractness— may have been a factor not only in the quality of modern Hungarian literature but also in the worldly success of so many Hungarians after 1900. I wrote "after 1900" because this, too, is something that we can recognize only in retrospect: the extraordinary and varied success of a generation of 1900 coming out of Budapest. For it was around that time that from the gymnasiums and the universities, from the bourgeois homes of Budapest and the gentry families of this then fairly obscure and relatively small nation an extraordinary generation of scholars, scientists, writers, thinkers, inventors, philosophers, financiers, *faiseurs,* painters, composers, musicians— a generation of Nobel Prize winners and mountebanks (in some cases, perhaps the same persons were both)—came into the outside world that knows the names of many of them even now, while it knows the names of some of the best of them not at all. In the succeeding tragedies and vicissitudes of Hungary many of them left to seek their fortune and acquire their fame elsewhere. And some of the seeds of those tragedies and vicissitudes were already there in 1900.

Three generations and nearly ninety years later the Budapest of 1900 looks better than it was. In 1920 the Budapestian culture of 1900 was excoriated by many Hungarians, and very definitely by the official public philosophy of the nationalist and counterrevolutionary regime. Fifty or sixty years later, the officially Communist and Marxist government of Hungary has found it proper not only to permit but also to promote the commemoration and the celebration of monuments and of people, and the publication of the arts and letters of that bourgeois era, through historical reconstructions that are suffused with respect and often even with admiration. But, then, much of the same has happened with the reputation of Vienna in 1900 (or with the urbane and bourgeois civilization of much of the Western world at that time). Who, in 1920 or even in 1950, would have thought that "Vienna 1900" would be the subject of the most successful and fashionable exhibitions in New York and Paris; that it would become the subject of a spate of books by non-Austrians; and that the cult of Franz Josef and of the Habsburgs would become sacrosanct in Vienna, with public homage paid to it by Socialist governments in Austria? Yes, Budapest 1900, too, attracts us; but we must watch for the symptoms of an uncritical and, therefore, unhistorical nostalgia.

Still, 1900 was both a milestone and a turning point in the history of Budapest. It has a meaning that is more than chronological. It provides a contrast with Vienna 1900 and Paris 1900—two capital cities of capital importance for the culture of the Western world—about which so many books have been written. The *belle époque* is a pleasant nostalgic phrase, but the crisis of an older France and the breaking away from the ideas, ideals and standards of the nineteenth century had begun in Paris fifteen or even twenty-five years before 1900. In Vienna, too, 1900 was the end of the Austrian *fin-de-siècle,* with many of its interesting artistic and intellectual symptoms and alarming manifestations. In Budapest, *le mal* (if it was a *mal de siècle*) was only about to begin. Yes: in that sense, perhaps, Budapest was behind Vienna. But what is "behind" and what is "ahead"? Yes: the crisis of the old Liberalism, the breakdown of the old political and capitalist order and of the urbane social and financial equilibrium had come in Vienna seven or ten or twelve years before Budapest. It is, of course, not arguable that what happened in Vienna (and what was happening in some Viennese minds, too) would influence the twin capital, that junior one, the Budapest about which many Viennese in 1900 were supercilious. They (as had Freud, for example) looked down on Budapest and on its Hungarians, that semibarbaric country and place. But what the Viennese did not know—and how could they?—was that in 1900 in Budapest the breaking away from the nineteenth-century habits of thought, vision, manners and even speech was occurring even faster than in Vienna, and in different ways. At the very moment when Budapest became the indisputable focus of Hungarian culture, a new generation of Hungarian painters, writers and composers sought and gained their inspiration from the Magyar countryside. The new Hungarian painters Ferenczy, Hollósy, Rippl-Rónai and Csontváry had learned nothing from Klimt, Schiele and Kokoschka; the writers Krúdy, Kosztolányi, Ady, and Babits were very different from Musil, Trakl, Hoffmansthal; Bartók and Kodály had little in common with Schönberg and Webern. Only in the architecture of Budapest can we still see a definite Austro-German influence.

For Budapest 1900 was the noon hour. The zenith of its prosperity in that year coincided with the zenith of its cultural life; and a few years later—rather precisely, again, in 1905–06—the breakdown of its parliamentary and political order coincided with many of the first appearances of new forms, shapes, manners, expressions. A new generation of men and women were coming into their own. Some of the colors, sounds and words—the atmosphere, language* and music of Budapest—would eventually change. *"Les parfums, les couleurs et les sons se répondent"*†—there are few times and places in the world that illustrate that famous line from Baudelaire's *Correspondances* better than Budapest in 1900.

---

*With the new century, even Magyar spelling changed. In 1900 the Hungarian Academy of Sciences, after serious discussions and study, declared that the old Hungarian usage of the double consonant *cz* must give way to the more modern *c* (both corresponding to the sound *ts* in English).

> †Comme de longs échos qui de loin se confondent
> Dans use ténébreuse et profonde unité
> Vaste comme la nuit et comme la clarté
> Les parfums, les couleurs et les sons se répondent . . .

Urbane Hungarian poetry has always been influenced by French poetry, and perhaps especially around 1900. Baudelaire's *Correspondances* and Rimbaud's *Voyelles* had, for example, a great influence on the poet and novelist Dezső Kosztolányi, whose *tour de force* poem "Ilona," a poem playing with the vowels of that Magyar female name, surpasses *Voyelles* in its directness and in the beauty of its music.

2

The City

Only a few years before 1900 De Blowitz, the most celebrated and most cosmopolitan journalist in Europe, the
chief diplomatic correspondent of the London *Times,*
traveled from Vienna to Budapest. "I confess," he wrote in his
account in *The Nineteenth Century,* "that no city in the world holds
or interests me less than Vienna. . . . It is, let me say, as a town,
merely 'one of a dozen' . . . I showed my son, who was with me,
the powdery Prater with its hot inelegance of aspect, the leading
arteries of the capital, the cathedral, which is a little stiff in its lines
and *dépaysée* amid so fast-rushing a world, and the conventional
Government buildings, which complete the impressions of this
town, towards which converge reluctantly the multifarious and
heterogeneous elements of the most complex empire in the world."

On the other hand, Buda-Pest has for me an attraction, and
when on the morrow—a warm, bright day—I was at last permitted to instal myself in the shade high up on one of the
balconies of the Hôtel Hungaria overlooking the Danube, I

29

experienced one of the most agreeable sensations that I recall. Here the ample breadth of the stream diminishes the forces of the current, and the Danube passes majestically under the two imposing bridges which hide its courses where it bends far below beyond the town with the dimensions and the appearance of a stream opening out into the sea. In front frowns the ancient and lofty fortress of Buda, which formerly held Hungary abject and trembling under its cannon, and the Burg, formerly Imperial, where watched the implacable eyes of the conqueror. Both fortress and Burg, however, are to disappear for ever. A new royal *château* is going up near by, which will take the place of the old yellow barracks which serve now as a dwelling for the King of Hungary in this capital, finally recovered from the age-long domination of Austria. Below, the life of the river is unceasing; and the whole warm, brilliant, animated picture is most enlivening. . . .

Blowitz's dislike for Vienna was odd. "Every time I return to (Vienna)," he wrote, "I am struck by the feel that the older it grows the more improvised its appearance." But Budapest was much more improvised. Its antiquities were inconsiderable. It was a booming modern city, swelling and smoking.

The best thing about Budapest was its situation. It is the only large city on the Danube through which that majestic river flows in the middle. Five-sixths of Vienna are to the south of it (the same is true of Belgrade); you can spend months in Vienna without being aware of the great stream. Budapest is almost evenly divided by it. Moreover, the Danube (which is not, and never was, blue) is just the proper width at Budapest, about a half-mile wide. Thirty miles north of the capital, the river takes a turn and bends straight to the south; that Danube bend has been a painters' paradise because of the proportions of river and hills and land, less romantic but more charming than the beautiful valleys of the Rhine or the Hudson. As in the case of Venice or New York, in 1900 the best and also the cheapest way to arrive in Budapest was by boat. The first sight was that of the industrial suburbs, but above them the mountains of Buda already promised grand sights; then came a bosky island, after which the Danube bends slightly and the entire panorama of the city revealed itself at once, in a pearly, blue-gray light of the day. The proportions were splendid, since the presence of the great river was not diminished by the rows of buildings on the left and the rising hills on the right bank. The scene was majestic but not awesome. It is as if the Danube had been invented for the esthetic purposes of the city, which, of course, is not the case (except that one of the great architects of nineteenth-century Pest, Ferenc Reitter, had devised a plan in 1865 to divert half of the stream through a broad canal, flowing in a vast semicircle between high masonry walls, to rejoin the mother stream in southern Budapest. It is perhaps fortunate that this ambitious plan was not followed).

In 1900 the large graystone river walls and quays had been built. Three of the seven great bridges spanning the Danube were already there; the fourth one, Elizabeth Bridge, still an enormous warren of wooden scaffoldings, was under way, to be completed two years later. In 1900 the contrast between Buda and Pest was greater than it is now; indeed, greater than even a few years later. The Royal Castle would be completed in 1905. It does not compare with the Hradčany in Prague. Its great courtyards and southern and western façades, which are not visible from the Danube and from the Pest side, have good eighteenth-century details and proportions, baroque rather than classical, in the Austrian manner (it was said that Franz Josef had insisted on that). It would soon have a fine terrace above the river, around the equestrian statue of Prince Eugene of Savoy, whose armies reconquered Buda from the Turks in 1686. Yet that royal palace was low rather than massive, ornamental rather than soaring, the main portion capped by a strangely ugly cupola studded with stony warts, a suggestion of an old Magyar warrior's semibarbaric helmet*—representative not of Habsburg baroque but of the then Hungarian nationalist new style, perhaps symptomatic of the nation's and its government's split-mindedness about Hungary's place within the Dual Monarchy. But, again, the general effect was very impressive because of the perspective. The Castle Hill (Várhegy) is not much more than three hundred feet high, but seen from the Pest side it seems higher. The view of it from the promenade above the Pest quays or from the windows and balconies of the hotels is one of the incomparable sights of capital cities of the world: the buildings of Castle Hill beckoning from Buda, with the theatricality of the scene further enhanced by the stately slow bend of the Danube and by the classi-

---

*Gutted and burned out during the winter siege of Budapest in 1944–45, its restoration, after more than forty years, is almost completed. The new cupola is simpler and better than the old one.

cal Chain Bridge arching above the river from the busy quays of Pest to the greenery and the stone parapets of the Castle Hill walls and to the neoclassical portal of the Castle Tunnel. From that bridgehead in Buda a steam-powered elevator on an inclined plane rose to Castle Hill.

Castle Hill was District One among the then ten districts of Budapest. It is the most famous, the most old-fashioned, and perhaps the most beautiful portion of the city now, infested with tourists so much that private automobiles have recently been excluded from it. It had none of that fame and crowds and traffic in 1900. It was a historical and architectural jumble. Jumble, not jungle: for it was not cramped; it preserved a quiet and ample sense of spaciousness. There were the newly rebuilt Royal Castle, the newly rebuilt Coronation (Matthias) Church, and the undulating white stone parapets, the Fishermen's Bastion, invented by an imaginative Hungarian architect, overlooking the sea of houses in Pest and the enormous Parliament building. In 1899 a foreign visitor who could not have been more different from De Blowitz (whom he almost certainly detested) arrived in Budapest. He was the strangely brilliant Jérôme Tharaud, whom the French Ministry of Public Instruction had sent to Budapest for an instructorship in French at the university. He disliked the new monumental buildings: "I find the Middle Ages of the Anjous and the Corvins, here in Budapest; but all of it new, aggressive, blinding one's spirit and one's vision." But this ironic and sharp-witted young Frenchman was comfortable and respectful in the presence of the older, modest nobilitarian houses of the Castle district. There were a few new government buildings in its square (that of the National Archives, for example), but the rest were mostly houses and small palaces built before 1830. Compared to all of this *bric-à-brac héroïque,* Tharaud wrote, "how much I prefer the old sleepy streets, the old yellow houses, simple but of a good period . . . in their interior courtyards, in their rusted wells I can hear the murmuring of history better than amidst that false medieval décor, *ce faux décor moyenâgeux.*"*

This was, I repeat, not the most fashionable quarter of Budapest in 1900. Portions of these houses were medieval, having survived the siege of Buda and the Turkish occupation. The arcades and

---

*Tharaud was enchanted with his discovery of a perfect Biedermeier remnant, the Ruszwurm pastry shop and tearoom in one of the side streets of Castle Hill, a living 1830 period piece. It is pleasant to record that it still exists.

courtyards were eighteenth-century or older, the façades somewhat newer—graystone or that particular yellow stucco that character-ized much of the Habsburg domains as far west as Milan and as far east as Cracow. Their portals and doorways breathed a cool, shad-owy quietness. In their courtyards were wells and grandfatherly old plane trees. Their cobblestoned sidewalks and streets breathed the air of historical autumns. Their beauty was more provincial than urban; and so were their velvet silences in the night, with an occa-sional plashing of a fountain with its mineral-iron smell.

Here lived the oldest inhabitants of the capital. That First District was, like the rest of Buda, conservative and traditional; certainly not assertively Hungarian. In 1900 a considerable number of people in Buda still spoke German. (Many of the names of the streets, hills, meadows of Buda had been German; they became transformed into Magyar by municipal decree, in 1847 and again in 1873). Yet, in spite of their sometimes Austrian designs and South German ar-chitects, these buildings, and their atmosphere, acquired the aristo-cratic, rather than patrician character of a Hungarian baroque—yet another illustration that Lamarck was not entirely wrong and Dar-win not entirely right: for in life, historical life, acquired character-istics *can* be inherited (or, to paraphrase Wilde, nature, and espe-cially historical nature, has a way of imitating art).

In 1900 two other portions of the First District deserve descrip-tion. One of them still exists today, the other was razed sixty years ago. The Krisztina (Christina), named after its parish church, was a Catholic bourgeois district, still mostly inhabited by the older middle classes, by families of officials and artisans with German names, on the western slopes of Castle Hill, beginning to be filled up with a few new apartment houses. The first trolley line in Buda ran there, leading to the South Station from where in 1900 the trains of the Danube-Save-Adria Company puffed away to the southwest. It was the terminus and starting point of the proverbial Trieste night express, going from Budapest across the Croatian mountains to Trieste and Venice. Many newlyweds, including this writer's parents and grandparents, boarded its wooden sleeping cars on their first (or second) wedding night en route to a honey-moon in Venice.* Tucked away in the gardens and the courtyards of the Krisztina were open-air establishments: taverns, wineshops,

---

*In 1900 this well-known train left Budapest at 8:00 P.M. and arrived in Venice at 2:15 P.M. the next day. (In 1988 this train trip takes more than an hour longer.)

essentially restaurants, because food could always be had there. Their few remaining examples are the precious survivals of an older Budapest even now. In some of these places, with their simple tables bedecked under large plane, locust or walnut trees, were Hungarian versions of the Viennese garden restaurants in Grinzing or Hietzing, fabled for their small orchestras and the young green Heuriger wine; but the differences were at least as important as the similarities. Due to the mild climate of Budapest, dining outside in these garden restaurants ("greenery restaurants" in Hungarian: *zöldvendéglő*), late in the evening, could begin in early May and last till the end of September. Much of the wine, poultry, vegetables and fruit were homegrown. The peaches and certain varieties of the grapes grown within a mile of the Buda taverns were the most reputed ones in Hungary. Some of these garden taverns depended not only on the locals but also on their habitués coming over from Pest. Around 1900 The Marble Bride was the most famous. But The Marble Bride—like The Trumpeter, The Green Barrel, The Golden Duck, The Rose Tree, The Seven Owls and The Red Frog (some of them in the Second District)—was reputed not only for its cooking and for the agreeableness of the summer evenings under its leafy trees. It also had comfortable rooms inside, not only in order to accommodate its guests in the event of a sudden chill or a rainstorm or for a family reception. On cold, crisp Hungarian winter days, these rooms would be wondrously cozy, with the lovely evenness of the heat coming from large tile stoves in the corners, and with the pleasurable contrast that the susurrating, warm, food- and wine-scented interior provided to the crackling and invigorating cold winter air outside.

The other, now vanished portion of the First District was the Tabán, on the southern slopes of the Castle Hill, between it and the Gellért Hill that was topped by the pancake-flat barracks and casemates of the Citadella. The Tabán stretched away from the Buda entrance to the new Elizabeth Bridge. That Tabán was truly ancient, unadorned by new buildings and undisturbed by innovations. It was also moderately unsanitary and, in places, disreputable. During the eighteenth century a motley population of Serbs, Magyars, Greeks and gypsies lived there, most of them rivermen. They made their living out of the barges, boats and ferries and by fishing on the Danube; later by transporting grains and food. Their commerce came from the south, from the more primitive and in part still

Turkish-ruled Balkans, rather than from the Middle Danubian Europe of Austria and South Germany. They were involved in all kinds of trade, including an episode or two of white slavery. The Tabán had a share of taverns, gambling dens and whores. On its edges stood the two famous Turkish baths of Buda, the Rudas and the Ratsian (Rácfürdő), built by the Turks atop the surging warm springs that are so munificent below the soils of Buda. By 1900 much of that racy population was gone, but the Tabán was still there, catering to men with a liking for good cheap dishes, good cheap wine and (I think in a few instances) good cheap women (though the more famous whorehouses were now on the Pest side). With its swaying oil lamps, unpaved streets and roughly stoned sidewalks, rambling and curving between the one-storied (and here almost always whitewashed) stone houses and hovels with their red tile roofs, with its tiny wine gardens and the ripe mixture of its smells, including the heavy scent of apricots and plums from its nearby orchards in the spring and summer, the Tabán was a very romantic place. It had been discovered, here and there, by habitués of old-fashioned things and places even in 1900 when the taste for times past was so much less than what it was to become later, and when it was but a miracle that some of the older and worthier buildings of Budapest were not razed by the orders of an otherwise exemplary and efficient City Planning Council of Public Works.

In 1900 Buda consisted of three districts, and Pest of seven. As in most capital cities of Europe, the city had grown out of a center in concentric circles, even though the nineteenth-century way of urban expansion, that along railroad lines, was already in the making. Beyond and below Castle Hill, which formed the inner half-circle of Buda, and largely to the north of it, was the smaller Second District, Viziváros, "the Water Town." Farther to the north came the Third District of "Ancient Buda" (Óbuda). Surrounding all of them were the Buda hills, which in 1900 administratively still belonged to the First.

The Water District had some of the characteristics of the First, in that it was old, introverted, provincial. Except for some of the vegetable-garden suburbs of Buda, it had the largest remnant of a German artisan population in 1900. It was one of the two smallest districts of the capital, stretching for about a mile on the Buda side of the Danube, between the already existing Chain and Margaret bridges, with many of its narrow streets marching up the humps of Castle Hill. It had been inundated during the last great Danube flood, in 1838. Its people were conservative, and suspicious of the milling, blooming Pest across the river. There could hardly have been a greater contrast between two districts than between the Water District in Buda and the Leopold District straight across from it in Pest: the first one the oldest, the second the most modern one in Budapest; the first still inhabited by old families of German artisans, the second filled up by more-or-less prosperous Hungarian Jews. And *that* was where the future was in 1900, across the gray-green flow of the Danube, less than half a mile across, where dozens of semipalatial apartment houses had risen, and even these were dwarfed by the nearly completed Parliament, a gigantic mass whose very name meant more than mere parliament or even national assembly or congress. It was the *Országház,* a word translatable into English only incompletely: The House of the Nation; or, perhaps, The Palace of the State. Yet the people of the Water District had a full share of the improvements of the booming city. In 1879 they had become beneficiaries of one of the finest municipal waterworks of any city in the world; before that they had plenty of troubles with their wells. Along the quay of the Danube clanged and clattered a trolley line. Between the two great bridges flanking it, the Water District was more approachable than ever before; and a row of those neo-Renaissance apartment buildings had begun to rise, across from that impressive row on the Pest side above the quays. Further inland were plenty of open markets and one-story houses with their green, close, leafy gardens, and restaurants such as The Green Barrel or The Trumpeter.

North of the Water District, beyond the Buda end of the Margaret Bridge, was Rose Hill (Rózsadomb), partly within the Third District of Ancient Buda (Óbuda). The Turks who ruled Buda for a century and a half (from 1541 to 1686) brought with them little that remained enduring, save for two things: roses and baths. Four hundred years ago one of the Turkish officials of Buda became famous because of his love for the rose garden he had planted along the slopes of that hill. (He was the only Turk after whom a street is still named in Budapest.) By 1900 Rose Hill was about to become fashionable again. In 1900 (and in some places even now) a large part of Buda was still very sparsely inhabited. By 1900 in the outer districts of Paris—Passy, Neuilly, Auteuil—smart streets and apartment houses had come into existence; the smoky swelling of London already included Richmond and Kew; and even in booming Berlin, the European capital city with the largest municipal area, the West-End and the villa districts along the lakes had lost their rural character. But one of the charms of Budapest in 1900 was this mixture—or, rather, compound—of provinciality and cosmopolitanism.

It contained orchards, the green breasts of the Buda hills, and beyond them the fields and forests stretching up to veritable mountains, still within the city boundaries, the highest of them, St. John's Hill (Jánoshegy), more than 1,700 feet above sea level and more than 1,300 feet above the Danube. Some of these hills in the southwest, among them Eagle Hill (Sashegy), were still solid with vineyards. Others were dotted with the white apparitions of houses and villas, easily visible from the Pest side, human additions to the landscape that hardly compromised its agreeable vistas. Trolley lines had already snaked their iron ways out to the meadows and valleys of the Buda hills, even beyond the large country-town–like open market of Széna (Haymarket) Place. On Sundays the trolleys would be full with families from Pest who had packed up for a picnic in the faraway Augarten (Zugliget) or in the Hüvösvölgy, a veritable country outing. On weekdays in the spring they would carry loads of schoolchildren with their teachers. There, too, old taverns such as the Boar's Head or The Shepherd's Pretty Wife, often found around one or another well-known spring, served as meeting places and often had wooden benches and trestle tables. Since 1872 a cogwheel railway, built by a Swiss firm, has crawled and puffed up every half hour to the highest crest of the Buda mountains, the Schwabenberg, or Svábhegy.

Along the upper slopes of these high hills a few wealthy families of Pest had their villas built, among that of the most famous Hungarian novelist, Mór Jókai. Unlike some of the neoclassical and semibaroque mansions of the city, these villas were architecturally undistinguished. Most of them were spacious wooden chalets, with large and often glassed-in verandahs, not very different from Austrian and South German types. But, then, they were meant to serve only as summer residences, whereto these fortunate families would repair from the heat of Pest and the Danube plain; and the view from them was infinitely breathtaking. Infinitely: because across the silver-colored ribbon of the Danube lay the sea of houses and buildings in Pest, none of them more than four or five stories high, and beyond them the great flat plain of Hungary, stretching under the sun eastward to an unbroken, seemingly endless horizon. Breathtaking: because the scene was arcadian, with green meadows, copses and gardens with their occasional clumps of habitations undulating downward to the Danube: a green fugue of a landscape, here and there dotted with white and red roofs, and coming to rest against the almost toylike protuberance of Castle Hill when seen from above.

The Third District, Ancient Buda, was perhaps less interesting in 1900. It was the most ancient part of the city, but only archeologically, rather than historically speaking. There had been at least two major Roman settlements in Ancient Buda, and by 1900 the excavations of Aquincum had begun.* These Roman legions may have been the first to discover the hot springs in northern Buda. In 1900 Budapest was not yet a seasonal spa, though its springs were well known. Two of the oldest mineral baths were, as we have seen, in the Water District: one of them was on Margaret Island; another one in Pest; but two of the most famous ones were in this Third District, again with their atmosphere of provincial charm. The Empire Baths and the St. Luke Baths were set in yellow-stuccoed late-Empire buildings, with swimming pools overarched by trees and containing small restaurants; the salty smells of steam and cabin-wood mixing with the pleasantly bitter odor of freshly tapped beer.

The population of Ancient Buda had hardly grown during the nineteenth century. It contained a large shipbuilding factory, the oldest synagogue in the city (though few Jews were living in Óbuda around 1900), and a number of cheap taverns, some of them known for the Danube fish dishes they served. Of all the districts of Budapest it was the most provincial one, reminiscent of a Danubian village of bygone days, with its one-story houses, crooked streets and peasant-baroque churches.† Most of these houses were heated with wood stoves; in the winter the pleasant smell of woodsmoke, different from the acrid coal-smoke of Pest, wafted through the Óbuda streets. They were inhabited by fishermen, craftsmen, a

---

*The Aquincum Museum was built in 1894. Before that, some of the excavated Roman tablets, stones and capitals were stored in a restaurant (Frindt's tavern).
†In 1867, 77 percent of the houses in Buda and Pest had one story; by 1905 only 50 percent, but most of these were on the Buda side. In 1900 some of these districts were still patrolled by night watchmen (bakter) carrying lanterns.

goodly number of shipwrights and carpenters, and surprisingly many bootmakers and cobblers. Here, too, a fair portion of the population was still German-speaking, with a few remnants of Greek-Orthodox Serbians. A part of the Third District ran up the northern segment of the Buda hills, a portion that in 1900 was still wholly agricultural and not residential, including vineyards producing mostly white wines (the southwestern Buda hills produced both reds and whites).

We are now crossing the river. Across the Óbuda quays (already mostly paved by 1900; along the main one ran the narrow-gauge tracks of a commuter rail line to the north) lay Margaret Island, perhaps the best-known island along the entire 2,000-mile length of the Danube. In 1894 Blowitz was taken there for lunch. He called it "Sainte Marguerite's Island, pearl of the Danube, nest of flowers, sweet odours, and cool air, whence and whither the white steamers go—a spot unequalled by any one of the public gardens of any of the great cities from the Vistula to the Spree." (Why only from the Vistula to the Spree? Public gardens more beautiful than Margaret Island existed in many places of Europe, but few of them were on an island.) It had a curious history that came to fruition only a few years before 1900. In the Middle Ages the island had a cloister called The Isle of Hares (where Saint Margaret was a nun). Its ruins were excavated only in the 1890s. For centuries the island was uninhabited (whence perhaps Isle of Hares) because it was difficult to reach. Sometime in the early nineteenth century it became the property of a Habsburg archduke who was the Palatine (a unique Hungarian title corresponding to something like Viceroy) of Hungary. He built a small hunting lodge for himself, and another one in the late-Empire style, again stuccoed in Habsburgian yellow. After about 1860 the island could be approached by a small white river steamer from Pest (appropriately named "Swan"). Soon half a dozen of these public-service boats, called "propellers," appeared, crisscrossing the river to and fro, ferrying from one small floating dock to another, carrying passengers and occasional excursionists. Later in the nineteenth century a small hotel was built on Margaret Island and a public bath was opened near one of the springs. Writers, including the greatest poet of Hungary, János Arany, came to the island to rest under its giant oak trees. A few years before 1900 steeply angled stone levees were run around the island to protect it from high water. The channel between a small wild islet near the southern tip of the island was filled up. In 1901 the island was connected with the Margaret Bridge and thereby with Buda and Pest. That bridge, planned and built by French engineers in 1878, was the least attractive of the bridges over the Danube, resting flat on heavy piers, with a fairly ugly French-Victorian kind of railing, angled in the middle, at which point that spur leading to the island was added to it, in the form of the lower part of a wide Y. By that time almost all of the island had been landscaped. It had a restaurant and a confiserie, both open-air, of course, and a large rose garden. (It was only in 1908 that the city officially purchased the island from the Archduke Joseph Habsburg.) A solitary horse trolley ambled from the southern tip of the island to the hotel at its northern end. A booth at the entrance of Margaret Island exacted a ticket from its visitors: its price was small, yet it sufficed to keep the proletariat of Budapest away.

And now we come to Pest, the eastern half of the city, younger and less beautiful than Buda: yet the dynamic engine that made Budapest famous, and where eighty-three of every hundred of its peoples lived in 1900. Imagine a Paris where the inhabitants of the Latin Quarter, of Montparnasse and—more important—of the Faubourg St-Germain had translated themselves to the other bank of the Seine: where *tout Paris,* that is, the men and women who matter, went to live on the *Rive droite.* * There was but one old portion of Pest, and that only partly old: the Inner City, the Fourth District, Belváros, the smallest one. Partly old: because few of the buildings of the Inner City dated before 1800. There was only one architectural monument, the Inner City Church, some of whose walls were truly medieval. In 1900 it was not yet certain whether it would be allowed to exist, since it nearly blocked the entrance of the broadened roadway to the Elizabeth Bridge. (Not until 1910 was the Inner City Church declared a historic building.) Partly old: because one-half of the Fourth District, that between the Elizabeth and Franz Josef bridges, was the older portion of it, and in a stage of slight decay. But the Inner City reflected, as in a microcosm, the Budapest charm. It was a perfect compound of the ingredients of what was old and what was new: on the one hand the rather magnificent apartment houses, shopping streets, clubs, restaurants and hotels, the *confort cossu et moderne;* on the other hand the sights,

*By 1900 the word—or, rather, the abbreviation—"Pest" had become synonymous with Budapest in everyday Hungarian parlance. *"Megyünk Pestre"* ("We're going to Pest") meant "We are going to Budapest."

sounds and airs of an older Danubian commercial city, still inhabited by a solid *vieille bourgeoisie.*

The finest hotels of Budapest were here. The old Archduke
Stephen and The Queen of England had been pulled down. But
along the Danube Corso stood the modern Hungaria and the Carlton and the Bristol. Near the sweeping bridgehead of the Chain
Bridge, the small, jewel-like and partly neobaroque Budapest Ritz
was about to be built, eventually bearing the pompous name of
Dunapalota (Danube Palace). That bridgehead and the large place
before it were marked by recent history. There in September 1848
the Austrian commissioner, Count Lamberg, was torn from his
coach by a Pest mob and hacked to death. Yet less than twenty years
later it was in that square that Franz Josef chose to take the coronation oath as King of Hungary, in a supreme, exotic and colorful
scene of national pride and reconciliation.* On the northern side
of the square stood the neoclassical building of the Hungarian
Academy of Sciences where—again, not unconnected with a royal
gesture of generosity—the great national poet Arany had his sine-
cure as its secretary. In 1900 two impressive, though not really
attractive palaces of finance were rising, that of the First Commercial Bank and of the Gresham Insurance Company. Except for the
small Catholic and aristocratic quarter within the Seventh District,
this was the loyal conservative portion of Pest. (By coincidence,
many of its streets, places, squares and bridges bore the names of
the Habsburg family: Gisela, Maria Valeria, Dorothea, Elizabeth,
Palatine Joseph, etc.) The hotels had their entrances on Maria
Valeria Street. Their terraces stretched out under their awnings
along the Corso, which was the promenade above the lower loading quays of the Danube.

The Corso, with its row of hotel terraces, coffeehouses and restaurants, was high enough over the quays so that the murmur of a
thousand people talking and the music of the bands in the afternoons muffled the clangor and the noise of the wharves, save for
the occasional hooting of a passing steamer and the shorter, shriller

*In 1867 the ceremonies of the coronation were divided between Pest and Buda.
When, in December 1916, the last Emperor-King was crowned in Budapest, the
ceremony took place in Buda only: the necessity of making a special gesture to the
people of Pest no longer existed. Unlike in June 1867, the day of that last
Hungarian coronation was dark and ominous: the weather was ugly, the King's
horse slipped, and the crown nearly fell from the King's head.

hoots announcing the departure of a "propeller."* Farther inland, two squares away, opened the most famous shopping promenade of Budapest, Váci Street. This was a narrow thoroughfare between many kinds of smart shops; another promenade, at times with what Saki would call "a fevered undercurrent of social strivings and snubbings." From Váci Street many older and narrower mews and streets opened up (one of them housing the Vadászkürt, "Hunter's Horn," an old-fashioned inn patronized by the older aristocracy and the higher country gentry on their visits to the capital). Most of the buildings in this part of the Inner City were built between 1810 and 1850. This meant that their façades and proportions were neoclassical and Empire, with none of the late-Biedermeier, early-Victorian or Second-Empire ornamentation. Some of them had fountains in their courtyards, and statues gracing the alcoves and thresholds of their inner stairways, all classical Floras and Venuses. But by 1900, already dozens, if not hundreds, of new buildings stood among them, reflecting the eclectic architectural atmosphere of Budapest. Even at noon, in high summer, the Inner City was a dappled mix of golden sunshine and cool flannel shadows; the predominant colors dark gray and pale yellow, punctuated here and there by linen awnings and the colors of the many flower stalls; the predominant odor that of the peculiar, and perhaps unique, Pest Inner City mix of fresh cool paper-smell and warm burnt coffee-smell, occasionally enriched by a whiff of lilac water (or was it heliotrope?) when passing one of the many barbershops.

Farther south, between the in 1900 still unfinished Elizabeth Bridge and the Franz Josef Bridge, both Váci Street and the broad cobblestoned quay lost their elegance. But it was there that the older Inner City atmosphere was still extant, in houses inhabited by grain dealers, shoemakers, fishmongers, etc., with its acidulous odors of leather and wine—and, in winter, with the agreeable pungency of freshly made sauerkraut, surely not a matter to be sneezed at. Behind the university quarter, which was relatively new in 1900, were some of the small Empire buildings of the high aristocracy, among them their exclusive club, the National Casino. These few assymetrical house blocks of the Inner City District and of the southwestern portion of the otherwise very different Sev-

---

*Later the electric trolley line No. 2 was built along the edge of the Corso, an unfortunate concession to the needs of public transport, in existence even now. It should have been run along the lower quays.

enth, or Elizabeth, District formed what the literati of the city sometimes called the Saint-Sulpice of Budapest because of its occasional palaces owned by some of the great Catholic aristocratic families: Eszterházys, Károlyis, Wenckheims. It had a touch of the Faubourg St-Germain because of its Catholic seminary and its reserved, almost haughty quietude. This portion of the city straddled the Museum Ring, on the south side of which were the shops of numerous antiquarian booksellers, and the end of which debouched into Calvin Square, where stood the largest, though architecturally indifferent Protestant church of Pest.

In 1900 the great general design of Pest had been in existence for nearly thirty years. Its main lines can be described and imagined without much difficulty. There was a broad semicircular sequence of boulevards, starting from the Margaret bridgehead and ending at what in later years would become the bridgehead of a new commercial bridge to the south. This was the three-mile-long Budapest Ring, each part of which bore the name of a Habsburg: Leopold, Theresa, Elizabeth, Joseph, Francis. Within this semicircle was a flatter, more elliptical curve of boulevards running from where the Leopold Ring met the Theresa Ring (at Berlin Square, next to the great West Station) to the Franz Josef Bridge. This inner ring was composed of three portions: the Váci, the Carl and the Museum. All of the Inner City (the Fourth) District and most of the Leopold (the Fifth) District were between this inner ring and the Danube. There was one more dominant feature in this basic outline of an entire city. Imagine this semicircle as if it were the speedometer of an automobile; and now imagine the needle of the speedometer standing at forty. That was the position of the widest boulevard of the city, Andrássy Avenue, cutting a broad swath across the ring of the boulevards. It was meant to be—and to some extent, it resembled—the Champs-Elysées. It was laid out in 1872. Fifteen years later it was lined by an unbroken row of buildings from beginning to end, nearly two miles long.

Andrássy Avenue was typical of the grandiloquent verve of modern Pest. It was wonderfully straight and wide (nearly 140 feet), though not quite as wide as the Champs-Elysées; also, the original idea of flanking it with two tree-lined promenade islands was not followed, except along its eastern third. Underneath it, in a square tunnel, ran the first underground electric subway line of Europe, completed in 1896, with its comfortable yellow coaches, and an inimitable smell of varnished wood and of the ozone of direct-current electricity. (It is perhaps symptomatic, though surely coincidental, that its terminals were next to the most famous pastry shop of Budapest, Gerbeaud's in the Inner City, and near a very well-known restaurant next to the Zoo in the City Park. The original coaches of this Franz Josef Underground Line lasted for eighty years; Gerbeaud's is still in existence.) Starting from the edge of the Inner City, the first portion of Andrássy Avenue was typical of the Central European *Gründerzeit,* the building wave of the prosperous period 1874–90: monumental apartment houses, Germanic-neoclassical rather than Victorian, the palatial mansions of insurance companies and, in 1884, the Budapest Opera House. There were rathskellers, coffeehouses, restaurants, a couple of small theaters; and where Andrássy Avenue crossed the Ring boulevards, at Octagon Square, an array of coffeehouses on the sides of the octagon, with their great plate-glass windows and terraces jutting out on the sidewalks. Then came the less attractive middle section, until another Champs-Elysées feature, the Rond-Point of Budapest, formed another bulge in the avenue. From there the last half-mile of Andrássy Avenue marched straight to a kind of Etoile—without an Arc de Triomphe, but with a semicircular monument commemorating Hungary's kings and heroes—alas, not unlike the grandiloquent and sepulchral Victor Emmanuel monument in Rome, that nineteenth-century period failure.

Beyond that, Andrássy Avenue ended and the City Park, Budapest's Bois de Boulogne, began. But well before the reach of the Bois, on both sides of the Andrássy a villa district had grown up. On that sandy soil where but a few years before 1900 there were hardly more than a few copses of young willow saplings, an eclectic mix of neo-Renaissance, Italianate, Victorian and neobaroque two-story houses appeared, with an occasional Germanic medievalism cropping up here and there. Here lived some of the richest and most respected Hungarian Jewish families, some of the Magyar aristocracy and a few diplomatic families (including that of the Consul-General of Her Britannic Majesty). That these people preferred to live amidst these flat clearings rather than amidst the greenery of the hills of Buda says something about the urbane attractions of Pest in 1900. Farther on, the City Park included a zoo, a castle, a lake with skating in the winter and boating in the summer, a bath, a circus, and a parade of coaches and carriages in between, on Stephanie Avenue. But apart from the few villas and restaurants on Stephanie and Hermine avenues, the City Park was a big, dusty expanse resembling the Retiro in Madrid rather than the Bois de Boulogne in Paris.

Of the ten districts of Budapest we have five more to describe, inhabited by perhaps as many as three-fourths of its population. And we can do this fairly fast because there was not much that was particularly distinguished in these five teeming districts on the Pest side. Relatively—but only relatively—the most interesting among them was the Fifth, the Leopold District, divided by the Leopold Ring into its older and newer portions. The older part was dominated, indeed, overpowered by the enormous Parliament, in 1900 only two years away from its final completion. The other large edifice in that district was the massive Basilica of Pest, begun in the 1850s, Saxon-Germanic and not particularly beautiful. Around the Parliament stood some of the government buildings, ministries and courts, and the apartment houses of the newer bourgeoisie, buildings sometimes reminiscent of Wilhelmian Berlin, except for the many coffeehouses and the very un-Prussian atmosphere of the streets. Some of the more attractive apartment houses came into existence as the Neugebäude—a kind of Austrian Pentagon, a large military building of barracks—was being demolished, and stood around the new squares and in the new streets. In 1900 the Leopold Ring was a kind of urban frontier. Beyond it were brickyards, empty lots, carriage sheds and many big factory chimneys disfiguring the sky. Yet it was there, north of the Leopold Ring, that the city would grow fastest, with entire blocks of new buildings shooting up during the ten years after 1900. On the north side of that Ring the Vigszinház, the Comedy Theatre of Budapest, was already standing (1896)—another pompous building whose stubby exterior, however, did not at all correspond either to its finely proportioned interior or to the sprightly brilliance of the performances of its actors and actresses.

The Theresa, Elizabeth, Joseph and Franz districts—the Sixth, Seventh, Eighth and Ninth, respectively—were a sea of houses, with a teeming population: the Theresa north of Andrássy Avenue, the Elizabeth south of it, between the Andrássy and the Rákóczi, the latter a commercial boulevard, ending at the East railroad station. Jews amounted to about one-third of the Theresa and Elizabeth districts. Elizabeth District was the most crowded of all, with 67.6 inhabitants per house in 1900 (the city average was 44.2). Although there was no ghetto in Budapest, the poorer Jews lived mostly in the ghetto-like streets between Carl and Elizabeth rings (including Király Street, whose population in 1900 was 70 percent Jewish); at the western edge of this portion of the Elizabeth District stood the eclectic, largely Moorish-style Central Synagogue of Pest, built in 1859.*

Except for the many new grand buildings on the Ring, the many coffeehouses and restaurants, two or three of the eighteenth-century small baroque churches (especially the St. Theresa and the St. Roch), the National Theater and Opera, there was little that was remarkable about this portion of the city. Its appearance (as distinct from the aspirations of some of its inhabitants) had nothing romantic about it. Many of its streets were crowded, smelly, dark and sometimes disreputable: they included brothels and the fairly infamous "orpheum" The Blue Cat (patronized, among others, by the Prince of Wales, later Edward VII). In retrospect, parts of Joseph and Franz districts were more interesting in 1900 because they were older. They had a touch of the rural towns of the Hungarian plains, of Danubian and Eastern European cities. There one still found a motley array of old one-story houses, inhabited by various craftsmen: coachmen, bootmakers, tailors, wheelwrights, undertakers, tavern-keepers, bakers and the like. Some of them, especially in Joseph District, were the last remnant of the German artisan population of Pest. Their streets sometimes ended in spacious squares, with acacias and lindens and a few open-air taverns with oleanders in their tubs and good cheap yellow wine from the sandy soil of the Alföld. Unlike in Buda, their habitués consisted only of the locals.

These people were a mix of what may be called, surely with considerable imprecision, lower-middle and upper-lower class. To

---

*The Orczy House—soon to be demolished, north of the Carl Ring—was an enormous tenement building, an original investment of the Counts Orczy (of the high nobility) early in the nineteenth century. By 1900 it had become a sort of unofficial reception center—or, rather, a temporary dwelling place, a veritable warren—for the stream of newly arrived Jews from the eastern provinces of the Austrian Empire. Jérôme Tharaud, that extremely intelligent but also sharply anti-Semitic Frenchman, was appalled as well as fascinated by it; it served as the thematic starting point of his later book, dealing with the Jews of Budapest, entitled *Quand Israël est Roi* (published in Paris in 1921, after the Béla Kun regime had come and gone in Hungary). "These people of the Orczy House," he wrote, "transformed Budapest. From the once small bourgeois and provincial town they made an enormous capital city. One may dislike it, since its styles are a cacophonic mix of iron and brick and concrete; but one must give credit to their energy and to their verve" (p. 42).

the east of them stretched the already vast proletarian sections of Budapest, including the Tenth District, the Stone Quarry (Kőbánya). That was mostly proletarian, studded by the towering chimneys of giant factories, among them the great breweries of Budapest and the municipal slaughterhouses. Flanking them and between them spread and grew the rapidly multiplying iron webbing of the railyards, leading to the railheads of the West and the East stations. Under their smoky glass and iron domes, these were the largest railroad terminals of Eastern and perhaps even of Central Europe, except for the giant German stations of Berlin, Leipzig and Dresden. And beyond them the working-class suburbs in 1900 were growing even faster than the swelling metropolis itself, pulling hundreds of young peasants toward the edge of a great city for the first time in a thousand years. We will not ignore them: but their story belongs to the next chapter, devoted to the description not of a cityscape but of a humanity, to the peoples of Budapest in 1900.

The year 1900 was the world of the day before yesterday. Those who read Stefan Zweig's *The World of Yesterday,* published in 1942, were recipients of sentiments of respect and even nostalgia for the world of Vienna and Europe around 1900. Since that time the respect for bourgeois culture has spread widely, involving the esthetic nerve and eye. Most things that are bourgeois (and Victorian) have gained a reputation not only in Vienna and Budapest, but in London and New York, too. This includes the eclectic buildings of Budapest, and not only because they are period pieces. In the professional, and prosaic, words of recent architectural historians, "the sheer quantity of eclectic buildings provides a feeling of unity absent elsewhere . . . whereas in other cities the excellence of individual buildings dominates the urban scene, in Budapest the urban entity amounts to much more than the sum of its parts: the macroform of the city has become a work of art . . . an urban environment of a richness and variety which it took centuries to achieve elsewhere."

This was not how connoisseurs of buildings saw Budapest in 1900. Yet even at that time its planning and architecture evoked the respect of some of the most famous city planners and architects of the world. The German Stuebben, in his famous *Städtebau* (1907), described it as a "model city." He particularly admired the Budapest Council of Public Works (Közmunkatanács, established in 1870), which was modeled, to some extent, on the London Metropolitan Board of Works. In 1901 a United States government commission that was studying the redesign of Washington, D.C., came to visit six of the most important cities of Europe: Budapest was among them. It included the most eminent of American architects: Daniel Burnham, Charles F. McKim and Frederick Olmsted.

The eclectic presence is easy to justify. This was, after all, the end of the nineteenth century when many factors (romanticism, a consciousness of history, the rise of the moneyed classes) produced architectural eclecticism all over the world—neo-Gothic churches, neo-Romanesque country houses, neo-Egyptian railroad stations. In Budapest the neoclassical and neo-Renaissance styles continued to predominate until well beyond the middle of the century. Because of this, most buildings in Budapest escaped the excesses of early Victorianism (which was not true of some of the private villas). The works of the great architect Mihály Pollack were designed in a calm Empire style. The Chain Bridge was neoclassical, too, dominating the city more than any other architectural achievement. With the Redoute (Vigadó), built by F. Feszl in the late 1850s, began the eclectic period of public architecture in Budapest. By the end of the century eclecticism was not only represented by a variety of individual buildings; its various elements were incorporated within single buildings, here and there. But then the same thing was true of Vienna and Paris at the time. Unlike in Paris— but, *mutatis mutandis,* not unlike in Vienna, Barcelona, Madrid and Lisbon—Hungarian eclecticism included the neo-baroque style, too, for which Hungarians had a particular national as well as aristocratic attraction (we must keep in mind that in 1900 the word "baroque," in French and English, still had a pejorative connotation).

The architecture of Budapest, though not its city planning, lagged behind Vienna (and behind much of Western Europe and Scandinavia) in modernism. By 1900 in Vienna, Munich, Brussels, Paris, Barcelona, etc. the breaking away from a long architectural tradition had begun; indeed, the votaries and creators of *Jugendstil,* Art Nouveau and *Sezession* were out in force. In Budapest this would not happen until a few years after the turn of the century. The first eclectic-secessionist building in Pest was that of the Gresham Insurance Company. Between 1903 and 1906 came

Ödön Lechner's Postal Savings Bank, his Geological Institute and his Museum of Industrial Arts. Some of these buildings, as well as the interesting apartment house on Szervita (now Martinelli) Place in the Inner City, incorporated a unique Hungarian pyrogranite frost-resistant ceramic facing and siding, manufactured by the famous Zsolnay porcelain factory; but generally (at least in my opinion) Lechner's nationalist secessionism amounts to an interesting footnote in the architectural history of Budapest, not more. Some of it is reminiscent of Gaudí's churrigueresque and bizarre eccentricities in Barcelona and not of the determined simplifications of the Vienna modernists Loos and Hoffmann. It was not until 1910–11 that the first impressively modern buildings appeared in some of the Budapest side streets. Their architects were Béla Lajta and Károly Kós, who (again, in my opinion) deserve to be better known.

In 1900 a peculiarity of the public architecture of Budapest was its monumentalism. Peculiarity, because the tendency to the colossal was not typical of Hungarian architecture either before or after the turn of the century. But at that time it was in full—if perhaps unfortunate—accord with the trend of the times: with the excessive and grandiloquent outbursts of Hungarian national pride. Its ingredients were a strangely optimistic (strangely, because the Magyar national character inclines to pessimism, not optimism) and also understandably (but perhaps not excusably) myopic feeling of Hungarian omnipotence. The enormous financial outlays for these monuments of architecture were, again, consequences rather than causes of prevalent sentiments. In 1895 the largest stock exchange in Europe (or perhaps even in the entire world) was built in Budapest, an extremely ugly pile of a building designed by Ignác Alpár; yet the volume of trade in the Budapest exchange did not come close to that of Vienna, for example. When the plans for the enormous new Parliament building were first presented in the old House of Deputies in 1883, the otherwise thrifty, careful and puritanical Prime Minister, Kálmán Tisza, pronounced that in this case "there must be no place for caution, calculation and thrift." As the symbol for the constitution of Hungary, the Parliament building must be monumental and resplendent "to the eyes of our friends and foes alike." Indeed, when Imre Steindl's Parliament was completed in 1902, it was the largest parliament building in the entire world—and an eclectic combination of Magyar-medieval,

French-Renaissance, Westminsterian neo-Gothic, with a neobaroque ground plan, and much polychrome inside. It had no less
than twenty-seven gates; eighty-four pounds of twenty-two-carat
gold were used in its decoration. Oddly enough, it has not proved
to be a failure. More than eighty years later it still "fits" very well
into the Budapest cityscape; architecturally it has stood the test of
time.*

Many of the monumental buildings (and apartment houses) completed around 1900 were similar to those of the Berlin of William
II, whether consciously or unconsciously. This was true of the large
building of the Palace of Justice (Kúria), completed in the Millennium Year of 1896, across from the Parliament, with its two stun-
ningly ugly Wilhelmian square towers; and of the the edifices
erected by the team of F. Korbl and K. Giergl, for example, the
twin Clothilde Palaces (1899–1901). Because of the palaces' relative narrowness, allowing for the breadth of the roadway flanking
the approach to the new Elizabeth Bridge,† the vista and the perspective they allowed remains commendable; the two buildings are
not. Something of the same was true of the Comedy Theatre (Vigszinház; 1896), with its chunky Leipzig look. Meanwhile, a lot of
demolition was going on in Budapest—some of it necessary, some
not. The first includes the gradual razing of the Neugebäude; the
second that of the old City Hall in 1900.

The rebuilding and addition to the Royal Castle (Alajos Hauszmann) began in 1896 and was finished in 1905. This was Austro-
Hungarian, rather than German, in its style. To the north of it, the
neo-Romanesque Fishermen's Bastion on the parapets of Castle
Hill, startlingly sepulchral-white in 1902, proved to be a strange
but enduring success. Between 1892 and 1896 the Coronation

---

*Tharaud in 1899: " . . . newly built on the model of Westminster on the banks
of the Danube, by those Hungarian architects, with their bizarre passion for
medievalism, without reason." But Patrick Leigh Fermor, in 1934: "Built at the
turn of the century and aswarm with statues, this frantic and marvellous pile was
a tall, steep-roofed gothic nave escorted for a prodigious length by medieval
pinnacles touched with gilding and adorned by crockets; and it was crowned, at
the point where its transepts intersected, by the kind of ribbed and egg-shaped
dome that might more predictably have dominated the roofs of a Renaissance town
in Tuscany, except that the dome itself was topped by a sharp and bristling gothic
spire. Architectural dash could scarcely go further."
†Completed in 1902, it was then the largest single-span bridge in the world.

(Matthias) Church was not only rebuilt but substantially enlarged, in a neo-Gothic style, again somewhat Germanic in inspiration, as was its heavily polychromed interior, an unhappy combination of somber dark spaces and sometimes strident colors. While the early-Empire and yellow-stuccoed Sándor Palace, the residence and office of the Prime Minister on Castle Hill, remained modestly beautiful, the palace of the Ministry of Finance (S. Fellner) was monumental and eclectic, only second in height to the Coronation Church.

By the 1890s the influence of German finance and commerce had replaced the French influences of two decades before, when not only some of the fledgling Budapest banks and the railroads had been financed by Paris banks but when the Margaret Bridge (Emile Gouin, 1878) and the West Station (De Serres, 1874–78) were built by French architects of the Gustave Eiffel school. West Station was the largest railroad station in Europe before 1880, when the Berlin Anhalter Station surpassed it in size. Another Germanic feature in the cityscape of Budapest was the sudden burgeoning of statues and monuments. For once we may trace the original source of that impulse—which, to be sure, corresponded with the national inclinations of the time—directly. In 1897 William II visited Budapest in the company of Franz Josef. He was impressed by the flourishing city, but that voluble monarch was also compelled to remark that there were few statues, *Denkmäler,* around. The press took up that imperial intimation, and Franz Josef gave 400,000 crowns from his privy purse to the city of Budapest for the purpose of commissioning ten statues of historical significance.* Thereafter came the sudden prodigious peopling of the places and squares of the city with statues and monuments of Hungarian historical figures (and of two non-Hungarians: Eugene of Savoy and George Washington). Whereas during the forty-five years before 1896 twenty-

---

*In 1899 a significant relocation of a monument took place. The monument commemorating General Hentzi, in one of the fine squares of Castle Hill, had stuck in the throats of Hungarians for nearly fifty years. Hentzi was the Austrian defender of the fortress of Buda against the independent Magyar army in 1849; he fell in the siege; the monument was erected in his memory by the then victorious Austrians. In 1899 Franz Josef agreed, probably reluctantly, to have it removed to the inner park of a cadet school in one of the outer Buda districts. There it remained, unlamented and invisible.

six statues had been erected in Buda and Pest, of which more than half were of modest size, from 1896 to 1910 no fewer than thirty-seven appeared.

It must not be thought, therefore, that in 1900 the cityscape was altogether disfigured by ephemeral and monumental period pieces. The Parliament, Elizabeth Bridge, Royal Castle, etc. were true architectural achievements. They have not only "grown" on the city to a state of eventual agreeableness, like golden fungi on trees or green patina on copper roofs. There were, for example, the fine buildings of the architect Miklós Ybl, foremost among them the Budapest Opera House, completed in 1884, near-perfect in its appearance as well as in its interior, and even in the modesty of its perspective—merely and properly set back from the row of houses on Andrássy Avenue but by a few dozen feet, with the result of a perfectly harmonious setting. Knowledgeable people concluded then, as now, that this opera house surpassed in beauty Garnier's in Paris as well as the Vienna Opera. It was smaller than the famous Vienna *Oper* by two hundred seats, but its interior design was better. It also had more modern equipment: fire curtains and a metal backstage inspired by the then recent memory of the disastrous fire of Semper's beautiful oval-shaped opera house in Dresden. It was also the only authentic opera building in Central Europe at the time, since both the famous Vienna and Dresden opera houses that had been destroyed or damaged by fire were reconstructions.

One of the aspects of the late nineteenth century, evident in many of the surviving photographs, is the relative absence of crowds. Ortega y Gasset began his twentieth-century classic, *The Revolt of the Masses,* with that observation. He must have remembered Barcelona or Madrid; and his observation is amply documented by the photographs of Budapest, too, around 1900. Yet Ortega's point was not universally valid. Photographs as early as 1880 show us large crowds and tremendous traffic jams in London, New York, Chicago and Paris. Why do we have relatively few pictorial evidences of large crowds and traffic jams (except, of course, for great mass gatherings on ceremonial occasions) in Budapest, in that fastest-growing and already very crowded city in Europe? One element is the relative thinness of its vehicular traffic, compared to London, Paris and Berlin at the time. There is also some evidence that the photographers of its street scenes preferred to take their pictures at hours of the day when their projected vistas were relatively open, free of many people. But these are not sufficient explanations. What we may gather from all kinds of evidence, including the prose and the reminiscences of sensitive writers of the time, is something like this: the crowding of Budapest was there in the houses rather than in the streets, it was interior rather than exterior. Except for some of the promenades, people spent a large amount of their time indoors.

On one level the modern building boom of Budapest was such that at times people spoke of the "American" Budapest.* "American tempo" was a journalistic cliché at the time. But on another level city life in Budapest and life in America could not have been more different, save perhaps for the tenement dwellers in New York; but even in Manhattan, with its tenements and apartment houses, people had more space than their social counterparts in Budapest. In 1900 families who owned their houses in Budapest and lived in them were a very small portion of the population. Most people, except on the highest and the lowest reaches of the social pyramid, rented apartments.

That was not peculiar to Budapest in 1900; it was so in most large cities of the continent, from Madrid to Moscow. There was the frequent combination of businesses, stores, shops and apartments in many of these houses, especially in the better districts: shops or stores on the ground floor, offices sometimes on the first floor, and apartments higher up. (As a consequence of this, too, the definite separation of business from residential districts, so typical of American and English cities, did not exist, except for the villa districts, with their houses surrounded by small gardens.) There was an enormous difference in the place, size and comforts of apartments in the newer houses. They ranged from veritable palatial apart-

---

*A famous building bore the name New-York. This was somewhat unusual at a time when hotels, restaurants, etc. all over Europe still had a predilection for French and English names. There were dozens of Hotel Bristols in Europe at that time (why Bristol?) and hundreds of "Londons." (The most respected German newspaper in Budapest, a kind of combination of the *Wall Street Journal* and *Neue Freie Presse,* bore the title *Neues Pester Journal.*) In Kolozsvár, too (the greatest city of Transylvania), the best and most famous hotel and restaurant bore the name New-York. A lower-class neighborhood in the Eighth District of Budapest, infested here and there by the criminal element, was called Chicago (Csikágó) in Budapest argot—not because of its population but because of its fast construction.

ments, with *enfilades* and galleries, spread across entire floors of large buildings, to foul-smelling cramped warrens, mostly in the Sixth, Seventh, Eighth, Ninth and Tenth districts, hardly different from a Whitechapel or a Lower East Side tenement, the way "the other half" (and, in Budapest, more than half) lived. But unlike in London or New York, there was relatively little moving about in dynamic Budapest. Once a family found their dwelling place, they would stay there,* even when the extent and speed of the Budapest building boom was at its peak. The number of buildings had doubled in twenty-five years, from 1869 to 1894. In 1895 alone, 595 new apartment houses were built containing 12,783 rooms. In this respect, too, 1900 is an appropriate benchmark. The year 1899 had been a turning point in the construction boom; after that the pace of building began to slow down. During the next six years 775 new houses were built, although containing more and more rooms.

Whatever the shortcomings of these apartment houses, they were not ramshackle buildings. The speculators, builders and contractors could not get past the regulations of the Council of Public Works. These building regulations were the strictest in Europe. Among other things, they allowed no exceptions about the minimum and maximum plot sizes, setbacks and heights of buildings. Consequently few new buildings were more than five stories high. All of the "Americanism" of Budapest notwithstanding, there were no high-rise buildings, let alone skyscrapers. Hence the cliché "a sea of houses," especially when seen from the Buda side, was fitting.

The plan of many of these apartment houses resembled that of most Central European cities. They were rectangular or quadrangular, built more often than not around an inner courtyard. Behind the portal door (locked at night) was the janitor's lodge, under the doorway. The stairways were often wastefully wide, though perhaps not only for esthetic reasons: there was no other way to haul large pieces of furniture to the upper floors. Often there was a

---

*Here is another example suggesting the insufficiency of legal categories and of economic statistics. Renters of apartments acquired a sense of permanent possession that was often as strong—and longer-lasting—than that of an American home-owner. My maternal grandparents lived in the same apartment for almost sixty years, 1892 to 1951, through two world wars, a siege of Budapest, three foreign occupations, two Communist regimes and two revolutions. My paternal grandparents lived in a large apartment of their family house for sixty-three years, 1868 to 1931.

second, dark and narrow stairway called the servants' stairs. A peremptory sign was posted at the entrance: "For servants and porters the use of the main stairway is forbidden." The best, and largest, apartments were usually on the first or second floors above ground level, with their doors opening from the stair landing. Cheaper apartments were usually farther up, often entered from the courtyard side, along the open iron-railed gangways. In most cases, a narrow entrance hall was flanked by a closet and lavatory on one side, and by the kitchen on the other. Behind the kitchen was the miserably cramped cubicle for the cook or domestic servant, with a window opening at a dark and dank light shaft, and sometimes without a window at all. (In many lower-middle-class apartments that was missing: the maid slept in the kitchen.) The drawing or living rooms were the most spacious, invariably looking out on the street. Bedrooms were small, as were bathrooms. Of course there were many exceptions to this rough, and surely imprecise, sketch of a layout. Yet it was fairly typical of the apartment buildings erected between 1865 and 1914. The differences consisted in their sizes, locations and appointments. Many middle-class apartments consisted of not more than one living room, one bedroom and kitchen; entire families lived there, with the children sleeping in an alcove or on sofas in the same bedroom with their parents. The existence of a separate children's room often marked the difference between the upper and lower middle classes. The richer, more elegant apartments along the Danube, on the squares of the Inner City, along the first section of Andrássy Avenue, in the villa districts and in some places in Buda, had a minimum of four rooms, and sometimes seven or eight. Doctors, lawyers and important businessmen usually combined their apartments with their offices, seldom with a separate entrance. A well-trained chambermaid would lead patients or clients to the family father's receiving room during his appointed office hours, customarily in the afternoon.

The existence of at least one live-in maid was the division separating middle-class and lower-class families. In 1900 that division line corresponded, by and large, to three rooms. Slightly more than 50 percent of domestic employees lived with families whose apartments had three rooms or more. A surprisingly large proportion (36 percent) of two-room families still employed a maid. In the lower-class districts, the Seventh to the Tenth, overcrowding was endemic and at times horrifying. There were often four or more people living in a single room. In 1893 the city authorities declared that unhygienic overcrowding meant any room harboring more than four people. In 1869 the average room in Budapest harbored 3.2 persons; in 1900, 2.6. At that time there were more than 200,000 inhabitants of Budapest living in such conditions, and municipal housing had not really begun. The incomes of the slum landlords were often larger than those of more palatial real estate.

As late as 1900 the interior décor of the houses and apartments of Budapest was, by and large, not very different from the Viennese décor of the time. Even in the palaces of the magnates, there was nothing very special about the furniture, save perhaps for the opulence of the silver and crystal table settings. The pompous dining room of the Károlyis' palace seems not much more than a replica of those in the mansions of the European aristocratic families (or even of the newer industrial magnates) in Paris or London, or in some of the older princely cities of Germany. Except for ancient family portraits in oil, the quality of the paintings on the walls was not exceptional. Because of their high, often beautifully stuccoed or coffered ceilings, the mansions of the magnates gave an airier impression than those of the bourgeoisie (but the ceilings of the apartments of the latter, too, were high and elaborately stuccoed, at least around their corners). The impression of an upper-middle-class interior in Budapest in 1900 corresponds to late-Victorian styles, stuffed and heavy. And the same thing was true of the interiors of many public places. The nobly proportioned rooms of the National Casino (the club of the old aristocracy) do not seem to have been crowded, whereas the coffeehouses were, indeed, at many hours of the day. We get the same impression from the surviving photographs of the restaurants, rathskellers, beer halls and confiseries of that time. It is perhaps significant that in 1900, 60 percent of the coffeehouses in Budapest were in the districts inhabited mostly by the middle-middle and lower-middle classes.

In 1900 many of the sidewalls of the city were disfigured by enormous advertisements with bizarre large letterings. Meanwhile, one of the attractive characteristics of the streets of Budapest was beginning to disappear: the variety of its shop signs. A remnant of the earlier custom of a now vanishing century,* these often pretty

---

*In 1900 there was only one large department store in Budapest, the Parisian (damaged by fire three years later); but the Les Halles of Budapest, the central food market, was already in existence, largely unchanged even now.

and imaginatively crafted wrought-iron and gilt signs enlivened the streets, especially in the Inner City, Castle Hill and Water districts. In those narrow streets they were not only indicators to the different shops; they lent a charming, individual, old-fashioned, inviting quality because of their various designs and various heights, in summer among the window boxes of red geraniums, in autumn creaking in the wind, and rimmed by snow in winter. There is now only one street in Europe where the city fathers have chosen to preserve them, in the Getreidegasse in Salzburg, which, however, is an early eighteenth-century European town and not, like Budapest, a nineteenth-century one.

I n 1900 Budapest was the destination for most of the foreign visitors to Hungary. Tourism to Hungary was only in its beginnings, amounting to about 130,000 visitors in 1895. It nearly doubled by 1912: 250,000. (Ninety years later the annual number of visitors would amount to perhaps 10 million—to a Hungary two-thirds smaller than before World War I, besides being governed by an official Communist regime, with its consequent restrictions of frontier and visa requirements.) In 1900 there were about fifty hotels, of all kinds, in Budapest. In 1902 the first new type of a modern pension appeared.

Many of these visitors were attracted to the pleasantness of a modern city and to the agreeableness of its site. Elsewhere in Hungary—especially in Transdanubia, in the mountain regions of Upper Hungary and in Transylvania—there were many pretty, old provincial towns, often still partly medieval, but in 1900 that was not where travelers were drawn. Like Paris (rather than Berlin), Budapest was the central hub of the national railroad network. The express trains from Vienna (and the Orient-Express), equipped with a comfortable dining car, reached Budapest in four hours and forty minutes. (This rail journey took four hours in 1987.) Beginning in 1892, the reforms of the Minister of Transportation, Gábor Baross, led to a very rapid extension of the national railroad network (and also to a new, cheaper schedule of fares). The railroad mileage had grown from 7,025 miles in 1890 to 10,632 in 1900, and the number of locomotives from 1,680 to 2,917. By 1900 all of the locomotives were being built by the Hungarian state engine factory. In 1900 one of these won first prize at the Paris World Fair. The Hungarian National Railroads (MÁV) were separate from

Austria, and 85 percent of the lines were those of the MÁV. The rail density of Hungary (in length of track per 100,000 people) came just after France, ahead of Austria, and even of the great railroad network of imperial Germany. Accordingly, the passenger traffic increased nearly seventeen-fold during the thirty years before 1900. There was a phenomenal increase in freight traffic, too: from 3 million tons in 1866 to 275 million in 1894. As was the case almost everywhere else in Europe at the time, there were three classes for coach passengers (in Wilhelmian Germany there were four). The two great terminals, the West and the East stations, were, as we have seen, among the largest and most modern ones in Europe, completed in 1878 and 1883, respectively. Their external platforms, sidings and branch tracks were constantly being extended, nearly doubling in ten years, in part because of the increasing traffic of commuters. The commuter rail line (HÉV), independent of the national system, began in 1888. In 1900 it sold 3 million tickets. From 1896 to 1913 it became electrified, and its traffic increased thirteenfold.

By 1900 Budapest had become the largest port on the nearly 2,000-mile stretch of the Danube. The national fluvial transportation company (MFTR) overtook the Austrian DGT in volume. River transport was cheaper than rail transport, both for passengers and freight. There was a pleasant overnight trip from Vienna to Budapest on the large white-painted paddle steamers; the cabins of First Class were very commodious. The increase of freight traffic to and from the Balkans was also due to the regulation of the Iron Gate narrows on the lower Danube in 1896. The Danube boats were interesting to watch. Their funnels were slightly angled and hinged since they had to be bowed down to pass under the bridges. The funnels of the freight steamers were higher than was customary at the time; the silhouettes of the passenger boats were portly and broad-hipped. Except for the earlier mentioned "propellers" ferrying passengers to and from Buda and Pest, they were paddlewheeled. The barges were pulled rather than pushed. Shortly after 1900 the construction of a large freight harbor, with docks primarily for the purpose of loading and unloading agricultural goods, began to the south of Pest.

Automobiles were still rare in 1900. The old Vienna-Budapest highway was only partly paved. The first motorcar (a Benz, owned by a visitor) puttered along the streets of Pest in 1895. By 1905 there were 159 private automobiles, and the construction of the Hungarian-made Marta taxis had begun. Some of the private automobiles were electric ones: high-wheeled, boxy, resembling elegant hansom cabs, with tufted plush seats and small glass vases affixed to the interior window frames, usually holding a single rose. (One of these, the electric car of the president of the First Commercial Bank, Leó Lánczy, graced—if that is the word—the streets of Budapest for nearly forty years: a trademark of sorts.) In 1896–97 János Csonka, an excellent engineer, designed small electric cars for the Budapest postal service. In 1900 the Royal Hungarian Automobile Club (KMAC) was founded. Of course, most of the private traffic in 1900 was still horse-drawn. It consisted of private carriages, licensed and numbered one-horse and two-horse hack coaches (the *konflis, fiáker*), and unnumbered ones. In 1904 there were 856 one-horse, 456 two-horse and 539 unnumbered carriages. The last were the most expensive ones, hired not only for special occasions but by people who were loath to give the impression that they did not possess a private carriage of their own.* On Sundays, except in midwinter, the smartly curving Stephanie Avenue in the City Park was the place for the carriage corso, not unlike that of Hyde Park in London. The equipage and the occasional mounts of the aristocracy and of some of the upper classes were espied and followed with great interest by the assembled families of the carriageless and horseless.

The first electric streetcar ran along a half-mile stretch of the Ring, starting from the West Station, in 1887. By 1900 electric trolleys had replaced almost all of the horsecars. The total length of electric trolley lines grew from 110 miles in 1896 to nearly 200 miles by 1905. The upper classes eschewed these, perhaps because of their frequent crowdedness, unwilling to rub elbows with the proletarians of the city (trolley fares were cheap). Exceptions for their limitations of patronage were the lines running to the outer districts of the city, the elevated lines to Castle Hill, the cogwheel

---

*It is interesting, and perhaps significant, that left-side drive was the rule in Hungary (until 1941, when the German military requested that it be changed to the right). This may have been yet another result of the wish to assert Magyar independence from Austria; and there were Hungarians who argued that it was a natural consequence of the habit of Hungarian horsemen, whose sabers and scabbards hung on the left, to be lifted by the right arm when needed.

railway to the Svábhegy, and the earlier mentioned, spacious, clean and comfortable Franz Josef underground line.

By 1900 most of the public services of Budapest, including its public transportation, were already municipally owned, governed and financed. Budapest, like Vienna, was served by city waterworks that produced truly excellent water. In 1899, for the first time, *all* of Budapest had been piped for municipal water. This was a great change from earlier decades, when the filtration of the water of the Danube, especially in Pest, was insufficient and unsanitary. (As late as 1888 there had been a small typhoid epidemic in Budapest.) The quality of the Budapest drinking water was so good that by the 1890s some of the companies bottling the celebrated mineral spring waters of Buda and of Margaret Island decided to shift their marketing to exports. Indeed, unlike in many other European cities, mineral water was disappearing from the daily tables of Budapest, save when its bottles were meant to accompany wines. The average inhabitant's consumption of water increased considerably, from 157 liters per person in 1896 to 231 liters in 1910.

In 1900 most of the streets, houses and rooms of Budapest were still gaslit. Around dusk the lamplighters, with their long poles, were a common sight on the pavements. The purification and densification of piped gas had made progress, which was a great help for housewives and their cooks. Gas-fired stoves and ranges in the kitchens had begun to replace the dirtier and more laborious coal-fired ones; gas-fired hot-water tanks (so-called geysers) were installed in the more modern apartment houses. The first electric streetlights appeared in Pest as early as 1873. Electric lighting took a great surge upward during the glamorous illuminations of the Millennium exhibition. In 1900 the ratio of private electric light to gaslight was one to four; and it was not until 1909 that electric streetlighting replaced the gaslights in most streets. The city electric power stations were thoroughly modern at that time, even in the design of their architecture. The municipal fire service of Budapest was excellent. The city suffered no serious fires for over a decade. The number of mailboxes doubled in the decade before 1900; the increase of letter traffic was very considerable (from 3.6 million in 1895 to 14.2 million in 1913). The first telephone in Budapest was installed in 1881 (its inventor, Tivadar Puskás, was highly esteemed by Thomas Edison). He invented, too, a telephone news-and-music service, a kind of forerunner of radio: begun in 1893 with 500 subscribers, by 1900 it numbered 6,437 (the peak number). By 1890 long-distance calls to Vienna were possible; by 1900 such connections were extended to Berlin. Private subscribers were still few, about 6,000. (By 1913 there were more than 27,000).

Mention must be made of a fairly unusual municipal service, the city ambulance corps (Mentők), reliable and much respected to this day. Its establishment was a consequence of the tremendous improvement of the standards of medical training in Budapest, where the medical school of the university had come up to the highly reputed standards of Vienna. There was much progress in public health services, including the standards of medical care and of medical equipment in the public hospitals of the city. At the same time, the middle and upper classes depended much less on hospitals than on the services and house calls of family doctors; and such house calls were available to all classes of the population. When the middle and upper class people needed operations or more intensive medical care, they took a room in a private sanatorium.

To this general and statistical portrait of the progress of municipal services in 1900 belongs mention of the establishment of public comfort stations in Budapest. They were serviced by old women, public employees who were in charge of the cleaning and of the keys to the private toilet booths, dependent on a pittance of a municipal salary and on tips. These sheet-metal pavilions, invariably painted pea green, were more private than the *vespasiennes* of Paris. Tar paint was applied to their urinals, attempting to drench, or at least overcome, the foul smell of their interiors, usually with indifferent results. There were thirty-two of them in 1893 and fifty in 1902, often hidden among the trees and copses of the public squares.

The year 1900 was a turning point for Hungary and for Budapest.* But we can see this only in retrospect. No one knew then what was to come: that the outbreak of the Great War in 1914 would mark the end of an era for Hungary and Budapest that had begun around the time of the Compromise of 1867. It was then that

---

*Its "noon hour" was literally that: from the Citadella a cannon shot marked the exact noontime every day, at a time when public clocks in the streets of Budapest were still few and not always dependable.

the glorious rise and prosperity of the city began—another illustration of the condition that material prosperity is a consequence of
psychic, social and political climates, rather than the reverse. Two-
thirds of this 1867–1914 period had passed by 1900. The seeds of
troubles were already there—socially, politically, psychologically.
They had begun to appear in the 1890s, somewhere near the half-
mark of those forty-seven years. Yet historical life has its momentum: the self-confident progress went on with increasing speed,
largely unaware of the turn of the road; and so it was only a few
years after 1900 that the speed began to slacken somewhat and all
kinds of troubles had grown enough to appear on the surface. The
still largely untroubled climate of Budapest in 1900 reflected the
generally still prevalent confidence of its leading classes. But only
a few years after 1900 the symptoms of a malaise—in the literal
meaning of the word, an uneasy ill feeling—began to clutch at the
hearts of people. It was there in national and city politics: by 1904
at the latest, the difficult, though generally accepted, equilibrium of
the Compromise was broken. We can glimpse this from the rhetorical question posed by Prime Minister István Tisza in the Parliament, in 1904: "Just contrast the picture of our country in 1866
with that of 1896! Thirty years of such flourishing, such growth,
such increase of material, spiritual, moral and intellectual capital!
Should it be so easy to tear out such thirty years from the life of a
nation?" The tone of this statement was not plaintive—Tisza was
too severe a character for that—but it was censorious, as well as
regretful; and that regret already depended on the perspective of
retrospect.

In sum, the grounds for optimism were no longer solid, even
though material progress was continuing. And that progress was
still considerable. Within Hungary at large, the main national prod-
uct, wheat, was more than double in 1900 what it had been thirty
years earlier; the yields per acre had doubled, too; so had the cattle
population. What happened by 1900 was that Budapest finance had
caught up with the growth of agricultural and industrial production.
In the 1870s many of the capital investments in Budapest (and the
industries of Hungary at large) still depended on Parisian and
Viennese banks; but high finance had come to Budapest by 1900,
so that Budapest had become the banking center of Eastern Europe.
The number of Hungarian banks alone increased from eleven in
1867 to more than 160 in 1900. During the same period their
capitalization increased fivefold. Some of these banks, such as the

First Hungarian Commercial and the Hungarian Credit Bank, were now in the same league with the great Central European financial institutions—as indeed their palatial buildings showed. Savings institutions grew, too, from twenty-nine in 1867 to 455 in 1890. Sixty percent of the machine industry of the country was in Budapest. Some of these were very modern: the Ganz factory, for example, was well known in Europe; its manufactures included the first electric railroad engine in the world, delivered to the Valtellina railroad in northern Italy. The number of industrial establishments, ranging from small machine shops to the great Manfréd Weiss works,* more than doubled during the four years from 1896 to 1900 alone (from 11,796 to 28,980); the number of industrial workers in Budapest rose accordingly, from 63,000 to 100,000 within four years, and to 177,000 during the following decade.

Before 1900 Budapest was the largest city of mills in the entire world. (In that year Minneapolis passed it.) Wheat from the great plains of Hungary and the grain products of the Balkans were turned into flour in the great mills of Budapest. But many of the successful entrepreneurs who had begun their careers as grain traders earlier in the nineteenth century and then become founders and owners of the mills were switching their interests, enterprises and capital to other investments around 1900. The Hungarian export of flour, predominant in Europe in the 1870s, was beginning to decline, even though after 1900 its volume and its destinations were still impressive. (Among other things, Hungary was the main exporter of flour to Brazil!) This was generally the case for other agricultural products, too. The big slaughterhouses of the Tenth District suffered from a plague of hog fever around 1900, and the phylloxera ravaged the vineyards of Buda in the 1880s. By 1900 these damages were recovered. In 1896 Hungarian exports were still three times those of 1874. But after 1900 the rate of this progress began to diminish.

There was compensation for this for Budapest, rather than for Hungary at large. The growing population of the city meant an increase of consumers; production followed consumption and producers consumers. Thus the agricultural ring around Budapest went on growing, despite the transformation of the city into an

---

*By 1913 the Manfréd Weiss works alone employed more than 5,000 workers; among other products, they exported munitions to Spain, Mexico, Great Britain and other countries.

industrial metropolis. The vineyards within the municipal boundaries still grew, from 355 acres in 1900 to 401 acres in 1910, even
though by 1900 few families of Pest owned their own vineyards in
Buda, a custom that had been prevalent as late as 1890. Into the
outer districts of the city a new agricultural population was coming.
Hundreds of thousands of peasants were leaving their villages in
search of better fortunes in the ring around Budapest. Some of
them went to work in the factories, a country-to-city migration that
was typical of the nineteenth century throughout Europe, though
this happened in Hungary later than in Western Europe; but many
of them worked to produce and sell vegetables, fruits and other
foods for the people of the new metropolis. This new increase of
the population had a definite effect on the demography of the city.
Even more than in other cities at that time, Budapest had not only
spread out along concentric circles, but the farthest suburbs (except
for the residential villa districts) were often those of the poorest
people. From 1890 to 1910 the population of Hungary increased
by nearly 20 percent, of Budapest by 79 percent, and of its suburbs
by nearly 238 percent. It was thus that from the Great Compromise
to the Great War, from 1867 to 1914, Budapest was the fastest-
growing city in Europe, even though after 1900 the birthrate of its
population had slowed down.

I t was a European city. No Viennese would say in 1900 what
Metternich had suggested eighty-five years earlier, that Hungary
belonged to the "Orient." For a Viennese to go to Buda or to Pest
in, say, 1820, was an expedition. By 1900 a Viennese who had
some business in Budapest found it pleasant to go there, especially
in the summer. He may have been critical of Budapest, and of
Hungarian politics (as Viennese often were), but the criticism
would contain elements of respect and perhaps even of jealousy.
There were comforts and pleasures to be had in that city that were
at least equal to those of Vienna; prices were somewhat cheaper;
and their sojourn would be seasoned with a peculiar spice of Hungarianness, including a pungent soupçon of paprika. When in the
eighteenth or nineteenth century a traveler from Greece or the
Balkans was packing his bags to travel northwest, to Trieste or to
Vienna, he would say, "I am going to Europe." In 1900 he might
have said the same when going to Budapest.

It was, at least in some sense, a cosmopolitan city—and not only because of its hotels and restaurants but because so many of the people foreign travelers would meet spoke the languages of Europe. Most people knew German and many people spoke some French. This was not only due to the loneliness of the Magyar language, which has no relative among the great families of European languages, whence the frequent linguistic abilities of Hungarians; it was also due to the cultural appetites of the generations around 1900 and to the requirements of *bon ton* among the upper classes.

In 1900 Hungary, and Budapest, had an unusually good reputation in England. But some people saw things differently. Harold Nicolson was a small child when he was brought to Budapest by his father, who had been appointed Consul-General there in 1888. Harold's memories were vivid. "He certainly remembered the Budapest Legation [it was a Consulate-General] in Andrássy Avenue, a little house with a statue of Flora or Pomona in the pediment of the street front, and a terra cotta fountain in the garden. . . . He remembered how with white knitted gloves he would brush the first snow from the privet hedges which lined the alleys at the entrance to the public park, and how, beside the benches of the park, in the dark Danubian air which smelled of sulphur springs and yellow leaves, he would pick up and suck the little cardboard holders through which the Hungarians smoked their cigarettes. He remembered the tall, black water-tower at the end of the Avenue [in reality, it was farther out, at the end of Stephanie Avenue] round which the autumn gales howled, bringing cold, fear and sadness to little boys. He remembered the screech and clang of the trams as they rounded the corner; the doleful wail of factory-sirens at bed-time, and the interminable wind of the great bridge which led to Buda. He remembered too the scarlet devils of St. Nikolaus chasing each other round the cornice of his bedroom, when he lay ill with typhoid." He wrote about these things more than fifty years later in the London *Spectator,* in an article that was severely critical, indeed, condemnatory, of Hungary and Hungarians. In this Harold Nicolson followed his father. In his superb diplomatic biography of Lord Carnock, the former Arthur Nicolson, he wrote in 1930 that the four years that his father spent in Hungary "were four years of boredom. The stupidity of the Magyar aristocracy got on his nerves. Their arrogance disgusted him. . . . He carried away from

Hungary a deep distrust of Hungarian and indeed of Austro-Hungarian policy. This feeling became intensified with the passage of time. . . ." Such expressions were not usual for Nicolson's father. There was some talk that, while in Budapest, his wife was seduced by a Hungarian aristocrat. Because of what we know of the character and temperament of Catherine Nicolson this is very implausible. Why her husband, and her sensitive son, disliked Budapest so much we will never know.

3

The People

Buda-Pest!'' wrote Blowitz. "The very word names an idea which is big with the future. It is synonymous with restored liberty, unfolding now at each forward step; it is the future opening up before a growing people." A growing people indeed. During the last three decades of the nineteenth century Budapest—we shall see why Blowitz's usage of "Buda-Pest" was outdated in 1894—was the fastest growing city in Europe. From 1890 to 1900 its population increased by more than 40 percent. In 1900, with a total of 733,000 people, it had become the sixth largest city of Europe, and the largest one between Vienna and St. Petersburg. After 1900 the growth went on, but it was slowing down. In more than one way 1900 represented a zenith in the history of Budapest.

The theme of this book is not the history of a city but its historical portrait at a certain time, a portrait of its atmosphere, of its peoples, of their achievements and troubles. There is another reason for the brevity of the historical sketch that follows. Until the nineteenth century the two towns of Buda and Pest did not amount to much.

There was a tiny Celtic settlement on the northern reaches of Buda, around one of its mineral springs. The Romans made that place the headquarters of their Pannonian legion, naming it Aquincum. They seldom crossed the Danube. During the early Middle Ages Buda was scarcely a town; Pest a fledgling, semibarbaric village. Both were destroyed by a Mongol invasion in 1241. It was only during the fourteenth century that the kings of Hungary established their royal seat in Buda. On the Castle Hill of Buda a small Renaissance court was created by the redoubtable King Matthias in the second half of the fifteenth century. But two generations later Pest and Buda were conquered by the Turks. Buda was reconquered 145 years later by a Habsburg army composed of many volunteers and mercenaries from all over Europe. There were relatively few Hungarians among them. Most of Hungary had been torn, ravaged and depopulated during the century and a half of Turkish rule. Twenty-five years after the Turks had left, the population of Buda amounted to less than 13,000 and that of Pest to hardly more than 4,000. The two towns were separated by the wide and ungoverned Danube, unconnected save by an occasionally assembled and then again disassembled rickety pontoon bridge. Five hundred years after its medieval origins, Pest was still not much more than a semi-Oriental river village; Buda consisted of clusters of modest houses and vineyards.

In the eighteenth century the majority of the peoples of Buda and Pest were German-speaking. Some of the Habsburg emperors were not inimical to their Hungarian subjects and even to their aspirations; but the recuperation of the Magyar population, and the revival of its national consciousness, were slow. A considerable number of families from the Austrian crownlands and from the southern Germanies had come to settle in the two river towns, mostly in Buda. Buda and Pest were only 140 miles east of Vienna, but that was a distance between two worlds, one being in Europe, the other something akin to the Levant or even the Near East. In 1815, during the Congress of Vienna, Metternich was supposed to have said to one of his visitors as he pointed at the dusty road stretching away from Vienna toward Hungary that Europe ended there. But the extraordinary rise of Budapest, of Hungary, of the Hungarian people, and of Hungarianness was around the corner.

In 1799 Buda had 24,306 inhabitants and Pest 29,870, for a total of about 54,000; in 1890 the total was nearly 500,000, close to a tenfold increase. Berlin was the only European city that grew at a comparable rate (eightfold) during the nineteenth century (from 1800 to 1890 the populations of Paris and London increased by 3.4 times); and the famous eleventh edition of the *Encyclopaedia Britannica* would describe Budapest as "one of the handsomest capitals of Europe," which Berlin was not.

One hundred and seventy years ago the sudden eruption of Hungarian national consciousness and of Hungarian nationalism began. The extraordinary rise of Budapest depended on the extraordinary force of Hungarian nationalism in the nineteenth century: extraordinary, because it had much to do with certain characteristics—strengths as well as weaknesses—of the Hungarian national genius. The factor of national character is often eschewed by historians and social thinkers in our times; nonetheless, it is wrong and foolish to ignore, let alone deny, its existence. From Greece to Ireland, from Italy to Finland, as indeed in Hungary, nationalism proved to be the dominant political idea—and reality —of the nineteenth century. But there were elements in the Hungarian character that do not only distinguish a Kossuth from a Parnell or a Garibaldi or a Mavrocordato; they were ingredients, too, in the rise of Budapest. That rise in numbers surpassed that of other ancient capitals of newly independent nations, such as, say, modern Athens or modern Rome, but it was not a matter of numbers alone. It brought about a generation of 1900: writers and scholars, artists and savants, sometimes of worldwide fame. That was true of Vienna, too, but Vienna in 1900 was the continuation of a great urban and artistic culture that a century before had been already marked by a Mozart, a Beethoven, a Haydn; and by a European political culture manifested by a Metternich or a Kaunitz. In Budapest an urban and urbane civilization began to flourish at a time when Hungary was still largely unknown abroad.

The Hungarian national revival—the so-called Reform Age of Hungary—began to blossom after 1825. It debouched into the Hungarian Revolution of 1848. Much of this national revival was the inspiration, creation and exemplification of The Greatest Magyar, Count István Széchenyi (the epithet was bestowed on him by his contemporaries), who, together with other amazing achievements, inspired, planned and financed some of the first great buildings of Buda-Pest (including the Chain Bridge, the first permanent —and very impressive—bridge between the two cities). Yet his life, like the national revolution, ended in tragedy. The fiery and impolitic temperament of his countrymen deserted him. They poured their hopes into the more radical and sentimental nationalism represented by Kossuth. The result was the inspiring, but failed Hungarian War of Independence of 1848–49, during which Buda and Pest were twice occupied by an avenging Habsburg-Austrian army. Both towns suffered from the bombardments of a siege. But less than twenty years later, the Emperor and Empress of Austria and their cabinet chose to offer a Compromise to Hungary, the so-called *Ausgleich* of 1867, whereby Hungary received a very substantial share of the privileges and the independence that its leaders had demanded in 1848. In sum, Hungary got something like near-complete Home Rule. The official name of the Austrian Empire became Austria-Hungary. It was then that the dynamic increase of the population and the prosperity and growth of Buda-Pest began. In 1867 its population was less than 270,000; it more than doubled in twenty-five years. In 1870 it was the sixteenth largest city in Europe; twenty-five years later it was the eighth, larger than Rome, Madrid, Naples, Hamburg, Lisbon, Liverpool, Brussels and Amsterdam. It was the second largest city of the Austro-Hungarian Dual Monarchy, having bypassed Prague easily, and coming closer and closer to the size—and importance—of Vienna, in more than one way.

It did not become Budapest until 1873. Until then there had been three separate towns: Pest, Buda and Óbuda ("Ancient Buda," the smallest of the three). The reason for this was not only the broad dividing flow of the Danube. There were definite differences between their peoples, accounting for misunderstandings and even animosities on occasion. Buda (and to some extent Óbuda) was largely German-speaking, conservative, Catholic and loyal to Habsburg rule. During the 1848 Revolution many of its people did not share the Magyar nationalism and the radical enthusiasms of Pest. It was in Pest that the Revolution began; its leader, Kossuth, a Protestant, had come from northeastern Hungary. The Left-wing radicals of Pest distrusted Buda and its people. Mihály Táncsics, a political figure of the extreme Left, publicly opposed the unification of Buda-Pest in 1873; so did many of the people of Buda, though they were often careful enough not to voice these sentiments in public. To men such as Táncsics, coming from Cisdanubia, the southern plains, often Protestant and deeply anti-Habsburg parts of the country, Buda represented the German, Transdanubian, Catholic and antinationalist portion of Hungary, with its inevitable Habsburg connections. These mixed loyalties of the people in Buda (and of a considerable number of people in Pest, too) lasted for a long time. Some of its political and cultural elements were still apparent in 1900. But the proportion of the Buda people was decreasing. In 1850 the population of the dual cities was nearly even, with 45 percent of the people living on the western, Buda, side. Twenty years later this proportion fell to 25 percent. By 1900 only one of every six people of Budapest were inhabitants of Buda. In 1848, with its still unpaved streets, Pest was the dynamic side.*

Even more important than these changing proportions was the rapidly declining prevalence of the German language. Whereas almost everywhere else in Eastern Europe (and also in certain portions of Hungary) German people maintained their, at times, proud and even arrogant separation from the other populations surrounding them, in Budapest they allowed themselves to be merged with, and eventually absorbed by, the Magyar majority: they became part of a linguistic, cultural and even political Hungarianness. And so in 1872–73 there was relatively little open opposition, even in Buda, to the law creating the united municipality of Budapest (whose main municipal spokesman and parliamentary manager was, perhaps tellingly, a Hungarian Jewish patrician councilman, Mór Wahrmann). Twenty years later, in 1892—on the twenty-fifth anniversary of the Compromise, and of the Hungarian crowning of Franz Josef I (ceremonies that, in 1867, took place significantly in Pest as well as in Buda)—an imperial and royal decree proclaimed Budapest to be a *székesfőváros,* a capital and royal seat, equal in rank to Vienna.

On New Year's Day 1896 the bells of the churches of Budapest rang and rang. They were announcing the "Millennium." In 896, one thousand years before, the Magyar tribes led by their prince Árpád had ridden into Hungary from the east, to occupy the country and settle there. On a shining June day Franz Josef and the Empress-Queen Elizabeth arrived from Vienna to preside over the celebrations. They had a sense of occasion, as had their Hungarian hosts. Franz Josef wore a Hungarian hussar uniform. The melancholy Elizabeth, wan and beautiful, beloved by all Hungarians,

---

*But already during the five years before 1848 the population of Pest increased by more than one-third. Rents were, on the average, 40 percent higher than in Buda.

smiled through that long day of parades. (Their daughter-in-law, the archduchess Stephanie, carried and clicked her Kodak box camera, one of the first seen in Budapest.) There were the ceremonial thunder of cannons, green-trousered heralds blowing silver trumpets, military parades, and a long procession of cavalry bands and regiments from the ancient counties of Hungary, many of them caparisoned in eighteenth- and even seventeenth-century military finery. (In the regiment of County Heves rode the young Count Michael Károlyi, wearing a doublet of armor; twenty years later he would be the chief Hungarian gravedigger of the Habsburg monarchy, but who, including himself, would know that in 1896?) The municipality of Budapest had its own mounted delegation. (It included some of the great capitalists of the city, among others, the Swiss-born Haggenmacher, owner of the largest brewery, and two ennobled Jewish magnates, owners of mills.)

From Buda to Pest the King and Queen rode in a crystal-paned baroque coach from Maria Theresa's time. The holy object of St. Stephen's crown was brought to the still unfinished, monumental Parliament building. (There was a moment of anxiety: the hasp and lock of the crown's old iron chest were badly rusted. Two nobles of the royal entourage rode off to find a locksmith, who hastened to open it—after he had been dressed quickly in a tailcoat.) On the great open field to the west of Castle Hill (Vérmező: a Budapest Champ-de-Mars) oxen were broiled on giant spits for the populace. On the eastern edge of Pest a grand world's fair had been built in the newly laid-out City Park, with many impressive buildings, including a reconstruction of an entire late-medieval Transylvanian castle on the shores of the lake in the park. There were captive balloons, panoramas, a real military balloon ascending, the first movie newsreel made by a Hungarian, the brilliant blaze of electric illuminations, endless music. Budapest had nearly 6 million visitors that year, most of them from the Hungarian provinces. Within a few months the Gallery of Fine Arts, the palace of the High Court of Justice, the first electric underground tramway line, the last stretch of the Pest Ring boulevards were completed, and the building of the new wing of the royal castle had begun.

During the nineteenth century Budapest and Berlin were the two fastest-growing cities in Europe; and between 1867 and

1914 Budapest was *the* fastest growing one. Let us, for the last time, sum up the increase:

1720	about 11,000 people
1831	103,000
1867	280,000
1900	733,000
1910	880,000
1913	933,000

In 1867 Buda and Pest were the seventeenth largest city in Europe, by 1900 the sixth. The proportion of the capital city to the country at large was not unusual: the people of Budapest amounted to slightly more than 4 percent of the population of Hungary (the proportion of Paris to the rest of France, or of London to the rest of Britain, was larger). What was unusual was the comparison of Budapest with other cities of Hungary, of which the second largest, Szeged, amounted to only 12 percent of the capital city.

After 1900 the rate of rise was slowing down. The people of Budapest now had fewer children. To bring up children in the city was more difficult, burdensome and expensive than to bring them up in the country, where they would work in the barnyards and fields. The crowding in the apartments was a factor. There were two other developments, one negative, the other—perhaps—positive. The minds and habits of many of the families who had moved into the city were governed by their religion less than before. This happened not only among Catholics but also among Protestants and Jews. Large families were becoming rare. As in other European countries, notably in France, the availability of male prophylactics had nothing to do with this. Something like birth control was widely practiced among more and more married people, in one way or another. The, perhaps positive, factor was that the diminution in the number of children meant that they had become the subjects of increasing attention. More interest and more money could be spent on their education. Among the middle- and upper-class families it was taken for granted, after 1880 at the latest, that their children would not leave the family circle and would not begin to earn their way until sometime during the third decade of their lives. But among the lower classes, too, children were sent to school longer than before; and the requirements of the schools were such that young people could not really keep up with their studies while having a job on the side. Among the middle classes the often unspoken but generally observed belief reigned to the effect that their children, whether boys or girls, must not attain a social, educational or professional status that would be, even to the slightest degree, beneath that of their parents. Such family ambitions were not typical of the old aristocratic families. Yet, with all of their self-confidence and social position, their children, too, had to maintain not only the social but also the educational status of their parents, whence the frequent employment of private tutors, to which I shall return.

Some of these matters were not peculiar to Budapest in 1900. What was singular to it was the high rate of increase in its population even when a drastic decrease in the size of its families took place. One of these reasons was the continuous growth of the agricultural ring around Budapest. Another element was the great improvement in standards of health. In 1867 the Pest death rate was one of the highest among comparable European cities. Notwithstanding the conditions of urban overcrowding, during the twenty-five years before 1900 the death rate in Budapest dropped by half. Infant mortality also declined by 50 percent from 1869 to 1900. The mass killers of the nineteenth century, infectious diseases such as tuberculosis, were fading, while life expectancy was rising, though only slowly. In these respects, Budapest in 1900 had caught up with Vienna, which is remarkable when we consider that proletarian overcrowding in Vienna was less than in Budapest, and that the Viennese municipal health services were a model for much of Europe.

In 1900 the number of illegitimate children in Budapest was still unusually high. At least one of every four births was an illegitimate one. (The rate of illegitimacy was lowest among the Jewish and highest among the Greek-Catholic and Greek-Orthodox population of Pest, among the poorest newly arrived laborers from eastern and northeastern Hungary.) Another peculiarity in the composition of the population was the unusual imbalance between women and men: in 1900 1,088 females for every 1,000 males in the city. One explanation for this is the large number of domestic servants, who were almost all women (male servants, such as butlers or coachmen, existed only in the households of the aristocracy). As late as 1870 every fifth person in Buda and Pest was a domestic servant—a proportion twice as large as that in Vienna, and three times larger than in Berlin. One consequence of this was that among the poorer classes men and women married late. In 1900 among people over twenty years of age only 56 percent of males and 44 percent of females were married, a proportion much lower than elsewhere in the country. The rapid industrialization of Budapest caused a change after 1900. Because most of the industrial workers were young men, the average age of the population remained fairly young, younger than that of the generally aging urban population of other European cities;* but industrial workers now included many females, too. From 1900 to 1910 the number of women employed in domestic service rose by only 24 percent, while the number of those employed in industry rose by 37 percent. Whereas in 1880 only one of every three working women in Budapest was employed in industry, their proportion had grown to more than half in 1900, and to more than two-thirds in 1910.

The working classes were the largest portion of the people of Budapest; but by 1900 the *tone* of Budapest was that of a bourgeois city. Perhaps in all of Eastern Europe it was the *only* bourgeois city. There exists a descriptive novel about the Rumanian capital city of Bucharest around 1900 by the Rumanian novelist Ion Marin Sadoveanu. The differences between the atmosphere, people and habits of Bucharest and Budapest were not only immeasurably greater than those between Budapest and Vienna; it is almost as if the differences were larger than those of two neighboring nations; it is the difference of two civilizations.

But these are matters for which the illustrative evidence of statistics is no longer sufficient.† We are facing qualities of life, not quantities. The bourgeois classes of Budapest were a minority in 1900, a numerically lesser minority than the proportion of corre-

---

*It is significant that the characteristics of internal migration and of external migration (that is, of emigration) in Hungary coincide on one point. Around 1900 most of the young people who came to Budapest to seek their fortunes came from the same counties and regions (mostly from the north of Hungary) wherefrom most people were leaving for America.

†The Budapest City Office of Statistics was one of the most reputed in Europe, led by a great statistician, József Kőrösy, whose important (and pioneering) works in modern urban statistics were also published in Paris and in Vienna. It is melancholy to record that one of the ablest successors at the head of that office of the Jewish Kőrösy, after 1920, was the determinedly anti-Semitic Alajos Kovách.

sponding classes in Vienna or Paris. Yet their influence—not only their material or financial but their mental influence—was dominant. Evidence for this existed on all kinds of levels. There was the prevalence of bourgeois buildings, that sea of apartment houses. The rooms of the working classes compared, of course, most unfavorably in both comfort and sanitation with those of the bourgeois; but the working classes, too, lived in apartment houses, for the first time in their lives. The clothing of the great majority of the people of Budapest, including the working classes, also followed middle-class standards and habits by 1900. Unlike in most provincial cities of Hungary and in other large cities of Eastern Europe, peasant clothing and other rural habits were disappearing fast. By 1900 the street wear of most industrial working men in Budapest was that of the dark sack suit. It was the custom of some of the advanced workers, especially of foremen, to wear a black derby even at their workbenches or lathes. The cloth cap or the beret were still rare. This conformation to bourgeois fashions was more frequent among the men than among the women of the lower classes. The broad skirts, boots and black kerchiefs of the Hungarian peasantry were worn not only by the older married women of the working class; they were ubiquitous among the women and girls of the factories and of the agricultural suburbs; and they were the off-duty clothing of most of the domestic servant girls.*

As late as 1850 foreign travelers to Hungary found the eating and drinking habits (habits, rather than manners), and the seasonings (rather than the materials), of Hungarian national dishes exotic at best and barbaric at worst. In this, as in so many other matters, there was a considerable change by 1900. The cuisine of Hungary, certainly that of the middle and upper classes, had become more refined, more "European." Much of provincial Hungary lagged

*There was no coincidence between the development of Hungarian architecture and of Hungarian fashions in clothes. Neoclassical and Biedermeier architecture (and Biedermeier fashions among the women of Budapest) were still dominant at a time, before 1850, when male clothing was often pronouncedly national and Hungarian. And when after 1900 Hungarian national elements appeared in the very styles and forms of buildings, the bourgeois uniformity of European styles of clothing had become ubiquitous (except for the very occasional ceremonial *díszmagyar,* of which see p. 99).

behind. Before we go further, we must observe a peculiar condition that still begs an explanation. This is that in Hungary, as in so many nondemocratic and partly feudal societies, there was not much difference in the diet of the otherwise so very different classes. Many of the same national dishes were preferred, and beloved, by peasants, bourgeois and nobles alike. We may see this phenomenon also in Italy, Spain, Austria and Poland, whereas in democratic nations such as England or the United States the cuisine of the upper, middle and lower classes was (and often still is) different. I am leaving aside the obvious regional differences and the fact that, as in so many other matters, France does not fit into this scheme, all of the avowed differences between its *haute cuisine* and its *cuisine bourgeoise* notwithstanding. Yet France must be mentioned because by 1900 the French influence on Hungarian—more exactly, on Budapest—cooking had begun to appear, though the influence of Viennese cooking on the bourgeois households of Budapest was obviously greater.

Food in Budapest was relatively cheap. Hungary was, by and large, the food bin of the Dual Monarchy. Consequently, even the poorest segments of the population in most of the country (there were severe exceptions, especially in the northeastern, Ruthenian-inhabited part of the kingdom) ate better than the poorest people elsewhere within the Habsburg domains. (This would become evident during the First World War, toward the end of which undernourishment and near-famine in Vienna were worse than among the poorest people in Budapest, when the Austrian government as well as people had grown very resentful against what they saw, rightly or wrongly, as the privileged and selfish agricultural policies of the Hungarian government.) In 1900 only one Hungarian staple dish was well known outside Hungary, even as far as the United States: goulash *(gulyás)*. Many sins, from misspelling to miscooking, have been since committed in its name. *Gulyás* was originally a soup, rather than a stew, with pieces of mutton in it, and flavored with the inevitable Hungarian seasoning, paprika.* It was the frequent, if not standard, midday dish of Hungarian shepherds and cattle drivers on the great plains of the country. Ladled out in a bowl, it would appear on the tables (or be held in the laps) of the

---

*The origins of paprika were Turkish. On Hungarian tables in 1900, as now, one found three shakers: salt, paprika and pepper; often only the first two.

poorer people in Budapest around 1900, but on the tables of the majority only infrequently.

What is more important, a small but essential change in the overall food consumption took place in the two decades before 1900. Beef replaced mutton (including in the *gulyás*), mainly because of the large expansion of cattle-raising in Hungary at the time, and the consequent decline in the prices of beef products (especially those of the less expensive cuts). Another overall change, especially in Budapest, was the increasing quality and variety of vegetable dishes. There was the extraordinary expansion of the agricultural ring around Budapest, wherefrom came most of the vegetables (and dairy products) consumed by the population. As late as 1900 meadows were still within the municipal boundaries of the city and a few cattle were raised there. The habit, probably Viennese in origin, of cooking vegetables in a roux of flour and lard and seasoning them quite imaginatively had spread among all classes of the people of the capital city, to the extent that certain vegetable dishes (and not only as accompaniments to meats) had become preferred, and even beloved, staples of the national cuisine.

All of this was made easier by the widespread availability of gas-fired kitchen stoves in the apartment houses of Budapest by 1900. The name of these stoves *(sparherd)* suggests they were first imported from Vienna. There were other Viennese influences, spreading beyond the confines of the bourgeois households of Budapest at the time. Some Viennese staple dishes (thus unseasoned with paprika)—for example, boiled beef, a local variety of the then celebrated Viennese *Tafelspitz*—had become standard and beloved national dishes (Krúdy devotes long paragraphs in his books to describing it with naturalist, rather than impressionist precision). The preparation and consumption of veal, too, had become more common by 1900. There was a definite Viennese influence in the developing national appetite for certain desserts and sweetmeats. In the second half of the nineteenth century the reputation and influence of the bakeries and confectioners of Vienna were overtaking those of Paris: Viennese desserts and pastry shops became the best in the world. Before that time desserts were not a strong suit in Hungarian national cooking; in many traditional Hungarian desserts the pastry was cooked and not baked. By 1890 some of the confiseries of Budapest were equal to the Viennese ones, foremost among them Kugler, later Gerbeaud, proudly situated on a central square of the Inner District of Pest, where it is even now. But these rich desserts were baked daily in tens of thousands of household kitchens, too; and, as in so many other fields of endeavor, Hungarian ingenuity resulted in the creation of interesting, and sometimes richer, variants of Viennese *Torten.* * On a more mundane level, there was relatively little difference in the prices and varieties of the daily bread and rolls consumed by the peoples of Vienna and Budapest. One of the differences was the more widespread, and cheaper, rye bread in Budapest, consumed by the poorer classes: they spread lard over these large aromatic slices of bread, sprinkled with salt and paprika.

The sequence and the number of meals, was, of course, not the same for the richer and the poorer classes. Among the upper and middle classes, five daily meals were almost customary—an astonishing amount of consumption in retrospect, but then this was not atypical of much of Europe around 1900. Breakfast was what Americans still call continental—that is, coffee (with milk), rolls and butter, eggs rarely. "Elevenses" was, by and large, a male preserve: a small meat dish, perhaps sausages, washed down often by beer, consumed in a beer hall or coffeehouse; and substantial sandwiches, filled with meat or cheese, that children brought with them to school. The main meal of the day was usually served around two o'clock, when youngsters had returned from their schools: a substantial meal of three courses. Something similar to English afternoon tea or to the Viennese *Jause* was served around five in the afternoon: coffee, often with whipped cream, and pastries. This was the reverse of "elevenses": it was the favorite meal of the bourgeois ladies, sometimes surrounded by their relatives and visiting friends. Supper at night was lighter than the midday meal, sometimes consisting of a cold platter and accompanied by tea. Among the working classes, "elevenses" and afternoon coffee-and-pastry did not exist. Their breakfast and midday intake were, by necessity, frugal and coarse. At night their wives made do with at

---

*Baking with sugar rather than honey was the difference between European dessert-making and that of the Balkans and Near East. In Hungary sugar had replaced honey long before 1900, even though sugar—especially cubed sugar—was relatively expensive. A delicious Hungarian specialty of acacia honey was a breakfast or tea condiment.

least one substantial dish. They ate their evening meal earlier than the well-to-do citizens of Budapest.

The cuisine of Hungary is not one of the prime cuisines of the world (even in these times with their frenzy of gastronomic miscegenation there is not one first-class Hungarian restaurant in New York), but by 1900 it had risen to what we may assess as the first rank of second-class national cuisines—that is, after French and North Italian cuisines—having reached (and here and there even surpassed) the Viennese. With all respect due to the housewives and cooks of Budapest (and there is plenty of respect due to them, especially in retrospect),* we must state that the refining, lightening and judicious Frenchification of the cuisine of Budapest was mostly the work of a few serious restaurateurs who had followed the first great *maître,* Joseph Maréchal (born in France); they were József Dobos and János and Károly Gundel. Dobos, who, contrary to general belief, was not a pastry chef, created the first world-famous Hungarian dessert, the Dobos-torte (around 1890); János Gundel (of Swiss origin) started his restaurant in 1869. His son Károly followed in the family tradition, maintaining not only high standards but also creating many exquisite dishes of his own. In 1900 there were still few Hungarian dishes of cosmopolitan renown (one was the unique Hungarian fogas [*Lucioperca sandra*], perhaps the most delicate freshwater fish in the world), but the reputation of Budapest cuisine had begun to spread across Europe. François Coppée wrote an enthusiastic account of the chicken paprika he had consumed in Budapest; before that, Alexandre Dumas *père,* no mean gourmet, praised the paprika-laced Magyar dishes; and Edward VII on one occasion asked for a Hungarian chef to join his household in London.

In 1900 the number of public establishments, ranging from taverns *(kocsma)* to the garden restaurants and fish restaurants of Buda to the coffeehouses and hotel-restaurants of Pest, was very large.† One reason for this was the availability of cheap labor. Another was

---

*In Budapest, unlike in most other capital cities of Europe in 1900, fine cooking was not an absolute monopoly of women. Two kinds of men were creative cooks on occasion: a few members of the aristocracy and a few Hungarian writers. The occasional gastronomic articles in the literary journal *A Hét,* under the pen name "Dame Emma" (Emma Asszony), were recipes by anonymous Hungarian authors.
†The more famous restaurants in Pest were Wampetics (in the City Park), the Hangli on the Corso, the Transylvanian Winery and the Viennese Beer Hall on Andrássy Avenue; in 1910 Gundel's Restaurant would replace Wampetics.

the crowded and inadequate dwelling conditions: many men preferred to spend a portion of their day (and, sometimes night) in
such public establishments, often conducting business there. In
1900 Budapest had nearly six hundred coffeehouses.* Of all public
establishments, the coffeehouses had increased fastest; as in other
cities of the Dual Monarchy, they fulfilled the social function of
men's clubs of the middle classes, and their restaurative function
had broadened, so that in many of them full-course meals were
available to customers at almost any hour of the day. We shall
return to a description of the function and atmosphere of some of
these coffeehouses in Chapter 5, dealing with the cultural life of the
city, in which these coffeehouses had a definite place. Here we must
conclude this account of the sumptuary habits of the people of
Budapest around 1900 with a brief summary of their intake of
liquor. We have seen that the quality of the municipal water was
unusually good; and alcoholism in Budapest was not as excessive
around 1900 as in many other capital cities of Europe. The bourgeoisie, especially the Jewish families among them, put a great
emphasis on sobriety. In 1900 the reputation of an alcoholic meant
social unacceptability. Most of the wines consumed were local, with
a predominance of whites. The large breweries of the Tenth District produced lager beer of a quality comparable to the famous
Vienna and Pilsen brews. A somewhat unusual habit was the consumption of rum, rather than other cheap distilled spirits, among
the poorer classes; this was especially prevalent in winter among
coachmen and drivers. Rum was cheap because it was one of the
byproducts of the large Hungarian sugar refineries that had come
into being during the last decades of the nineteenth century.

We come now to the social problems, and diseases, among the
swelling population of this smoky, but hardly somber capital city.
Considering the constant swelling of that population by all kinds of
multifarious, rootless and adventurous elements, criminality in
Budapest was surprisingly low—proportionately very much lower
than in other capitals of Eastern Europe. In 1900 there was still a
fairly recognizable division between habitual criminals and the rest
of the population. It was certainly recognizable by the police (partly
because the Budapest underworld habitually sought shelter in rec-

*"Coffee" meant café au lait or Turkish coffee. In 1900 espresso did not exist in
Budapest. A few decades later the brewing of espresso, and small establishments
called Espressos, became very common. They are Hungarian staples now.

ognizable portions of certain districts). Thus, at least statistically, the proportion of unsolved crimes—that is, of unapprehended criminals—was very low, too. We have seen that this was not true of illegitimacy. The Magyar name for illegitimate cohabitation was that of "a wild marriage" *(vadházasság)*. We know little about the number and extent of abortions, which were unlawful at the time and severely punishable. What we know is the widespread habit— and not always among the poor—of farming out babies, illegitimate as well as legitimate ones, to wet nurses. Many peasant women eked out this kind of living in the agricultural ring of suburbs. But "farming out" may not be the proper term. The Hungarian word for these women was often that of "angelmaker" *(angyalcsináló)*, suggesting abortion.

As in other capital cities of the time, prostitution in Budapest around 1900 was widespread. Its first serious municipal regulation —for moral as well as for sanitary reasons—was attempted by the city authorities in 1885. In 1867 there were forty licensed and inspected brothels in Buda and Pest; in 1906 there were twenty-one. At least one of these, in Magyar Street, was famous as well as luxurious, frequented by men of the aristocracy as well as by distinguished foreign visitors.* Its madam (Mme. Róza Pilisy) was a remarkable woman, with literary interests (she was in love with Gyula Krúdy). Whorehouses existed in almost every district of the city. There were many independent streetwalkers, some of them licensed and subjected to periodic medical inspections. Many were not. I cannot ascertain their numbers, even approximately, but it seems that the extent of this social vice differed little from what it was in other European cities at the time. There was another, melancholy aspect. The *filles* of Budapest were a national commodity of export. Perhaps because of their physical attractiveness, perhaps also because of the relative refinement of their habits, they were sought eagerly by the *souteneurs,* and by the cabaret owners and

---

*In 1907 a group of MPs from the House of Commons known to be sympathetic to Hungary visited Budapest. The government wined and dined them. One or two of them took the liberty (or rather the opportunity) to run up large bills, including a visit to the establishment in Magyar Street, where they refused to pay, charging the cost of their fornications to the host government. An unpleasant scandal ensued.

their wealthy customers, in the far eastern reaches of Europe—
especially in Constantinople and, most of all, in Tsarist Russia,
wherefrom the sturdier and luckier of these night-blooming flowers
returned with a modicum of fortune. Around 1900 they were so
well liked in Moscow and St. Petersburg that Russian argot had a
special word for them: the *vengerka,* meaning a Hungarian girl of
light morals.

Many of these young girls started their public careers not on the
streets and avenues of Budapest but in the orpheums. The Budapest
orpheum was a mix of nightclub and café chantant; catering to all
kinds of customers among the native population, it depended only
partly on visitors or tourists. The coffeehouse, tavern, theater, orpheum and circus were the main places of recreation for the people
of Budapest, whose character was often gregarious, and for whom
a modicum of entertainment outside their homes was a definite
necessity. By 1900 Budapest had a year-round circus under a fixed
tent in the City Park (the scene of Ferenc Molnár's later famous
play, *Liliom*.)

Interest in sports was only in its beginnings in 1900. The people
of Budapest are athletic (as early as 1896, at the first Olympics in
Athens, they won a number of gold medals). Horse racing was
introduced by the great Széchenyi in the 1830s; in 1900 there was
a track for flat races and another one (curiously named Tattersall)
for harness racing. In 1900 going to the races was the favorite
pastime of many people (perhaps less of the bourgeoisie than of the
aristocracy and of the working classes). Some of the most reputed
jockeys were English or Irish, many of whom settled in Budapest
after their careers in the saddle. The legendary Kincsem, a Magyar
mare, was the horse with the longest unbroken winning record in
Europe and England in the nineteenth century. There was plenty
of hunting, shooting and riding in the Hungarian provinces, but
little of that within the boundaries of Budapest. One of the few
outdoor sports was skating on the rink of the Budapest Skating Club
on the City Park pond, a favorite meeting place of young people
of the upper-middle class. Sculling and rowing on the Danube were
still rare in 1900; swimming on Margaret Island, later so popular,
did not yet exist. Apart from a very minimum of calisthenics, there
was nothing in the way of organized athletics or sports in the
schools. An old Hungarian game called *longa méta* (the name came
from Latin), a game similar to stickball or even baseball, was still

played by children in the empty lots of the city. By 1900 it was being replaced by soccer. The first soccer clubs had come into existence. Soon they would be organized into a league. Within a decade their Sunday games would attract large crowds. By 1910 soccer was popular enough so that famous actors and actresses were game to appear on the field, in order to start off an important match by punting the ball; there exists a photograph of the elegant Lord Mayor of Budapest, István Bárczy, in a top hat and Prince Albert coat, kicking off the ball with great verve and an agreeable smile.

In 1900 the class structure of Hungary was highly articulated and complicated. The class structure of Budapest reflected this national stratification, but its proportions were different.

Budapest was largely urban; Hungary was still half-feudal. There were, at that time, two aristocracies in Budapest: the older land-owning one, and the newer financial one. But the employment of the word "aristocracy" is inaccurate since it applies to both groups only in a broad sense of the term. In Hungarian usage, "aristocrat" meant a member of the high nobility: a prince, count or baron. A "financial aristocrat" could be respected or envied, but the term was hardly more than an epithet. It even carried within itself a pejorative sense, a touch somewhat critical. Around 1900 the high nobilitarian and the financial aristocracy could coexist and even collaborate or commingle on occasion; but the financial aristocracy—including those of its families who became ennobled by the King—was well aware of its relative social inferiority compared to the old nobility. After the French Revolution the brilliant French writer Rivarol overheard a socially ambitious emigré, in the company of aristocratic emigrés in a Hamburg boardinghouse, beginning a sentence with *"Nous aristocrates"* ("We aristocrats"). Rivarol cut in: "That usage of the plural is very singular." No financial aristocrat in Budapest, even if ennobled, even if in possession of the title of baron, would ever have said "we aristocrats," no matter when.

The old nobility were the great landowner magnates of Hungary. They held a very large proportion of the Hungarian land. By 1900 the value, and the income, of their large estates had begun to decrease; but that decrease was uneven and they were not, as yet, threatened by the full devolution of feudalism into capitalism.

There were only a handful of Magyar princely families. (Franz Josef elevated many counts, even more barons, but only one Hungarian prince, Tasziló Festetics, who did not live in Budapest.) The divisions among the high nobility lay elsewhere. There were a few non-Hungarian counts and barons who had very large estates, mostly in northern and western Hungary, and often resided in Vienna but seldom, if ever, in Budapest. There were the members of the old Hungarian nobility who held positions in the high ranks of the Austro-Hungarian government, many of them in the diplomatic service. There were other members of the Hungarian high nobility, mostly of eastern Hungary and Transylvania, whose estates were smaller and who were considerably less wealthy than the others. And the best known, and perhaps the most respected, were those high noble families that were long and deeply rooted in Hungarian history, families whose members had associated themselves with the causes of Magyar patriotism and independence both before and during the nineteenth century—Batthyánys, Széchenyis, Eszterházys, Andrássys—even as all of them were unreservedly loyal to the Dual Monarchy in 1900. During the nineteenth century this was the group that, in addition to their great country houses, chose to establish their houses in Pest (unless they possessed ancestral houses on Castle Hill). Their patriotism and political interests were the sources of that choice. The urbanization of Budapest and its culture contributed further to that inclination. A few of them took part in the government of the city; one of them, the eccentric Count Frigyes Podmaniczky, served as the vice-president of the Council of Public Works. They had their own club, the National Casino, which remained restricted and exclusive, its membership dependent almost exclusively on birth. They married mostly among themselves; the sources of their wealth and income were still predominantly land and forestry in 1900, but their intermarriages with the financial "aristocracy"* and their financial and political interdependence with Budapest high capitalism had already begun.

Still their ways of life were quite distinct. For one thing, the sons and daughters of magnates were educated at home by private tu-

*In 1900 such intermarriages were still few; they involved those of aristocratic men and the daughters of rich, often Jewish, families; the opposite was rarely the case.

tors, often till their twelfth year. Then their sons were customarily sent to the gymnasiums of certain religious orders, and their daughters to convent schools till the age of seventeen or eighteen. Most of these families were Catholic; they often employed a family priest. There was sometimes a small private chapel not only in their country houses but also in their small palaces in Budapest. They were more cosmopolitan than the other classes. They had connections with other European noble families, often well beyond the frontiers of the Austro-Hungarian Empire. They were taught French at an early age, which almost all of them spoke faultlessly and fluently. Their sons also learned riding, fencing, shooting and hunting. Their clothes were often cut by English tailors, one or two of whom traveled to Vienna every year for that purpose. Much of this was not very different from the lives of other continental noble families of the period. Yet there were differences, sometimes significant ones. In 1900 many of these Hungarian nobles no longer saw their Budapest residences as temporary or secondary. In Germany, Poland or Italy (the Roman aristocracy excepted) such families chose to spend little time in the national capital; often they had no house of their own there at all. In Budapest there was no such thing as a "season." Only during the high summer months could one be sure to find these families in their country seats, away from the capital. Nor was there a definite aristocratic quarter of the city, save for some streets on Castle Hill and in the streets around the Museum Ring. Furthermore, unlike in Vienna, many of these families were not indifferent to currents of urban and national culture. They frequented not only the Opera but also the flourishing national theaters. Unlike in the France of 1789 and other European nations around 1900, in this still half-feudal nation the hatred of the people for the high nobility was generally absent.

Yet we must not exaggerate their merits. Their patronage of the arts was limited. They had few remarkable collections. More important, surely around 1900, was the fairly idle condition some of the younger men of these families, who had no taste either for the management of their estates or even for the diplomatic service. The careers that members of such families had espoused earlier—that of high military or high civil-service positions—no longer drew many of them. Perhaps one of the reasons for this was their liking for the pleasures of Budapest. A frequent vice among them was gambling. It was after years of remarkable dissipation, and after more than considerable losses in gambling, that the Károlyi family helped to launch the young Mihály Károlyi's career in politics. He became a national figure soon, mostly because of his vocal proposition of radical and "modern" ideas. In 1919 he became the President of the Hungarian Republic, with disastrous results,* his character being marked by the same kind of irresponsibility as that of the erstwhile gambler. Among the high nobility the women were, generally speaking, more sedate than the men. They were more religious and conservative. The fiery Hungarian temperament notwithstanding, extramarital scandals among the high Hungarian nobility were relatively rare at the time. There was little of the raffishness of the Edwardian aristocracy among them, perhaps because life, and the diet of daily pleasures, in nineteenth-century Hungary had been less constrained than in Victorian England.

Beneath them on the social scale stood the families of the Hungarian gentry. People regarded them, as they regarded themselves, as categorically superior to the financial aristocracy (and not only because many of the families of the latter were Jewish or Jewish in their origins). In this respect, the society of Hungary resembled Poland in some ways and England in others. The gentry families, especially in Budapest, had less money than the financial aristocracy and less than much of the bourgeoisie. But then in Hungary an unusually large proportion of people were "nobles"—according to some estimates, as many as one of every ten people as late as 1848 —mostly because of a peculiar constitutional law dating back to the early sixteenth century. They lived on the land; they had many petty privileges and constitutional rights; their titles—true, stretching the category somewhat—were the Hungarian equivalent of a *von* or a *de.* In essence, they were a *petite noblesse terrienne,* with a fierce desire for independence, both personal and national, and with many acquired handicaps and inherited vices. The word "gentry," borrowed from English (*dzsentri* in Hungarian), did not

---

*His wife, née Katinka Andrássy, was beautiful, nonconformist and raffish. She shared her husband's advanced ideas. Some people called her The Red Countess. She went into exile with her husband, returned with him after the Russian occupation, went into exile again, returned to Budapest after her husband's death (above the Riviera, in Vence, in the 1950s), where she lived as a kind of ancient *grande dame,* respected by the Communist regime, receiving fellow-traveling intellectuals. She died only a few years ago, in the same year that a movie was made about her life.

become current until the 1880s. There was at that time a proud and widely accepted idea in Hungary (corresponding with some of the ideas that Englishmen had about Hungary at that time) that the Hungarian constitution resembled, if not paralleled, that of England. (Like England, Hungary had no written constitution; there was, too, the chronological near-coincidence of the rights that the nobles of England had extracted in 1215 from their king in their Magna Charta, and Hungarian nobles from their king in the Golden Bull of 1222.) There was the widespread belief that the main representatives of English and Hungarian freedom were the independent landed gentry class, with its inherited sense of traditional freedoms, practice of self-government, and taste for country life. We need not analyze the validity and the shortcoming of this agreeable, and not entirely untruthful, comparison except to say that at the very time the word "gentry" became widespread in Hungary the social structure of England and Hungary could hardly have been more different. By 1880 the Hungarian petty nobility was in considerable, and often grave, financial and material decline. They were in trouble for many reasons. Their land values and yields, the quality and the profitability of their agriculture could not compete with that of the larger, better-run estates. As Győző (Victor) Concha, the thoughtful author of *the* book on the Magyar gentry, wrote, among other things: most of the English gentry *still* wishes to live in the country, but the Hungarian gentry *now* wishes to live in Budapest. Many gentry families had migrated to Budapest, without relinquishing their sense of pride and importance, and without giving up what remained of their estates and of their, alas, often run-down country houses. But they did not wish to go into commerce, finance, industry or business. What was open to them was a new source of income: that of civil service positions. Outside Budapest leading governmental positions remained in the hands of the gentry, in many ways as late as 1944. In Budapest the centralization of government, and the establishment of many government institutions, included other possibilities. The Austro-Hungarian, as well as the particularly Hungarian, civil service consisted of twelve grades. Members of the nobility, functioning as ministers, ambassadors, chief judges, generals, etc., were in Grades 1 to 3; the jobs occupied by the gentry usually spread from Grades 4 to 10. These jobs gave them authority, security and pensions. But they were not a moneyed class, and their income meant less and less as the nineteenth century drew toward its end.

Consequently they were inclined to become critical and jealous of the more successful and rising people of the capital, perhaps especially of Jews. But there was more to these nascent animosities than mere financial frustration and material envy. The gentry saw themselves, with some reason, as the truly national and historical class, the flag-bearers of Hungarian independence. They were apt to be critical of most features of the 1867 Compromise with Austria. They looked down on most private occupations, including clerical and even executive ones. For every Hungarian Jew employed in the governmental, civil or municipal services there were eight non-Jewish civil servants, usually from the ranks of the gentry; among white-collar employees in private firms the ratio was nearly the reverse. In Budapest the number of state and municipal employees increased fivefold from 1867 to 1900. There was, too, a rising need for auditors and accountants. The sons of the gentry were uninterested in such jobs. As late as the 1870s they were filled by clerical arrivals from Austria and Germany. Meanwhile, the gentry were becoming less sure of themselves. Sometime after 1890 the term and meaning of "gentry" in Budapest—though not yet in the provinces—began to overlap with another term, that of the "gentlemanly middle class" *(úri középosztály),* suggesting at least an increase in their identification with urbanity. A decade later another change came that is significant, and perhaps ominous, in retrospect. People began to refer to their class as "the Christian middle class," "Christian" in this sense being a negative adjective, meaning, simply and squarely, non-Jewish.*

It was thus that while there were few evidently and predominantly "gentry" districts in Budapest in 1900, there were certain gentry streets and predominantly gentry houses. We know more about the lives of the Magyar gentry than of the aristocracy because of the many novels (and even studies) that dealt with the sometimes

*There were, too, suspicions and animosities extant between Catholics and Protestants. While the aristocracy was predominantly Catholic, the gentry was both Catholic and Protestant. (The Protestant population of Hungary amounted to 25 to 30 percent of the total.) These religious affiliations were represented in politics. Most Hungarian Protestants were nationalists and anti-Habsburg. Even among the gentry, marriages between Catholic and Protestant families posed certain difficulties, mostly because Catholic families insisted on the Catholic baptism and religious upbringing of children in mixed marriages. Since 1895 the Catholic Church could no longer insist on this as a condition of legal marriage, but the religion of the children had to be determined by a contract *(reverzális).*

tragic, sometimes tragicomic fortunes of that class. Many of these dealt with the amplitude of their pretensions and the emptiness of their purses. Their prime chronicler was the writer Kálmán Mikszáth, but he wrote mostly about their lives in the small towns of the provinces. The lives and the workings of the minds of the gentry civil servants in Budapest were more complex. The best thing we can say about them is that they were strong-minded and proud, with a genuine inclination for aristocratic habits of *sprezzatura*. Their shortcomings were those of a narrow nationalism that had grown out of the older, county-related patriotism, and a consequently narrow nationalist cultivation that was as intense as it was shallow. It included their fondness for gypsy music, for nationalist literature, for declarative rhetoric, whether in poetry or in politics. Their sons were now, for the first time, required to have a university degree (usually in law), for the purpose of acquiring a civil service position; but their education was often rigid and narrow. This middle class was much less cosmopolitan than either the aristocracy or the Jewish bourgeoisie. For them and for Hungary this was ultimately disastrous, since they had eloquent ideas but insubstantial illusions about the world and about other nations, with fatal consequences for Hungarian politics and the destiny of the nation. Yet this class represented a bridge between the city and the country. They brought some of the agreeable atmosphere of the countryside into their Budapest houses and apartments. There was something in the atmosphere of Budapest in 1900 that was both provincial and gentry-like: the "green" restaurants of Buda, for example, or the erect bearing of their often beautiful young daughters at the university balls, or even some of their other habits, good and bad (including dueling), that some of the men of the urban bourgeoisie were inclined to emulate. For the latter the aristocracy was too far above them in the social atmosphere, whereas the gentry were, after all, almost within hailing distance. This, and perhaps only this, explains how the Magyar gentry in Budapest represented something similar to the squirearchy of England: proud rather than fashionable, they seemed to represent the essence of the race.

Thus three factors—all of them mental, not material—placed the gentry above the financial aristocracy in the estimation of people even in 1900, at that time of the peak of capitalism, in the Money Age. One of them was the still accepted idea that the gentry were the standard-bearers of Hungarianness, the prime representatives of the nation. The other was race: the gentry were not Jewish, whereas the financial aristocracy were largely Jewish, at least in their origins. Yet anti-Semitism is an inadequate explanation for this. Had many of the financial aristocracy not been Jewish, this social hierarchy would not have been different, because of the low Hungarian esteem for commerce and finance. A country gentleman was more respected than a banker—at least as long as he paid his bills (even after a long delay) and left good tips. The bankers knew that. What mattered was a certain style of behavior and of bearing.* Consequently, many men, rather than women, were attracted to some of the gentry habits and adopted them. The financial aristocracy and many families of the upper bourgeoisie bought country houses and estates; they sought a noble predicate (about which later); on occasion their sons fought a duel or two. But there was a certain reciprocity. It was not merely the usual reciprocity of the attraction of wealth for birth and of birth for wealth. It was a reciprocity of attitudes. The wives and daughters of the gentry took notice of the cosmopolitan elegance of the women of the financial aristocracy and adopted their fashions and clothes when they could afford them; and some younger sons of the gentry took interest and pleasure in the intellectual and cultural commerce of Budapest because of, not despite, its cosmopolitanism. In 1900 the elements of a fatal discord and division between the urban and the populist, between the commercial and the agrarian, between the cosmopolitan and the nationalist, between the non-Jewish Hungarian and the Jewish-Hungarian culture and civilization of Budapest were already there. But the break had not yet come. Their coexistence was still fruitful. Notwithstanding the differences and the jealousies, the misunderstandings and the animosities were often below the surface; and the flourishing of Budapest around 1900 was the outcome of that.

Above the middle-middle and lower-middle classes stood the wealthy citizenry of Budapest: a class to which "financial aristocracy" and "patricians" would be equally applicable in 1900, despite the occasionally still extant shades of difference between these terms and their subjects. By 1900 a historical development had caused these differences to fade. Because of the old Hungarian

---

*A typical Hungarian conversation, reported by my mother. She said to a family friend, "You seem to be a bit downhearted." He: "Ah! If I could only afford to live the way I live!"

attitudes and, perhaps, of the Hungarian temperament, the national disdain for commerce and finance lasted for a long time. In the first half of the nineteenth century the financiers, manufacturers, wealthy traders and artisans of Pest and Buda were mostly non-Magyar families. During the eighteenth and early nineteenth centuries, Greek families, taking advantage of evident commercial opportunities together with their chance of emigrating from the domains of the Ottoman Empire, established themselves in Pest. These families (Haris, Sina, Nákó, Sacelláry, Lyka, Mannó, Agorasztó, Muráthy became their Magyarized names) were among the first of the Pest patricians.* Around the middle of the century other enterprising foreigners came to Buda and Pest and soon established fortunes there, mostly in the building and manufacturing industries: the Norwegian Gregersen; the Swiss Ganz, Aebly, Haggenmacher; an occasional Rumanian (Gozsdu) or Serbian (Petrovics, Vrányi, Grabovszky, Bogosich, Mocsonyi—again, Magyarized names). But most patricians in Buda and Pest were still German. It was a largely German patriciate that ruled the city governments of Buda and at times even of Pest. Some of these families (Luczenbacher, Wagner, Wurm, Heinrich, Röck, Drasche, Dreher, Kauser) were not only respected; they became both Magyarized and wealthy. Most of them were builders and manufacturers. Around 1830 a few Jewish families began to rise. Their names (Wodianer, Ullmann) have an honorable place not only in the financial history of Pest but also in the political and cultural history of Hungary. They identified themselves with the 1848 Revolution and the War of Independence, often at great risk to their fortunes and freedoms. Most of their fortunes had come from the grain trade. After 1867 things changed, and not only because the law establishing the emancipation of Jews in Hungary passed with a large majority. From grain-trading some of these families shifted their interests and investments to mills and distilleries, industry, textiles, ultimately from manufacturing to finance. Thereafter other Jewish entrepreneurial families (Hatvany-Deutsch, Herzog, Strasser, Kornfeld, Weiss,† Chorin, Fellner, Tafler-Györgyey)

*Few Hungarians know that the name of one of the first famous mayors of Pest, Boráros (a *very* Hungarian-sounding name), had been Greek originally (Voraros).
†The successive generations of this richest (and eventually most prominent and ennobled) family moved from grain markets to real estate and then to light metal industry (the manufacture of canning), finally (around 1900) to heavy metal and

joined their ranks. By 1900, after Budapest had become the largest financial center of Europe east of Vienna, these banks were directed mostly (though not exclusively) by members of the Jewish financial aristocracy.

Much of this was reflected in the politics of the city. What happened in Budapest from 1870 to 1900 reflected, as in a microcosm, the rise and the decline of the overall relationship of capitalism with liberalism in the world. In 1871–72 the Parliament passed a law according to which half of the city deputies—two hundred men—would consist of the payers of the highest taxes on the city rolls. This was not such a crude materialist step as it might seem in retrospect. To the contrary: at the time this was a progressive and liberal step forward. Its purpose was to reduce the influence of the feudal elements in the city assembly, including the presence of the ancient entrenched guilds. In 1871–72 people saw this reform of the city assembly as being "antireactionary." Still, there was some opposition to it, to the effect that the original proposal of the law was slightly revised. The presence of the highest taxpayers in the city assembly would not be automatic; they would be elected from among the 1,200 highest taxpayers. The precise, painstaking researches of the superb urban historian of Budapest, Károly Vörös, reconstructed the devolution thereafter. For about fifteen years there was no radical change in the general profile of the highest taxpayers, that is, of the richest people in Budapest.* There were many aristocrats among them, many of the German builders, and a number of rising capitalists.† After 1888 the Budapest building boom changed this. The old patriciate was beginning to disappear from the rolls of the highest taxpayers. At the same time the newer kind of capitalists—owners of real estate, mostly of houses—was rising. In 1888, 211 of the highest taxpayers came from the latter group; by 1903, 466. By 1900 house-owning landlords constituted the largest group among the 1,200 leading taxpayers: 34.05 per-

---

steel production, including munitions, ordnance, armaments and even airplanes. Their social concerns (they provided soup kitchens to the indigent population of Budapest during World War I) and their patriotic dedication were outstanding.
*An important caveat: as elsewhere in the world, statistics of taxation—i.e., the figure of *declared* taxes—were not always, and not inevitably, an accurate reflection of true assets or income.
†The ratio of the highest taxpayers between liberal Pest and conservative Buda remained substantially the same for more than twenty years: one to eight. By 1912 the share of Buda had dropped to one in twelve.

cent. After them came the category of merchants: 21.85 percent. No other group amounted to more than 10 percent. (The third group were bankers: 8.46 percent and factory owners: 7.14 percent.) The composition of the wealthiest class in Budapest had changed drastically. The problem was no longer that of the remnants of the feudal order; it was that of the largely unbridled capitalist order, or disorder.

This was a sociological phenomenon, not very different from the rise of urban capitalists, including Jewish ones, in Berlin, Vienna or Paris around 1900. But there also existed a cultural condition in Budapest that was perhaps unique. The assimilation of this financial aristocracy in Hungary was among the most complete in Europe.* It was not only that (as elsewhere) some of these families had intermarried with the gentry and with the aristocracy. It was not only that some of these families had converted to Christian religions during the nineteenth century—and, so far as we can tell, out of deeper convictions than mere social ambitions. The ambitions, habits and even manners of the financial aristocracy conformed to those of the gentry—to the upper families of the gentry, rather than to the nobility. By 1890 it was almost *de rigueur* for the financial aristocracy to acquire a country estate—which they managed well, often with more consideration for their tenants and peasants than the landowners of other classes. In Vienna, Berlin, London or New York the atmosphere and the tone of the drawing room of a Jewish financier was perceptibly different from that of a Gentile magnate. In Budapest and in the Hungarian country, these differences were subdued to the extent of being hardly perceptible: foreign visitors could not recognize them unless they were reminded of the social origins of their hosts. What we may see here, in retrospect, are certain admirable characteristics of a class of people who were seldom ostentatious or arrogant, who took great pride in the strict probity of their financial operations and in the cultural and moral standards within their families. Conversely—and this is another, perhaps unique phenomenon—respect for some of these families, with their well-established names, continued in Budapest for a long time. It survived the rise of middle-class and, later, of popular

---

*In 1900 the exclusively aristocratic National Casino had seven Jewish members (the Country Casino of the gentry a few more). They were not necessarily converts. This again was unique. The clubs of the aristocracy in Vienna, Paris and Germany would have no Jewish members.

anti-Semitism, lasting, in some ways, through the worst years of the Hitler period and the Second World War.*

That financial aristocracy was, of course, only the top layer of the Jewish population in Budapest. That population was unusually large, having grown from 16 percent in 1872 to 21.5 percent in 1900. Karl Lueger, the selectively but definitely anti-Semitic Mayor of Vienna, allowed to deliver himself of the epithet "Judapest" on occasion. (His dislike of Hungarians was stronger than his dislike of Jews.) During the last decades of the nineteenth and the first decade of the twentieth centuries thousands of Jews arrived in Budapest each year. In the beginning many had come to Budapest from the West, from the Bohemian and Moravian provinces of the Habsburg Empire. After 1867 many of them came from the East, from the more primitive villages of Galicia in eastern Poland, and from Russia. Until about 1860 Jewish traders and artisans in Buda and Pest were sometimes handicapped by discrimination. Their licenses and their trade were restricted by the older, mostly German guilds. Apprentices of the latter rioted against Jews in 1848. This was one of the reasons why almost all Jews in Hungary identified themselves with the Magyar national cause in 1848 and thereafter. The other reason was the ease of their Magyarization. Because of the earlier decrees of the Emperor Josef II, most of the Jews in Hungary had German names, but a considerable minority— one-third or more—Magyarized their names during the last quarter of the nineteenth century. There were a few identifiable Magyar-

---

*A recent and otherwise estimable study of this phenomenon by an American scholar (William O. McCagg, *Jewish Nobles and Geniuses in Modern Hungary*, Boulder, Colo., 1973) misses this. It is true that many of the leading Jewish families in Hungary sought ennoblement, and that Franz Josef, especially after 1867, granted them the noble title or predicate. During the second half of the nineteenth century about 120 Jewish families in Hungary received that; there were twenty-eight Jewish barons, though no Jewish counts. But this ennoblement was, again, a peculiarly Hungarian condition, because of the already mentioned widespread ennoblement of the Hungarian gentry. Since almost one of every ten people in Hungary belonged to that class, these titles meant less than a noble title elsewhere in Europe, or than a baronetcy or even a knighthood in England. They were not always equivalents to a *von* or a *de* (even though some of the Hungarian gentry, traveling abroad, were not displeased when they were taken for aristocrats). Ennoblement in Hungary meant a titular admission of a family of the *haute finance* to the *petite noblesse terrienne;* and that the financial aristocracy on occasion desired such an admission to the titular ranks of a much poorer gentry was a very Hungarian and very telling phenomenon.

Jewish family names and first names, but these were a minority. A smaller minority were recently arrived Jews from Eastern Europe who spoke Yiddish. Among the Jewish congregations the modern-liberal "Neolog" were predominant; Orthodox Jews were relatively few. Ninety percent of Austrian Jews lived in Vienna, whereas only about 20 percent of Hungarian Jews lived in Budapest. Most Jews in Hungary were dispersed, many of them assimilated within the Magyar population in the small towns of the provinces. There were, however, districts in Pest where the population was considerably Jewish, in a few streets 60 or 70 percent. In 1900 there existed, typically, and predominantly, Jewish clubs, Jewish coffeehouses, Jewish restaurants—but not exclusively so. The Leopoldstadt Casino of the Jewish upper bourgeoisie had a fair number of Gentile members. Political and popular anti-Semitism began to appear on the surface in the early 1880s, but it was not yet particularly popular in Budapest. Theodor Herzl, the founder of modern Zionism, was a Jewish man born in Hungary; but his career as a journalist, and his discovery of Zionism—from his shock of recognition that, because of ineradicable anti-Semitic sentiments, the ideal of total Jewish assimilation in Liberal Europe was an illusion—occurred in Vienna and Paris, not in Budapest. There were, of course, Jewish elements in Budapest who evoked popular dislike and distrust: usurious landlords, fast-talking schemers in business, corner-cutters, successful skaters on thin ice—and on thin paper. Yet as late as 1900 the large proportion of Jewish lawyers and physicians in Budapest inspired little resentment. Many people in Budapest would depend on these Jewish professionals, whose standards of learning and of practice were generally high. Few occupations were closed to Jews, most of these by unspoken custom rather than by fiat: certain positions in the civil and diplomatic service, for example. This does not mean that anti-Semitism did not exist at the time. Its expression and manifestations were beginning to surface within political parties and in cultural affairs, the descriptions of which belong to later chapters.

When we contemplate the large, broad, lower part of the social pyramid of Budapest around 1900 we are facing gradations that are perhaps less subtle but no less complicated than those distinguishing some of the relationships of the upper classes. There was one rather definite barrier separating those families who had at least one domestic servant and those who had none. It was this difference— not differences in income, and not differences in occupations—that divided what we may call the lower-middle class of Budapest from the working class. But even this line was less definite than before, say, 1880, when it may be said that the majority of the people of Budapest were engaged in serving a minority, in one way or another. The proportion of those engaged in domestic service began to decrease after 1900, while the proportion of industrial—and of agricultural—workers in Budapest was rising. The wages of domestic servants were increasing, too, though they were still abysmally low. The crowded conditions of the middle-class and lower-middle-class apartments allowed for less and less space for boarding even a single, and pathetically undemanding, peasant girl. More important was the rapid industrialization of the city, and the consequent opportunities of other, better-paying work. Industrial jobs now attracted tens of thousands of young men from the provinces. These jobs nearly doubled between 1890 and 1910. By 1900 they had brought about a new class: a fairly self-conscious Budapest proletariat, whose members (especially the men) rather quickly adopted many urban habits, from their clothing to their everyday language. We shall deal with the political consequences of this development, among them the rise of the Hungarian Social Democratic Party, in the next chapter, Politics and Powers. But evidences of this new kind of class consciousness were there in the daily life of Budapest. As early as 1868 a working-class speaker raised a serious voice of protest against the then new conditions; he said that the workers were no longer human beings, they had become mere material. In the 1890s the first strikes occurred, including a large strike by bricklayers in 1897. There were occasional demonstrations in the industrial districts, involving, among other things, demands for the reduction of the twelve- (sometimes fourteen-) hour working day. Closer to the inner districts, in some of the tenements the tenants demonstrated against their landlords. On other occasions the demonstrations of the working class approached the Inner City; they took place on and around the central sections of the Ring. Such occurrences were still infrequent in 1900, but the palpable presence of a new kind of working class was already there. There was a new kind of people in some of the streets and districts of Budapest, even though this was seldom visible in Buda and in the Inner District of Pest.

There were differences in class consciousness not only between domestic servants and factory workers but between either of them and the multiple layers of the lower classes, which included the considerable group of janitors and assistant janitors of the private houses and public buildings, the very numerous low-grade employees of the civil, municipal and other institutions *(altisztek)*, * including policemen, firemen, trolley conductors, street sweepers and garbagemen. Few of them were unionized in 1900. Even among factory workers only 8,666 belonged to unions in 1901, but six years later there were already 130,000 of them. Important differences separated foremen from other workers, and workers in some occupations from others. Printers had, relatively, the highest reputation and the highest pay. In 1900 there were nearly 8,000 printers in Budapest in 560 printing shops, many of them using modern machines. A list of the different occupations would be interminable; and it would not be very different from that of other European cities of that time. Perhaps only two disparate groups were peculiar to Budapest around 1900. One was the already-mentioned and still rapidly growing agricultural population, often within the metropolitan confines of the city. The other was the peculiar institution of the guild of red-capped porter-messengers *(hordárok)*, one of the few physical occupations that included many Jews. These were jacks-of-all-trades, their duties encompassing a wide variety, ranging from the discreet transportation of love letters to the carrying of heavy baggage.† And on the bottom of the social scale and pyramid lived the floating population of destitutes, amounting, perhaps, to two of every ten people in the burgeoning city. One of every three inhabitants of Budapest had no dwelling of his own: subleasers, many of whom were not even occupants of a cramped, airless chamber. They were renters of a bed or mattress for the night.

---

*Authority mattered more than income. On occasion, a low-grade municipal employee would demonstrate a brutal pleasure in asserting his authority—like a sergeant in the regular army.

†A 1900 story. A young journalist living in a rented room lost his lease. Repairing to his usual coffeehouse, he called in one of the porter-messengers he knew. The latter emptied the young man's room, piled his clothes, books, lamps, etc. on a wheelbarrow, which was left in care of a janitor; then the porter-messenger went out to find a suitable room to rent. Having found one, he pushed the wheelbarrow there, agreed to the conditions of the lease, and set up the room for his client; he hung his client's clothes in the closet and put the book the latter had been reading on the night table. Then he went back to the coffeehouse and told the young man, "Sir, here is your address."

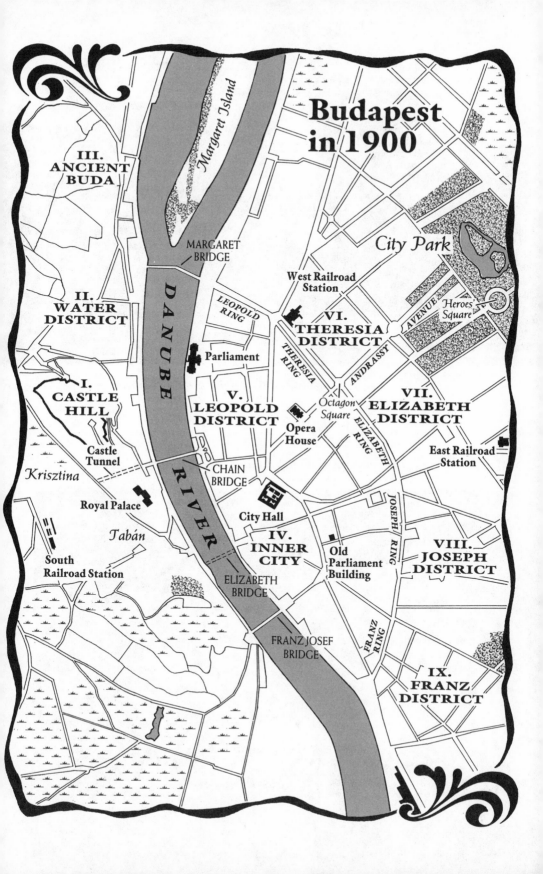

The catafalque of the painter Munkácsy.

The courtyard of the Royal Castle, the "Millennium" year.

*The promenade beneath the Royal Castle of Buda
(E. Balló: painter).*

The portal of the Tunnel under Castle Hill.

The inauguration of the—yet unfinished—Parliament in the "Millennium" year.

The Parliament.

*Budapest in 1900: in the foreground the scaffolding
of the Elizabeth Bridge, under construction.*

The Inner City as seen from Buda,
with the Chain Bridge in the foreground.

The still unfinished Royal Castle, seen from the Pest side.

The Budapest Opera House.

The Royal staircase and gallery of the Opera.

The Hungarian Academy of Sciences.

Váci Street, the main shopping street in the Inner City.

Fish Square, near the Elizabeth Bridge in the Inner City.
This square no longer exists.

The Elizabeth Ring.

The Corso of Pest above the Danube quays, with the
new hotels Hungaria, Bristol, and Carlton.

*Serpent—later Apponyi—Square, with the Clothilde Palaces.
The scaffolding of the Elizabeth Bridge is in the background.*

The new palatial row of villas at the upper end of Andrássy Avenue.

*The Emperor-King Franz Josef I and the Empress-Queen Elizabeth
drive away from the West Station, 1897.*

Hungarian political figures (including Ferenc Kossuth, far left) in ceremonial dress.

Interior of the Budapest apartment of the former Prime Minister Kálmán Tisza.

Interior of the apartment of Baron Gyula Wolfner.

Interior of the salon of an aristocratic house in Buda, owner unknown.

Terrace of a well-known coffeehouse on Andrássy Avenue, opposite the Opera.

Top: The Café New-York before its opening.

Bottom: Wampetics (later Gundel's) open-air restaurant in the City Park.

Right: A factory in Budapest (note the derby worn by one of the foremen).

T his was a very class-conscious society. In this respect Budapest was hardly different from the still largely feudal social structure of Hungary. This was manifest in the appellations (and not only in the titles) of the different classes and, consequently, in their usage in everyday language. In the civil service, for example, members of the first two grades possessed the title of *kegyelmes* (Gracious Sir, or Madam); of Grades 3 to 5, *méltóságos* (Dignified); of Grades 6 to 9, *nagyságos* (Great); and of Grades 10 and 11, *tekintetes* or *cimzetes* (Respectable). These English translations are inadequate, but not meaningless. To the contrary: these usages were widespread, accepted and used outside the civil service, involving many offices and occupations. Moreover, the Hungarian language possessed at least three ways of addressing people (like the Italian *Lei, Voi* and *Tu*). This involved not only nouns but also grammar and even syntax. It required considerable social experience and savoir-faire (or, rather, *savoir-parler*) to know how to address and to speak to one kind of person or to another. Some of these differences existed even between foremen and other workers. I wrote earlier that the general tone and picture of Budapest in 1900 had become largely bourgeois, and that this was already apparent in the clothing of the menfolk. (One of these changes involved the gradual substitution of shoes for boots; the latter had become rare, though not among the poorer women.) But there were many exceptions to bourgeois habits on the higher level, too—for example, the *díszmagyar* (festive-Magyar), the ceremonial outfit worn by the nobility (including the recently ennobled barons, as well as many of the gentry) on ceremonial occasions. It consisted of a rich, often jewel-bedecked and gold-chained short fur dolman or cape, usually draped around one shoulder, and a magnificent fur cap, topped by an aigrette. It was admired by foreigners; and, while not frequent, it was not an altogether rare appearance, since it was often worn not only on state occasions but at weddings and funerals and when the upper house of the Parliament was in session.

An example of the unbridgeable, and often tragic, class differences is found in one of the personal reminiscences, couched in a short story, of the fine Magyar writer Sándor Hunyady. During his year of military duty Hunyady, then a simple soldier, met Vilma, a beautiful peasant girl on a Sunday afternoon, when privates and maids on their only afternoon off kept promenading in one of the squares, eager to engage each other in conversation. (If the girl was agreeable, the custom was to put your hand in hers, and thereafter walk with your arm around her waist—a custom unimaginable among other classes.) They fell in love. A week or so later Hunyady (who was the son of a noted writer and a noted actress) was invited to supper in the apartment of a bourgeois family. Their maid happened to be Vilma. When she came into their dining room and saw Hunyady, who had sufficient courage and presence of mind to speak to her, she did not answer. She fled the house in an instant, never to return, and never to see Hunyady again.

But there was much social mobility in Budapest in 1900. It was social mobility that drew many people to it; and it was social mobility, too, that disturbed others, out of various motives ranging from respect for traditions to pulsations of envy, and often with a hardly separable human mixture of both. Here was the duality of the city: liberal in many ways, but with social democracy rising; bourgeois with feudal elements; urban with provincial features; a place marked by rapid and even astounding change, yet one in which the desire for stability was widespread. Historians must not overlook the dominant, though often invisible, sentiment of the nineteenth century, the desire for respectability, which involved all classes of the population. In Budapest, unlike in other cities of Eastern Europe and in many of the smaller towns of Hungary, it had become possible for the poorer classes to emulate and actually adopt certain urban and bourgeois habits and standards. Even for the working class this had become a desirable thing to do.

Another element in social mobility, in the relative democratization of the people of Budapest, was their schooling. Illiteracy declined, amazingly so. In 1870 one-third of the people of Buda and Pest were illiterate. By 1900 less than 10 percent were. Not only was illiteracy much lower in Budapest (and also in Hungary at large) than in Eastern Europe, but it was less than in many Western European countries: Italy, Portugal, Spain, lower even than in certain south-central *départements* of France.

An important element in social mobility, and in the consequent fulfillment of certain aspirations, was linguistic homogenization, the rapid Magyarization of the language and commerce of Budapest. It was a city where very many people still spoke German, yet it had ceased to be a predominantly German-speaking city for at least a generation. This duality reflected the complexity of the Dual Monarchy itself. As late as 1851 German was the main language of a slight majority in Pest and five out of six people in Buda. This was also true of the majority of Jews at the time. But after 1860 this changed. Among other things, German ceased to be the main language of the Jewish population. Generally speaking, Magyar-Jewish Pest was outstripping German-Hungarian Buda. As late as 1870 those whose first language was Magyar amounted to only 46 percent of the peoples of the two cities; but they had become a predominant majority in Pest, though not yet in Buda. By 1900 the number of those who spoke *only* German had fallen to 4.3 percent. (Those who spoke only Hungarian amounted to 38.7 percent.) Thus the majority of the peoples of Budapest was still bilingual, at least to some extent; but in 1900 those whose first language was Hungarian amounted to eight out of ten people, and those whose first language was German only to one out of seven. There were no more German theaters in Budapest. There was only one important German-language paper, the *Neues Pester Journal,* a kind of *Wall Street Journal* of the times, owned and edited by a Hungarian-Jewish newspaperman of great intelligence. In 1896 the most celebrated and loved long-ruling Lord Mayor of Budapest, Károly Kammermayer, retired. He was a typical descendant of the solid German patrician families, but throughout his public career he identified himself with the Hungarian national cause. His funeral, a year later, was accompanied by public mourning and ceremonies second only to that of Kossuth three years before.*

This rapid change from German-speaking to Magyar-speaking predominance produced relatively few animosities at the time. During the second half of the nineteenth century the city of Prague, too, changed from predominantly German-speaking to Czech-speaking, but the result was an increasingly tense and adverse relationship among Germans and Czechs in Bohemia and Moravia. In Budapest other animosities were appearing, but as late as 1900 they were still beneath the surface. In any event, these no longer involved troubles between the still German-speaking and the Magyar-speaking elements of the population. At any rate, the

---

*After 1896 came a rapid succession of lord mayors: Károly Ráth and József Márkus. Both of them died soon after their assumption of high office. But the old City Hall was demolished, too; the new City Hall and a new kind of city politics came into being after 1900.

triumph of the Magyar language was nearly complete. Many of the Slovak-language families, too (they were particularly numerous on the lowest levels of construction workers), ceased to speak their ancestral language. Their children would consider themselves Hungarian.

This was, by and large, the case with most of the thousands of recently arrived Jews from the East. In Budapest by 1900 (unlike further to the east, and in New York, for example) Yiddish-speaking among the Jewish population was relatively rare. Around 1900 a German- or Slovak-accented Magyar speech was not only more recognizable but it was even more often the butt of jokes than a Jewish-Hungarian accent. We find evidence of this in the literature of the period, including the comic weeklies and the newspapers. On the other hand, a certain kind of Budapestian street language was in full development, a kind of argot* that had both proletarian and *boulevardier* elements, with a sprinkling of often Magyarized Viennese, French, Gypsy, and even some Yiddish words and idioms. It is perhaps significant that in 1900 such elements of everyday speech had been adopted by almost every class, and perhaps especially by the younger generations among them. A conscious insistence in using the more ornate idioms and lengthier phrases, and the much slower pace and rhythm of the older Magyar habits of expression, was kept up only by the older families, and by others on certain official occasions. (As in Austria, there were many bureaucratic and ceremonial phrases and expressions in the official, governmental and military language. As in other matters, a displeasure with the quicker, more irreverent and more superficial habits of Budapest, including its speech, was sometimes evident among those of the gentry who had moved relatively recently from their country habitations to the capital city.

The rapid Magyarization of Budapest was a welcome thing, with many fruitful consequences to the national culture and literature. At the same time, it could contribute to a kind of Magyar self-centeredness, amounting to provinciality. The aristocracy and much of the bourgeoisie were aware of this. They knew that Hungarian was an orphan among the European languages, having no relationship to the great Germanic, Latin and Slavic language families. Thus, while Latin, German and some Greek were still required

---

*Argot, not jargon. The Hungarian word "jargon" *(zsargon)* at the time meant Yiddish-speaking.

subjects in the gymnasiums, private tutoring in European languages had spread from the aristocratic to upper- and middle-bourgeois families. Many of these had a German-speaking governess for their children. (Many of these *Fräuleins,* unmarried women from Austria or southern Germany, eventually became members of the family, confidantes of the woman of the house, staying on even after their erstwhile charges had grown to adulthood.) There was much private tutoring in French (which was a required subject in most of the convent schools for girls), just about none in English. There was another group of customary tutors: music teachers. The piano teacher (again, more often than not a woman) would ring the bell of the apartment door on a prescribed weekday afternoon, behind which door her student would cringe, conscious of not having done the prescribed exercises for the week, those endlessly boring difficult études by Czerny or Diabelli.

The social stratification of Budapest was manifested, too, by the different places of vacation. We have seen that some of the wealthier families owned or rented summer houses on the high hills of Buda, wherefrom in 1900 the head of the family could descend to his office in the city because of the recent improvements of roads and of public transit. But the very people who could afford such a second dwelling in the high summer months were, in most cases, the same people for whom a summer vacation abroad was a social requirement. "Abroad" meant Austrian or Bohemian watering places, the famous spas of Karlsbad, Marienbad, Ischl, Gastein, the Semmering, etc. Within Hungary there were few places where the standards of hotels would fulfill the requirements of the *haute bourgeoisie:* those in the Tatra mountains, in Pöstyén in northwestern Hungary, along the Adriatic coast, or in a few places along Lake Balaton, where soon the families of the gentry and the Jewish middle classes would establish separate places for themselves. Generally speaking, the farther abroad the vacation, the higher its social prestige. A family trip to France meant more than a visit to Italy, and a summer sojourn in the Swiss Alps more than one in the Austrian ones. In 1900 winter vacations were still rare, except for an occasional brief sojourn on the French Riviera.

In these respects the high nobility and the upper-middle classes had something in common. They were more cosmopolitan than the other classes. At least in cultural matters (and also in the extent of their loyalty to the monarchy) they were less nationalistic than the gentry. This was reflected not only in their linguistic abilities but also in their cultural interests. In 1900 the few considerable private collections of art existed in some of the houses of these people. Far more general and widespread was the theatrical culture of Budapest. In 1900 the city had at least six theaters, of which three had opened during the ten preceding years. Most of these, including the Opera, were frequented by all of the educated classes. A historical reason for this was the role that Magyar theaters, their actors and actresses, assumed already in the early nineteenth century, when they were visible and important instruments of the national revival. In 1900 the theatrical culture of Budapest—ranging from the quality of the playwrights, the literary erudition of the directors, the efficiency of the stagecraft, and the excellence of many of the actors and actresses—was on a very high level. In 1900 a celebrated actress (actress, rather than actor) was seen as a national asset. In some instances, streets and public squares were named after them. In addition to the cabarets and orpheums there was, too, a peculiarly Hungarian form of thespian culture, the *népszínmű,* a popular comedy often favored by the less sophisticated gentry and by the lower-middle classes. Their plays were nationalist, provincial and often shallow. (It is probably significant that in the last examples of this genre boy and girl no longer met at the end of a village garden but in a hotel hall in Budapest.) By 1900 this genre had begun to disappear, as had, too, the former German-speaking theaters.

In this portrait of the people of Budapest around the turn of the century it is perhaps not improper to say something about the relations of the sexes. The double standard, prevalent almost everywhere in the Western world at the time, was taken for granted in Hungary, too. Virginity and chastity of girls before marriage was not only desirable, it was *de rigueur.* For young men it was not. A sexual adventure of a married man was, on occasion, overlooked; of a married woman, customarily speaking, it was not. Unlike in other Catholic countries, after 1895 the legal possibility of divorce existed. In these matters there were no significant differences between Catholic, Protestant and Jewish families—and, somewhat surprisingly, not many differences between the upper and the middle classes. Most marriages were still arranged between families. It was unlikely that an engagement would take place without the family of the bride having some connection with, or at least substantial information about, the family of the groom. A broken engagement could amount to a tragedy, to an often wholly undeserved stain on the social prestige of a young woman; in many instances, she would give up the idea of marrying. It was difficult, nay, almost impossible, for a young girl to meet a young man outside the social circles arranged by her family, and outside acceptable places: the dancing classes, skating club, balls of the various university faculties, county balls (for the gentry), and perhaps a family introduction in the foyers of the Opera or the theaters. Unmarried girls were chaperoned everywhere, including on their shopping or even on their midday walk home from schools: the chaperones ranging from a governess or a stiff old unmarried aunt to a slatternly maid, since this practice reached down to the lower middle class.

Much of this was not different from life in Vienna or other European cities around 1900. There were, however, certain different nuances in the daily life and in the mental climate of Budapest that may deserve attention. We have seen that there were many illegitimate marriages and illegitimate children among the lowest classes, where illegitimacy was less of a stigma than elsewhere.* Yet the double standard was even stronger among the lower classes than elsewhere—when it involved life after, not before, marriage. An erring working-class wife would run the risk of being severely beaten by her husband, and of finding herself an outcast among her neighbors. Another condition in Budapest that was different from other cosmopolitan capitals of the world in 1900 was the relative absence of a demimonde—of a class of women of easy, rather than depraved morals, long-range mistresses haughtily above the short-range prostitutes. Save perhaps for the liaisons of certain actresses, *grandes horizontales* in Budapest in 1900 were rare. (We have seen that young women who were attracted to such careers had gone to seek their fortunes abroad.) Unmarried young men and married men satisfied their sexual desires with visits to various brothels, whose prices and arrangements ran from rich to poor, reflecting the social gradations of the city. Extramarital affairs would involve, on occasion, the wife of someone whom one knew—that is, from one's own social class. Since there were very few inns or hotels that would rent rooms during the day, it was very difficult to find a place for

*Interestingly enough, illegitimacy (as well as divorce) was occasionally overlooked among the gentry families (less so among the bourgeois ones). This was the case with the writer Sándor Hunyady, mentioned earlier, the love child of the author Sándor Bródy and of the actress Margit Hunyady, who was the daughter of Transylvanian gentry. Discriminations experienced by Sándor Hunyady in consequence to his illegitimate condition were minimal (perhaps because of his mother's high professional and moral reputation).

such assignations. (One of these was the Hotel Fiume in Buda, the other the Hotel Orient in Pest.) It was even more difficult, nay, impossible, to keep them secret because in spite of the growing population and the crowds, Budapest in 1900 was still a place where—at least within the confines of a class—everybody knew everybody.

A liaison of a man of the bourgeoisie with a shopgirl or modiste —a frequent practice in Vienna or Paris at the time—was relatively rare. So was the practice of part-time prostitutes. Another rarity in Budapest (and in Hungary) was the evidence of homosexuality among males. In all of the records, including those of the police and, even more significant, in the rich and gossipy journalism and literature of the period, we find very few examples of it. There are more—often cautiously suggested—evidences of homosexuality among females. The reason may have been that in Budapest around 1900 masculinity and virility were still very dominant; the supremacy of the male was unquestioned and unquestionable, sometimes to the detriment of feminine sensitivities.*

Whether optimists or pessimists, the people of Budapest, even in this bourgeois period, were expressive. They wore their minds, if not their hearts, on their sleeves. Their concerns, problems, strengths and failures were evident in their conscious expressions of all kinds, rather than suppressed or submerged on subconscious levels. By 1900 the change in the tone of the city, the rapid replacement of some of the older patricians by more and more parvenus and *nouveaux riches,* was perhaps the most disturbing development in the social climate; it would have baneful consequences in politics. Reaction against this development came through expressions of outspoken, rather than suppressed, envy. Yet that disturbance, too, was social rather than financial, psychic rather than material, because of the frequent cavalier (and, on occasion, nonchalant) Hungarian uninterest in money as such—something that may, again, seem to be reflected in the Hungarian idiom. How much money do you *make* a year? an American will ask. How much do you *earn?*

---

*The Magyar language—or, rather, its then prevailing usage—reflects this. Two equally frequent and acceptable words for one's husband were *férjem* ("my husband") and *uram* ("my master" or "my lord"). The second usage has now almost disappeared, but only during the last few decades. "Wife" in Magyar, *feleség,* however, has the lovely meaning of "my halfness"—a proper noun and not, like "my better half," a phrase.

(verdienen) ask the Germans. How much do you *win? (gagner, gag-nare, ganar)* say the light-spirited Latin tongues. *"Mennyit keresel?"* "How much are you trying *to gather?"* says the Magyar language, for reasons that its excellent three-volume etymological dictionary cannot really explain, except to inform us that the desire to achieve, the effort, was originally implicit in the verb *keresni.* "If I could only afford to live the way I live!" In 1900 that was not the problem of everyone in Budapest—surely not of the bourgeois classes, where financial probity was often unexceptionable, and who were seldom ostentatious. It was the problem—and the affliction—of Hungarian politics at large.

4

Politics and Powers

In 1900 the politics of Hungary were centralized in Budapest: more precisely, in the Parliament. Like that enormous building, then nearing its completion, this was a relatively new development. In the older Hungarian tradition much of the politics of the nation had concentrated in the counties and their assemblies. Even during most of the nineteenth century these somehow resembled the provincial *parlements* or Diets of late medieval and early modern Europe, in that their legislative and governmental powers meant little, while their local administrative (and social) powers were still considerable. Even more considerable was their rhetoric. These county assemblies were the places for the *petite noblesse terrienne* to blow off steam. Such had been the function of the *parlements* of France before 1788. But the social, material and intellectual characteristics of the Magyar petty nobility and those of the aristocracy, clergy and bourgeois of France were different. The Hungarian county assemblies were both less efficient and less democratic than comparable institutions in Western Europe. Precisely therefore the foremost Magyar Liberal political thinker and writer around the middle of the nineteenth century, Baron József Eötvös, friend and correspondent of Montalembert and Tocqueville, argued and fought for the necessity of political and administrative centralization, when classic Liberals elsewhere on the continent were often wary of centralization, as Tocqueville had been. Much of this had something to do with the peculiar inclinations of Magyar political rhetoric, which, in turn, was both cause and consequence of certain elemental inclinations of the Hungarian public, that is, political, character. When after 1867 the long overdue centralization of government and administration began to take place, many of the deputies carried their impolitic habits of political rhetoric from the provincial assemblies to the pompous vaulted halls of the national Parliament.

There was an allied development. "The Parliament," wrote Mihály Babits, "lies at the heart of every Magyar." Around 1900 the politics of the Parliament had become a national sport. "The existence and the security of the nation were no longer in question; to the contrary, the parliamentary battles raged around questions that had hardly any practical importance. Yet people now followed the party politics and the parliamentary scene with much greater interest than they had before. The Parliament played the role in public interest that was later taken up by the entertainments of the theaters and then those of spectator sports. It was the center of attention . . . so far as popularity went, [some of the] members of Parliament were the forerunners of film stars." This was written a generation later by the fine historian of Hungarian literature, Antal Szerb, whose history of Magyar literature *(Magyar irodalomtörténet)* is not only a classic but a sensitive and profound description of the historical development and of the successive inclinations of the Magyar mind. I am citing him because of this very condition: the problematic character of Hungarian politics in 1900 was a result of the problematic character of the Hungarian mind.

The Hungarian mind (as again Szerb wrote, elsewhere), "tends to monologue, rather than to dialogue."* This tendency does not, as is otherwise often the case, mean the monopolizing of conversation, since Hungarians are, by and large, good listeners. But this habit of the monologue, and the consequent and virtual absence of the dialogue, has had disastrous political consequences. Hungarians

---

*One result of this is agreeable: the national liking for anecdotes, and the frequent occurrences of anecdotes in Hungarian prose, sometimes on a high level.

are *not* a voluble people, *except* in their public speeches and state-ments. One of the reasons for this is the declarative character of the Hungarian language.* Expression dominates the thought—as a matter of fact, it often creates (and not merely completes) the latter. The Hungarian language is rational rather than mystical, lyrical rather than metaphorical; and there is little that is sly and secretive in the national character. But in public rather than in private speech, the sober and rational element in the Hungarian mind—and the terseness of the language—tend to be overwhelmed by the intoxication of rhetoric. There is little inclination to profit from a dialogue. There is little inclination to find satisfaction in compromise. There is an often yawning distance, not so much between thought and speech as between speech and action, be-tween the attraction of ideals and the contemplation of realities, between verbal energy and physical lassitude. The result is a fatal Hungarian tendency to self-centeredness.

During the nineteenth century the essential, and characteristic, pessimism of the Hungarian mind was overlaid often by a wholly impolitic optimism. That optimism was part of the dynamic rise of the nation on many levels, but it was naïve as well as myopic. That naïveté had many charming consequences in Magyar poetry. But its shortcomings were decisive. An example of it are the "works" and pronouncements early in the century of the Magyar historian István Horváth, who argued, among other things, that the Magyars had

---

*This may be related to the fact that in the Hungarian language the emphasis is *always* on the first syllable; and in everyday speech the lilt of sentences runs from high to low, downward—unlike in English. (". . . changes of sense are conveyed by a concatenation of syllables stuck on behind the first; all the vowel sounds imitate their leader, and the invariable ictus on the leading syllable sets up a kind of dactylic or anaepaestic canter which, to a new ear, gives Magyar a wild and most unfamiliar ring" Leigh Fermor, p. 33.) There may be a connection between this and the national character fault, excoriated often by great Magyar thinkers and writers: the brilliance of short-run effort at the expense of prudence and foresight. Their word for it is "straw-fire nature," since straw burns brilliantly but rapidly, leaving only a heap of black ashes. There are, however, two caveats to this otherwise plausible and illustratable thesis. The Finnish language is related to the Magyar, with a similar structure and identical emphases on the first syllable of each word; yet the Finnish and the Magyar national characters and temperaments are very different. The other caveat about the "straw-fire" metaphor is that persistence (rather than perseverance) is a Hungarian trait; and straw-fire is surely not persis-tent. Many of the most enduring achievements of the nation consisted of conserva-tive efforts of recovery and rebuilding after its worst disasters.

descended from Adam and Eve, and that the ancient Greek language was Magyar in origin. The fact that the absurdities of this near-maniac were accepted by the contemporary reading public (he was also a university professor from 1823 to 1845), "indicated the optimistic national self-portrait of the times," wrote Szerb a century later. This kind of optimism was the preparation for "the many shocking political mistakes of the succeeding generation." More than one succeeding generation were driven astray by their rhetoric of national self-confidence. Alas, that sometimes salutary sense of national self-confidence existed together with a wanting extent of self-knowledge; and with a wholly wanting understanding of the limits of national power, indeed, of Hungary's situation in Europe.

This was especially so in politics, and it was very evident around 1900. It was aggravated by the condition that much of the nation's politics were still in the hands of the Hungarian gentry, whose virtues were vitiated by their self-centeredness—meaning, among other things, their fatal ignorance of the world beyond Hungary (and often, too, of those worlds within Hungary that were not theirs). Their ideals, ideas and ambitions were already outdated, though they did not know this. The conservative Mably's *Observations on the History of France,* in 1786, were, *mutatis mutandis,* applicable to the Hungarian political class a century later: "The Third Estate is nothing in France because no one wants to be included in it. Every bourgeois among us thinks only of getting out of his situation and buying an office . . . and as soon as he gets it he no longer considers himself part of the common people." Substitute gentry in Hungary for "bourgeois" in France, and a parliamentary seat for "office" a century later: the statement is telling. The aristocracy and the gentry considered themselves—and were generally considered by others—as the "historical classes" of the nation. Yet their political talents were flawed. Again the evidence for this was there in the habits of Hungarian political rhetoric. For one thing, as late as 1900 the house rules of the Magyar Parliament did not allow the reading of speeches. Members had to deliver them extempore. There were two reasons for this: one the rule of "cloture," that is, a restriction of filibustering; the other, more traditional reason, the old Hungarian habit of public rhetoric. For a politician's reputation, the ability to make public speeches was what mattered. The result was often rhetorical flamboyance and nationalist brag, stuffed with hyperbole, and with few practical consequences.

Tocqueville once remarked that the main vice of aristocratic ages is pride, while that of democracies may be envy. To this we may add that there are societies in transition where we may find the unconscionable prevalence, or mixture, of both of these vices. This seems to have been typical of half-feudal, half-modern Spain and of half-feudal, half-modern Hungary; it was surely prevalent in the disorderly parliamentary politics of both. The national disinclination to dialogue was there in the ugly personal hatreds of some of the politicians. Unlike in older, feudal times, it was not so much that they carried their private quarrels into the political arena; to the contrary, they often allowed their political disagreements to poison their personal relations, degenerating into hatreds, duels, occasional physical assaults, even shooting. Around 1900 the level of rhetoric and the parliamentary habits of the Magyar House of Representatives were lamentable.* A decline in decorum, moderation and sagacity had occurred. In sum, the political situation in Budapest was disturbing at the very time the capital city was flourishing on more than one level, in more than one field of life, and not only materially. The politicization of Hungarian life ran at high tide. So ran the politicization of the Hungarian mind. That mind possessed, and still possesses unusual qualities, at times exceptional ones, but political ability has been a rare and infrequent asset among them.

Hungary, in 1900, was an independent nation, but not an entirely independent state. Many, probably most, Hungarians, including their politicians, neither appreciated nor understood the necessities for this limitation. They asserted that the independence of Hungary was compromised. To the contrary: the assertive independence of the Hungarian nation had been facilitated by a compromise—the Compromise, or *Ausgleich,* of 1867. This requires expla-

---

*From the memoirs of two principal Hungarian figures, a politician and a writer. Count Albert Apponyi: "Whenever three Hungarians talk politics, they form a party: one is President, the other Vice-President, the third becomes Secretary-General who regards it as his duty 'to make an important statement' on every occasion." Ferenc Herczeg: Mikszáth "told me bitterly: 'Don't forget—this is a country [and a Parliament] where no one remembers Deák [our greatest statesman] but where the memory of Sobri Jóska [a brigand] is extolled in heroic speeches."

nation; and a necessarily brief sketch of the history of the Hungarian state.

There was once a medieval Hungarian kingdom. Eventually it fell on evil days. Early in the sixteenth century, at the very time when the power of monarchs was rising elsewhere in the West, the kings of Hungary were impoverished weaklings, *rois fainéants*. But the catastrophe came from the outside. After their conquest of Byzantium and the Balkans the Turkish armies appeared on the Hungarian plain. In 1526 they annihilated the Hungarian army. The King perished on the battlefield. The remaining nobles offered the crown to the Austrian Habsburg monarch. That was how the dynastic connection of Austria-cum-Hungary began. The nobles thought, and hoped, that the Emperor-King Ferdinand (the brother of Charles V) would drive the Turks out. He didn't. He took the royal title and assisted in the defense of the western rim of Hungary —to keep the Turks away from Vienna. That was all. Buda fell to the Turks in 1541. For the next century and a half there were three parts to Hungary. There was the western and northern rim, largely free of the Turks, part of the Habsburg Empire. There was a large middle portion, including Buda and Pest, ruled by the Ottoman Empire. There also came into being a third Hungary, in the eastern part of the country, named Transylvania ("The Forest Country"), where Hungarian princes from time to time succeeded in maintaining a state of actual or virtual and sometimes nominal independence from Turks and Habsburgs alike. There were no clear and permanent boundary lines between these sovereignties and half-sovereignties. The hot rake of war went up and down Hungary for a century and a half. Most of the country was devastated and depopulated. Hungary was not able to free itself from the Turks by its own efforts. At the end of the seventeenth century the Habsburg imperial armies defeated the Turks, starting from under the walls of Vienna. Thereafter they drove them out of most of Hungary in about fifteen years. That was all to the good. But Hungary was now a Habsburg province. Many thousands of Germans and other settlers came to live on its empty lands. Those Magyars who detested this condition could do little. Yet the Austrian, Catholic, Habsburg governance was still better than life under the Turks. The population began to revive. Some of the nobles—the minor nobility, rather than the aristocracy—began to assert their independence, customarily in their county assemblies. Habsburg rule, while not always lenient, was seldom tyrannical. By and large, the people and the nobles respected the right of the monarchs in Vienna, to wear, allegorically, two crowns on their august heads: emperors (or empresses, as in the case of Maria Theresa) of Austria, kings (or queens) of Hungary. Even the most vocal patriots among the nobles were willing to offer their military services to these monarchs. Meanwhile, the Enlightenment, the Century of Reason, the French Revolution hardly touched Hungary, except on the mental edges of a few people and on the physical edges of the country—when, for example, Napoleon's army in 1809 penetrated into Hungary from the west for a few weeks and then withdrew, making peace with the Habsburgs.

Around 1820 came a change. National consciousness, that natural progenitor of the unruly twins of nationalism and independence, arose. Its rise was astounding, feverish and quick. Count István Széchenyi, an intelligent, melancholy and selfless genius, amounted to an entire generation of founding fathers rolled into one, but with one profound difference: unlike the American Founding Fathers, Széchenyi thought that the quest for a wholly independent Hungarian state was a perilous mirage, at least for the time being. He was very knowledgeable of the shortcomings and the petty vexations by the Viennese administration of Hungary; he was also profoundly aware of the wanting cohesion of the Hungarian kingdom, within whose borders lived millions of people who were not Magyars. Széchenyi's very great achievements notwithstanding— he was not only the propagator but the actual founder and builder of many modern Hungarian institutions—by the early 1840s he was overshadowed by the great national speaker Lajos Kossuth. There was no real or judicious dialogue between them. Kossuth was the more effective monologuist. In March 1848 the news of revolutions in Paris, Milan and Vienna arrived in Pest. The youth of the city rose on the 15th. A few weeks later the doddery Emperor-King, Ferdinand V, agreed to most of the Magyar demands for self-government. That was not the end of it. Those demands increased. At the same time, the Austrian government had an instrument at its disposal. The non-Magyar peoples within the borders of Hungary were restive. The Magyars wanted autonomy from Austria; they had no intention of granting autonomy to people who were not Magyars within the kingdom of Hungary. A Croat army, with Austrian help and equipment, marched up into western Hungary, toward Buda. Hungarian troops, raised and equipped out of almost nothing, turned them back. Then these Magyar brigades marched on Vienna, which was, temporarily, in the hands of Viennese radicals and democrats, the Court having fled to Innsbruck. Now it was the Hungarians who were turned back. The Viennese revolutionaries collapsed. The Court returned. The family made the senile Ferdinand abdicate. The eighteen-year-old Franz Josef I was made Emperor. An Austrian imperial army moved into Hungary, occupying Buda and Pest without much of a struggle. The 1848 Revolution seemed to be over. But it wasn't. In the spring a new Hungarian army, led by a superb general (Görgey), rose in the northeastern counties. It beat the Austrians. It reconquered Buda in a bloody siege. A national assembly, under Kossuth, took the final step and proclaimed the dethroning of the Habsburgs. Franz Josef traveled to Warsaw, to meet the Tsar of Russia there. The Tsar was willing to help, for many reasons, including the worrisome fact that Polish generals and officers were fighting on the side of the Magyar revolutionaries. Hundreds of thousands of Russian troops poured into Hungary. Görgey had to surrender. Kossuth fled the country. The Austrians executed thirteen generals of the revolutionary army and many other patriots. Thousands were imprisoned. The cause of Magyar independence was a rubble of ashes. The best Hungarians were full of bitterness and darkness. From 1848 the great Széchenyi found himself in a mental institution, though his mind would live through long periods of great bitter lucidity. In 1860 he killed himself.

Yet by 1860 the air in Hungary had become lighter. It was no longer oppressive. There were wholesale amnesties, though as yet nothing resembling a reconciliation with Vienna. The drift to prosperity became a current. Buda and Pest had begun to blossom. As in Milan, Venice and Prague under the Habsburgs, Austrian police rule went often apace with serious and enduring improvements in building, engineering and institutions. This, and the lightening of police rule over Hungary, was due less to Habsburg clemency (though the young Empress Elizabeth had an evident liking for Hungarians) than to the supple Austrian recognition of necessities, to the Austrian talent in maneuvering. Austria had lost a short war to Italy and France. It had to do something to reform the structure of its ancient, dynastic multinational empire. In 1860 the Habsburg Empire, for the first time, received a sort of constitution. It was heavily weighted in favor of its German-speaking peoples. It was not at all satisfactory to Hungarians. But the change in the political climate was more important than were the political structures. Freedom of expression, including political expression, had returned. Freedom of enterprise—that is, capitalism and industrialism—were now burgeoning in Hungary, especially in Pest. An old and wise national personage, Ferenc Deák, "The Sage of the Nation," took to his pen. In a prudent and principled way he suggested the need of a settlement, a pacification, an honorable compromise between the Hungarian nation and the house of Habsburg. His motto was an ancient Latin one: *peragit tranquilla potestas, quae violentia nequit* (a tranquil persistence of power may achieve what violence failed to do). Perhaps: but what helped was another external shock that altered permanently Austria's position in Europe. It was administered by Bismarck. In 1866 Bismarck's new model Prussian army defeated the Austrians in a lightning war. Bismarck wanted, but took, no territory from Austria.* What he wanted, and got, was the elimination of the Habsburg presence from the Germanies. Austria still remained one of the five Great Powers of Europe, but the structure and the direction of its peculiar multinational empire had to be changed. It was no longer a German *and* a Danubian empire. It remained the latter; and in the age of national consciousness, of national aspirations and liberal nationalism, Vienna had to take into account that within its domains its German-speaking peoples were a minority.

The outcome of this was the Compromise of 1867. It meant that Hungary became the junior partner of Austria. The official name of the Habsburg monarchy was now Austria-Hungary. That was the structure of "Dualism"—a term that the conservative, pessimistic, far-seeing Hungarian writer and publicist Baron Zsigmond Kemény first used in 1850. It meant Home Rule for Hungary. Almost everything that the Magyar liberals had demanded in 1848 was now embedded in a constitutional law. Hungary had its own parliament, administration, ministries and cabinet departments, even Hungarian regiments within the Austro-Hungarian army. Only three cabinet ministries—foreign affairs, army, finance—were "common" Austro-Hungarian ones, seated in Vienna. A joint bud-

---

*The Italians came in after Prussia; even though the Austrians defeated them, Italy got Venice and the Venetian province from Austria for a now united Italy.

get commission would determine Hungary's share of their expenses. This did not mean that the "common" portfolios were necessarily held by Austrians. They were often held by Hungarians, including the most important Ministry of Foreign Affairs. The Hungarian nation and people were relieved, indeed, joyous. In June 1867 Franz Josef's coronation in Pest and Buda was marked by scenes of exuberant enthusiasm. In 1867 only a handful of radicals, even fewer Magyar republicans, some of the non-Magyar nationalities, and, of course, the great Lajos Kossuth from his exile in Turin, Italy, sounded a discordant note. These notes were only a murmur then, though one with a persistent echo. Meanwhile the great liberal, capitalist, material flourishing of Hungary, and especially of Budapest, had already begun.

Peragit tranquilla potestas, quae violentia nequit. But that exercise of Hungarian political power was not tranquil. The national inclination to political rhetoric asserted itself. There were plenty of Hungarians who thought—or, rather, who convinced themselves—that the Compromise was unsatisfactory, that their rights were being trammeled and slighted. For a time this Hungarian "Left" (the contemporary parliamentary term for them was "Left-Center") remained an important element even within the governing Liberal Party of Deák, the one that had accepted and supported the Compromise. Gradually a kind of two-party system emerged in the Hungarian Parliament. The Liberals, also called the 67-ers, accepted the Compromise by and large; yet many of their members felt compelled to castigate one or another of its features in public rhetoric. The Independents, also called 48-ers, professed the demand for complete national independence, using it often as a stick to beat the governing Liberals; yet beyond speechifying, and other kinds of symbolic demonstrations, they did little or nothing to advance the cause of that mythical independence. From 1875 to 1890 the Prime Minister was Kálmán Tisza, a Protestant landowner and nobleman from eastern Hungary, with "gentry" as well as aristocratic family connections. After this original and eloquent member of the once "Center-Left" had become Prime Minister, he became prudent, calculating and moderate. He realized the inefficiency—the dangerous inefficiency—of extreme nationalist rhetoric. *Quieta non movere* (don't rock the boat) was the motto attributed to him by his opponents and even by some of his supporters. In 1890 he had to resign, almost in the same week when Bismarck left his office in Germany. As in the case of Bismarck's Germany, this was the beginning of a new political era.

The effective cause of Kálmán Tisza's resignation was symptomatic. It was A Constitutional Issue, meaning that it involved (as it would again and again) the complex matter of Dualism, that is, the status of Hungarian independence. The matter was complex not because the public law of the Compromise that had established the Dualism was especially complex or particularly vague; it was complex because the state of the national mind was complex. That state of mind was optimistic and grandiloquent, and beset by suspiciousness and jealousy at the same time. While Franz Josef was highly respected, Vienna and the entire relationship with Austria were not. Any reminder of the power of the latter—which, as we have seen, was effectively limited, both de jure and de facto—touched the raw nerve of the Magyar political nation; and that nerve was kept raw by the rhetoric of the politicians. During the late winter of 1889–90 two of those Constitutional Issues arose. One was the issue of Kossuth, the adored national hero, whose Hungarian citizenship had officially lapsed in 1889. This was meaningless in practice, since Kossuth would not return to Hungary. Meanwhile several Hungarian towns had elected him their honorary citizen. That Franz Josef and his government allowed (albeit reluctantly) such a thing speaks volumes of their relative liberality—and of their unwillingness to rouse sleeping dogs. Kossuth, after all, was *the* rebel principal, who had come close to destroying the entire Empire, who had declared not only the independence of Hungary but the dethronement of the Habsburgs, and who never relented in exile, sending messages to Hungary and articles to the newspapers. The other issue was the imperial and royal army. Franz Josef and the high command decided in February 1890 that general officers must be trained and appointed to the units of the joint army, even if they were serving in the specifically Magyar *honvéd* regiments. Characteristically, Kálmán Tisza attempted a compromise: a prolongation of Kossuth's citizenship, opposition to the army reform. He failed; his own party did not give him enough support; he had to resign. Even this explanation may be too simple. Many of the politicians who had turned against him did so because of their personal jealousies and ambitions. The very Constitutional Issues were their means, not their end. As so often happens, the effective causes and the real causes were different things. Such was the state of Hungarian politics in 1890. It was then—six years before the zenith of national pride in the Millennium Year of 1896, ten years before the zenith of national prosperity in 1900—that the Hungarian parliamentary and political system began to unravel.

The next Premier was Count Gyula Szapáry, an aristocrat of indifferent political talents. (Until the end of the Dual Monarchy in 1918 there was at least one member of the high nobility in every Hungarian cabinet.) In 1892 Szapáry resigned because of another symbolic fracas. June 1892 was the twenty-fifth anniversary of Franz Josef's coronation. Szapáry was in favor of a symbolic ceremony of an ultimate reconciliation: the official laying of wreaths at two monuments, one at the newly erected monument commemorating the Hungarian army of 1848–49, the other at the one honoring the Austrian General Hentzi, who had died a hero's death when he defended Buda from the besieging Magyars in 1849. It did not work. Szapáry was assailed from all sides. He had to resign. Another kind of compromise was made: the Budapest municipal council made Franz Josef and Kossuth honorary citizens, a gesture that was largely meaningless.

The new Prime Minister was Sándor Wekerle, a descendant of a German family, a political economist of considerable ability (the architect of the reform of the Hungarian currency, from the silver-based florin [*forint*] to the gold-based crown [*korona*] in 1892) who resembled Gladstone in some ways (including in his physical appearance) and whose biography is yet to be written. He got into trouble soon. The issue was the Hungarian *Kulturkampf,* the somewhat overdue passage of certain laws that would establish the priority of state over ecclesiastical (Catholic) authority in the registration and legality of civil marriages, including those contracted between members of different religions. There was another characteristic compromise or, rather, a trade-off: Franz Josef reluctantly accepted these liberal and, to some extent, anticlerical reforms,* but Wekerle had to go. His successor was Dezső

---

*This was a complicated business. In 1894–95 it amounted to another symbolic confrontation between Ultramontane Conservatism and Hungarian Liberalism, between Catholics and Protestants, between the Court of Vienna and the Parliament in Budapest, and even between anti-Semites and philo-Semites. (See p. 132

Bánffy, a martinet, who used every instrument (including the gendarmerie) to suppress manifestations of opposition to the government. Franz Josef did not like him ("I have no other choice, alas," he said). In March 1894 Kossuth died. His body was brought from Turin to Budapest. The funeral was awesome: three days of solid mourning, the city draped in black, even though Franz Josef refused to declare it a state occasion and the bells of Catholic churches did not toll. (The Protestant bells rang, and official mourning was proclaimed by the municipality of Budapest.) Soon Kossuth's son Ferenc returned to Hungary. He was instantly elected head of the Independence Party; but he was a poor politician, and a weak character. Bánffy, who had cared little for the Kossuth funeral, knew that. After an election marked by governmental intervention (and some corruption) he proclaimed a national political truce for the Millennium Year of 1896. It did not last. Two years after the Millennium the nation celebrated the fiftieth anniversary of the 1848 Revolution. The only concession made to Franz Josef was that the official state celebration would take place on April 11 and not on March 15. (April 11, 1848, was the date Franz Josef's predecessor had agreed to the Hungarian constitutional demands, but March 15, 1848, was the day of the Rising in Pest.) Later that year the Empress-Queen Elizabeth was stabbed to death by an Italian anarchist in Switzerland. The entire Magyar nation mourned her: she had liked the Magyars and was immensely popular among them. But this authentic effusion of monarchial sentiment was one thing; for meanwhile the political structure was badly frayed. The two-party system (if it was that) had already broken up into four or five sections. A National Party came into being in 1892, splitting off from the Liberals; and a Catholic People's Party in 1895. In 1898 Bánffy had to go. His successor was Kálmán Széll, an intelligent and moderate politician (and the late and revered Deák's son-in-law).

A factor in this breakup was the endless jealousies and personal quarrels among the Hungarian politicians, involving not only the governing Liberals but the opposition Independents, too, whose ranks were splitting off and reforming themselves ceaselessly. An-

---

about the beginning of the Catholic People's Party in 1894.) In the long run these laws were sensible and even acceptable to the Church, since they were judiciously drafted. (The standards of Hungarian legal science were high at the time. One of their results was the exemplary criminal code of jurisprudence [*Csemegi-kódex*].)

other factor was the rising criticism of the electoral corruption practiced, on occasion, by the government. This consisted of obstructing the campaigns of antigovernment candidates through all kinds of administrative legerdemains and even police and gendarmerie interventions. In the elections of 1892 and 1896 the Liberal majority began to diminish. By 1900, at the end of the century marked by Liberalism in the history of Europe, the Liberals were still the government party in Hungary and in Budapest, but not much longer. The Liberal Party—indeed, the idea of Liberalism—had weakened fundamentally. It no longer signified liberty, reform, progress; people regarded the Liberals as the remnant props of an antiquated system. The development of political vocabulary suggested this. Some people would now refer to the remaining core of the 67-ers, of the old party of the Compromise, as the "Ancient Liberals," *Óliberálisok.*

The turn of the century came and went. There were many occasions for national self-congratulation, perhaps especially in Budapest. There was little reason, or evidence, for satisfaction with national politics.* In 1901 the honorable members moved into the decorous halls of the monumental new Parliament building. Their conduct in those halls was often indecorous. In 1903 another Constitutional Issue arose. The Independents and other nationalists in the Hungarian Parliament demanded the exclusive use of the Magyar language for the command of Hungarian units in the joint army. This was a matter very close to Franz Josef's heart. He was convinced that in principle as well as in practice the army must remain supranational. It was, after all, the main defensive bulwark of the Dual Monarchy, and of its multinational state. In this the aged monarch was unwilling to compromise. Széll tried to delay matters, but his tactics did not work. He had to go. After a few months of a transitional cabinet Franz Josef appointed Count István Tisza, Kálmán's son, to the Prime Ministership.

Tisza was one of the greatest Hungarian political personages of the twentieth century: a statesman with a strong character and foresight. But that character was too rigid for the twentieth century. Were this book a history of Hungary and not of Budapest, a de-

---

*Or for satisfaction with Hungary's reputation in Vienna. In 1900 the heir to the throne, the Archduke Franz Ferdinand, married the love of his life, a Czech countess. At that time his interest in—and his planning of—politics began. He was bitterly anti-Hungarian.

scription of this odd, dark, conservative and predestinationist Protestant magnate—in some ways reminiscent of a Scottish Covenanter of the seventeenth century—would deserve at least a few pages. Here we must limit ourselves to the first years of the century, to the political crisis when the personality of Tisza rose above the hullabaloo of the Parliament. Like Bismarck, whom he admired, he was contemptuous of that hullabaloo. Unlike Bismarck, he did not have the means to rein it in, since in Hungary, unlike in Bismarck's Germany, parliamentary theatrics were popular. But Tisza tried. He forced new House rules that would limit the practice of limitless debate. He won that skirmish, but he lost his battle. The House was adjourned for twenty-five days. When the deputies returned some of them took the law into their own hands; they broke up the seats and the desks of the house that had just been built, of the Greatest Parliament in the World. Tisza lost the battle because he was less popular than the parliamentary vandals, who seemed to represent the national cause of political freedom.

Many of the leaders of Tisza's own party deserted him, too, going over to the "Coalition"—an absurd coalition of the most disparate men and groups, united only by their hatred for Tisza for the time being. Tisza had to call for elections. In January 1905, for the first time since the Compromise of 1867, the government party lost. The opposition, among them the Independents, had the largest number of seats. A normal transfer of power was impossible, not only because of the feverish state of political agitation within the country but also because the Independents and some of their Coalition allies still insisted on their opposition to Franz Josef's army decree. The critical essence of the matter was that these parliamentary squabbles in Budapest had revived the always latent anti-Austrian sentiments of the country, fanning its prevailing embers into visible flames. Now it was Hungary—Magyar public opinion, Magyar popular sentiments, Magyar elected representatives—who threatened the existence of the Dual Monarchy. For the first time, foreign governments began to pay attention to this. Some of them could not fail to notice that in the ensuing constitutional crisis the old monarch (Franz Josef was seventy-five) proved wiser and abler than the leading politicians of a nation that prided itself on centuries of a parliamentary tradition. For a few months Franz Josef tried to find an acceptable successor to Tisza, without avail. In June 1905 he appointed a loyal general, Baron Géza Fejérváry, as a nonpartisan Prime Minister of Hungary. Noisy demonstrations broke out throughout the country, in places amounting—at least rhetorically —to revolt. The Viennese authorities knew that. They actually drafted a plan *("Studie U")* for an eventual military occupation of Hungary. But this did not prove to be necessary. Fejérváry's honest hands were strengthened by a brilliant move suggested by his interior minister, József Kristóffy. That move was the proposition for universal secret suffrage. The right to vote would be given to all men over twenty-four years of age who knew how to read and write. "Since the Crown could count no longer on the support of the political classes, it had to seek support and allies elsewhere, that is, among the lower classes of the nation." Immediately the Coalition, the opposition, broke apart. Some of its members, including the Social Democratic Party, proclaimed their support of the democratic voting reform, if not of the Fejérváry government. Others did not. (Even Tisza opposed universal suffrage.) Franz Josef was wise enough to know (it is still difficult to ascertain precisely who his main advisers were in this matter) that the proposal of universal suffrage would frighten many, if not most, of the gentry politicians in Hungary, especially among the Independents. So it happened. After further months of demonstrations and disorders the Coalition gave in. By April 1906 the constitutional crisis was over. So was the Liberal Party of Hungary. Tisza himself proclaimed its end.

That was not yet the end of liberalism in Hungary, and in Budapest. But it was at least the beginning of the end of something more profound: of the often illusory but nonetheless dominant illusion of the parallel and allied progress of Liberty and Equality, of Liberalism and Democracy. It was also the beginning of the end of the almost universal goodwill that Hungary and Hungarians had enjoyed abroad, especially in England, where Hungary and its position within the Dual system had had a fine reputation. For a long time, this reputation prevailed among British Liberals as well as Tories; and to an entire generation of Irish political personages and writers Hungarian Home Rule (and the figure of old Deák) seemed a potential model. Conversely, we have seen that many people in Hungary admired Liberal England; that the architecture of the new Parliament building on the banks of the Danube incorporated some of the features of Westminster on the banks of the Thames; that politicians and writers made much of the comparison of the ancient Hungarian and English constitutions; that the Hungarian "gentry," as reflected in their own nomenclature, regarded themselves as somewhat akin to their English "counterparts." Kálmán Tisza himself was an Anglophile (without knowing English or ever having visited England), fond of quoting Nelson, Pitt, etc. in his speeches. (István Tisza did not know much English, though he had visited England once, for a short time.) There is a melancholy parallel in the political devolution of such different countries as Hungary, England and Ireland at the beginning of the twentieth century. After 1890 in England, and in Ireland, too, the old Liberalism—and the notion of Anglo-Irish Dualism, that is, of Home Rule for Ireland—began to unravel. Also, by 1905 the favorable image of Hungary in England began to fade rather suddenly. Main instruments of this change were the newspaper articles (and, later, other writings) of the Scots Liberal publicist R. W. Seton-Watson. In drawing attention to the often irresponsible behavior of the Magyar politicians he was not altogether alone, but he was a pioneer in drawing attention to the Magyar suppression of the non-Magyar nationalities. His "revelations" of this problem were not entirely detached or objective, but they were beginning to matter.* For *that* was the insoluble problem—a problem that most Hungarians, and most of their politicians, would not, and perhaps could not, face.

A round 1900 the Austro-Hungarian monarchy included at least eleven diverse nationalities, of which six were "magnetizable" —meaning that they were at least potentially attracted across the border to neighboring states whose peoples spoke their languages. In the 1890s ethnic conflicts in the Austrian crown provinces as well as in Hungary began to disrupt the political and social order of the Dual Monarchy.

From the geographical viewpoint the borders—that is, the shape —of the kingdom of Hungary were ancient and natural. They had changed little through the centuries. Almost two-thirds of these long borders, in a semicircle, marched along the crests and athwart the passes of the Carpathian mountains, separating the Danube basin from Moravian, Polish, Ukrainian and Moldavian plains: truly

---

*About this devolution the title of a recent excellent book by a young Hungarian historian, *Az elvesztett presztizs* ("The Lost Prestige"), by Professor Géza Jeszenszky (Budapest, 1986), is telling. He treats not only politics but the changing perception, and image, of Hungary among knowledgeable people in Great Britain.

natural frontiers, pleasing to the eyes of geographers and taken for granted by Hungarians. The rest were fairly reasonable natural frontiers, too, running along ample rivers and considerable valleys. But while the geographic shape of Hungary formed a natural unit, the ethnic composition of the country provided no such unity at all. In 1900 the Hungarian population amounted to barely half of the inhabitants of Hungary: 51.4 percent.* This condition was the outcome of a long history. Throughout most of their history the Magyar people had a relatively low fertility rate. The Magyars had not been the only inhabitants of the Hungarian basin. During the Middle Ages the density of population was lower there than in Western, Southern and even Germanic Europe. Thus the Magyars had allowed and, on occasion, invited other peoples to settle in its large, and often empty, valleys. Then came another drastic drop in the Magyar population during the ravages of Turkish rule, in the centuries when the population of Europe was beginning to rise elsewhere. During the eighteenth century, when Turkish rule in the Balkans had become somewhat softened and corrupt, more people moved from the Ottoman domains and Wallachia to a slowly reviving Transylvania and Hungary.

Sometime during the nineteenth century the national consciousness of Slovaks, Croats, Serbs and Rumanians began to awaken. The nationalism of the Hungarians, the Hungarian striving for independence, meant nothing to them; rather the contrary. Evidences of this were already there in 1848 during the Hungarian War of Independence. Croatian soldiery, bands of Serbians and Rumanian peasants rose against the Hungarians. The Compromise of 1867 did not change these animosities. Indeed, it solidified the Hungarians' rule. They were now the junior partners of Vienna, masters in their own house and country. In their treatment of the non-Magyars Vienna would not and could not interfere, at least not directly. There was only one constitutional exception to this. From the twelfth century the Hungarian kingdom included its sovereignty over most of Croatia. The Croatian portion of traditional Hungary consisted perhaps of one-tenth of it, comprising eight of its sixty-three counties. In these counties, unlike elsewhere, there was rela-

---

*Unlike in other Eastern European states at the time, these official statistics were fairly reliable. According to them, nationality was registered by the native language of the person—not by allegiance or religion or his own identification at the time the census was taken.

tively little mix of various nationalities. Save for the port city of
Fiume on the Adriatic, very few Magyars lived in the Croatian
parts. A Public Law of 1868, somewhat like the Compromise Law
of 1867, gave these counties a measure of autonomy somewhat
similar to what Hungary had received from Austria the year before.
Similar, but not identical: the autonomy of the Croat administration
from Budapest was more limited than the autonomy of Budapest
from Vienna. Consequently many Croats were not only anti-Magyar; the younger ones began to be attracted to the idea of a South
Slav, Yugo-Slav state, meaning union with the Serbs, those other
"southern" Slavs, despite the great differences between the culture
and religion of Serbs and Croats. In 1890 the 79th Croat Regiment,
stationed in Fiume, demonstrated against Hungarian rule. It was a
portent.

The other non-Magyar nationalities within Hungary were worse
off. They had no powers of self-government at all. The Hungarian
politicians did not merely take the rule of Hungarian mastery for
granted; they were convinced that there was no other way. This,
together with their historical doubts about democratic egalitarian-
ism,* was a reason for their unwillingness to introduce universal
secret manhood suffrage. Universal suffrage would have meant the
swamping of the Parliament in Budapest by a crowd of obstruction-
ist Slovak, Rumanian, Croat, Serb and other deputies. Kálmán
Tisza, who was in many ways a genuine nineteenth-century Liberal
(and, as we have seen earlier, originally a man of the "Left-Center"), declared in 1875: "There can be only one viable nation
within the frontiers of Hungary: that political nation is the Hungarian one. Hungary cannot become an eastern Switzerland because
then it would cease to exist." He intervened in a court case in
eastern Hungary to forbid the use of the Rumanian language. In
another case, confronting the old, proud and privileged German-
Saxons of Transylvania, he said that "a Saxon nation does not
exist." His successor, Bánffy, proclaimed that Hungary, "being a
unified national state, cannot tolerate political parties on the basis

---

*I write "historical" because this reluctance had deep and long roots, embedded
even in the Magyar language, wherefore it must not be simply attributed to
reactionary selfishness. The word "nation," in Magyar, in 1900 (and even later)
still had a special sense. It was not at all identical with *people* (as, for example, *Volk*
in German). It meant the lawful minority of nobles and petty nobles, that is, of
the "historical" classes.

of nationality." Among other things, Bánffy forbade the use of place-names in two languages, sometimes even on railway station signs in Croatia. His successor, Széll, tried to make some compromises, including the acceptance of financial aid from the Rumanian government to certain Rumanian schools in Transylvania. But the teaching of the Magyar language was a requirement in every school of the kingdom.

Still it would be wrong to attribute nothing but arrogance to this kind of Magyar chauvinism. Perhaps two things may be said for it in retrospect. One is the condition for the consciousness of nationality is a matter of growth, and not a mental or material constant. As late as 1900 there were hundreds of thousands, if not millions, of peasants within the Dual Monarchy who did not know what their nationality was. Their sense of nationality had not yet entirely crystallized. They spoke their native language, they had their own customs, but their sense of community was religious and often tribal, rather than national. The national consciousness of Hungarians was stronger because it was both older and more advanced than that of many others. The other fact to consider is that the Hungarian suppression of the other nationalities was not racial but cultural. The issue was language. Once a Rumanian or a Slovak spoke Hungarian, once his children would speak Hungarian as their first (and not necessarily their native) language, they would have few disadvantages, or none at all. The worst feature of the ruling Magyar discriminations involved education: attempts to reduce, or to suppress, the influence of non-Magyar schools (except in wholly non-Magyar Croatia). But even this policy was not entirely a bitter and cramped attempt of a threatened ruling nationality. It rested on the, in retrospect, unduly optimistic Hungarian belief in the assimilative powers of Hungarian language, civilization and culture. How many Germans had become Hungarians, in their language, culture, and loyalties, during the past century*— not to speak of the Jews! The Germans, the ruling people to the west of Hungary, and people who not so long ago had thought themselves superior to Magyars in their language and civilization! If their Magyarization came naturally to them, how much easier this

---

*"The Magyarization of the cultured German bourgeois classes developed undoubtedly on the intellectual plane, by means of Hungarian letters and literature; and this is something of which Hungarian culture may well be proud" (Szerb, p. 310).

must be for an illiterate* Slovak or Vlach (*oláh*—a Hungarian word for Rumanians).

The history of politics is the history of words. It is surely significant that "chauvinism" was a positive word in the vocabulary of many Hungarian politicians around 1900. That year the influential publicist Jenő Rákosi called for "a total Hungarianness, when every man in Hungary will feel in his innermost soul that he had become a Magyar chauvinist."† The same Rákosi, in a celebrated article, called for a nation of "thirty million Magyars."‡ It was both symptomatic and typical that this eloquent nationalist was German-born.

There had been, and still were, far-seeing Hungarian patriotic statesmen who saw things differently. They were conservatives, not chauvinists. They saw the dangers of rising nationalist sentiments even before these had crystallized. Széchenyi, first of all, saw that a complete break with the House of Austria, that is, the total independence of Hungary, was not only premature but a recipe for potential disaster. Kossuth would not and did not realize the necessity of equal, that is, democratic cooperation with the other peoples of the Danubian basin until his bitter defeat and subsequent exile. Yet even in the 1880s the profound, thoughtful and melancholy Béla Grünwald, a publicist and historian, believed that the non-Magyar peoples within Hungary were "not capable of an indepen-

---

*In 1910 illiteracy among Hungarians was 20 percent (in Budapest less than 9 percent), among Rumanians 67 percent and among Carpatho-Ukrainians (Ruthenians) more than 72 percent.

†Contrast this with the words of Franz Josef. During an important Crown Council in 1878 the monarch noted "the salutary rise of patriotism. But one must keep things within reason, lest such sentiments degenerate into political chauvinism."

‡From 1880 to 1900 the population in Hungary had been rising—though not, of course, at the astounding rate of Budapest—from 13.8 million to 16.9 million (18.26 million in 1910). The relative proportion of the Magyar population grew, too, from 46.6 percent in 1880 to 51.4 percent in 1900. During this time the proportions of the German and Slovak peoples in Hungary were decreasing; that of the Rumanians remained about the same. This occurred despite the relatively low—and already dropping—birthrate among Hungarians. One of the reasons for this last phase in the relative increase of Magyardom in the Danube valley was the previously mentioned assimilation of tens of thousands of non-Magyar families. Another element was emigration (after 1880, mostly to the United States). From 1867 to 1914 only three of every ten emigrants from Hungary were Magyars. The total number of emigrants from Austria-Hungary was about 2 million from 1892 to 1914, of whom one-fourth returned. There was little emigration from Budapest.

dent advancement"; that it was "the destiny of Magyardom to assimilate them, to absorb them into a superior people," thereby fulfilling the Magyar "duty to humanity, to elevate them as if we were the champions of civilization." There were a few Magyar politicians and thinkers who saw that this was an illusion. But their voices were not heard for more than another decade, until around 1900 when, as we shall see, some of these voices had acquired a new undertone, as well as a new kind of echo.*

During the 1890s there occurred sporadic anti-Magyar riots and demonstrations in Croat-, Slovak- and Rumanian-inhabited villages and towns. A conference of the non-Magyar nationalities met in Budapest in 1895. The nationalities now had a politically minded intelligentsia, often half-educated but not less vocal for that. Among the poorest and least educated people, the Carpatho-Ukrainians, or Ruthenians, religion was allied to national consciousness—indeed, their religion was identical with their awakening nationalism. Russian and Ukrainian Greek-Orthodox priests had begun to propagate the cause of the Russian Orthodox Church, luring these people away from their Uniate, or Greek-Catholic, hierarchs. This was not difficult since the liturgy and the rites of Greek-Orthodox and Greek-Catholic religions were just about identical. What attracted them to this propaganda was the lure of allegiance to their Russian brethren, away from the Western (Hungarian-, Polish- or Austrian-oriented) Greek-Catholic Church. In the 1906 elections more Serbian, Rumanian and Slovak deputies came into the Parliament in Budapest. But by that time the Liberal era in Hungarian politics was over. As in faraway Ireland or nearby Austria, the rise of nationalism meant the decline of Liberalism in Hungary, too.

The general crisis of nineteenth-century Liberalism has not yet found its general historian. Almost all historians and political thinkers have dealt with the devolution of Liberalism on the economic or social plane. But there was a deeper, emotional substance

---

*See p. 190ff. One rare example of Magyar self-criticism in 1898, from the pages of a satirical weekly (and a generally pro-government one!), contrasting the ideals of the 1848 revolutions with conditions fifty years later: "Liberty, Equality, Fraternity! . . . We have become tired of these . . . Equality? To make the peasantry our equal? Fraternity? No-no! Our Rumanian, Slovak and other Slav brethren must not hear this! . . ."

to that devolution. The Liberal ideas were losing their appeal not only to thinkers, but also to masses of the lower classes who were supposed to have been its beneficiaries. Economically speaking, the Liberal principles and policies of free trade and free enterprise had lost their novel ring of generosity and freedom. While industrialists and financiers were still profiting from them, many of their workers were left to fend for themselves in cold and dark places, unlit by the elsewhere brilliant arc lights of capitalist enterprise. Hence the emotional anticapitalism of the masses preceded their eventual, and partial, rational acceptance of socialism. After 1880 some of the Liberals in England and the Progressives in the United States began to comprehend this. Hence they moved away from classic Liberalism toward social reforms, toward the beginning of the welfare, or provider, state—toward the Lib-Lab ethos (or the lack of it). There was some of this among the Liberals in Hungary, too, but not much. My argument is that it did not matter much either. Had the Hungarian Liberal Party moved toward social democracy as had the British, its eventual demise may have come somewhat later, but, as in England, it would have come nonetheless.

One of the elements of its eventual demise was the emergence of a politically conscious working class. By 1900 in Hungary, and especially in Budapest, an industrial working class had come into being that was both larger and better educated than the working classes in other European nations east of Vienna. The first great May Day demonstration in Budapest took place in 1890, when perhaps as many as 40,000 workers marched in the City Park. The Hungarian Social Democratic Party was founded in that year (one year after the Austrian one). During the next ten years its influence grew. There were a few significant strikes in the factories of Budapest. Yet on May 1, 1900, a rainy day, the planned Socialist demonstration fizzled. In 1900 the Hungarian Social Democrats were not yet a strong national party. (*Népszava,* their first daily newspaper, appeared only in 1904.) There were at least two reasons for this. One was the pronounced urban character of the party, with many Jews among its leaders. Yet the poorest workers in Hungary were peasants, not factory workers. Among some of the peasants in certain parts of the country, a tradition of agrarian socialism had already taken root. Since this is a history of Budapest and not of Hungary, this is not the place to describe the moving, at times pathetic, and sometimes deeply religious sentiments and manifestations of this Christ-like socialism of the poor peasants. In the 1890s they were often suppressed by the government and by its local police instruments with even greater force than that directed against the occasional strikes and working-class demonstrations in Budapest. There was thus a lack of coordination—indeed there were disagreements—between the agrarian and industrial socialists in Hungary. The other reason for the relative weakness of the Social Democrats was the customary Magyar political syndrome: personal jealousies and discord among the leaders of the party, leading to splinterings and factions.

It was nationalism, more than socialism, that destroyed the Liberalism of the nineteenth century. By nationalism I do not mean the perhaps insoluble problem of the non-Magyar nationalities in Hungary. The masses of the Magyar people, too, were more nationalist than liberal (as, among others, the Social Democrats would find later: more nationalist than internationalist, that is, race- rather than class-conscious). But, then, this was a worldwide phenomenon: the nationalist illiberalism of the rising democratic masses. In Austria, for example, the old Liberal and the young radical nationalists split in the early 1880s. I write "young" because, as events showed, most Austrian students were no longer liberal. They had become nationalist radicals of the Right, not of the Left. In Budapest, too, such a movement was discernible among university students by 1895 at the latest. From their earlier liberal nationalism they had moved in the direction of a radical nationalism that evidently included anti-Semitic sentiments. In 1897 pan-German nationalism exploded in the Vienna Parliament. Facing not only parliamentary violence but popular violence in the streets, the Austrian government had to retreat. The parliamentary and popular disturbances in Budapest in the 1890s were less dramatic, and the parliamentary explosion in Budapest would not come until a few years later. But a new kind of Right was rising in Hungary, too, as the Liberal Party had begun to erode.

Anti-Semitism, for instance, was part of anti-Liberal nationalism, not the other way around. The sudden, almost revolutionary rise of Karl Lueger's "Christian Social" Party in Vienna in 1894–95 was part of an awakened Austrian-German populist nationalism that had protean manifestations around that time. While Judaeophobia in the past was a deeply rooted and largely religious prejudice, the now emerging anti-Semitism was national, racial and populist. Its

object was not the phenomenon of strange people wearing outlandish garb, following outlandish rites, and living in isolated ghettos.
Its objects were the emancipated, assimilated and, on occasion,
even Christianized Jews, in charge of finance, journalism, and other
profitable and politic professions, often hardly distinguishable in
their language and habits from other Viennese, sometimes even
physically indistinguishable from them, but to some of the latter,
somehow not *really* Viennese in their ambitions and practices. Karl
Lueger understood the potential power of such sentiments. He also
understood that his church had condemned both materialistic socialism and materialistic capitalism, in Leo XIII's *Rerum Novarum*
encyclical in 1891, for example. Lueger was a convinced opponent
of untrammeled capitalism (which, among other things, had led to
the mismanagement of some of the Viennese municipal services),
and a somewhat less categorical opponent of Jewish "power." The
people of Vienna, including tens of thousands of former Liberals
(and also Socialists), voted him into office in 1895. He turned out
to be an excellent and efficient Lord Mayor. In addition, he re-
solved not to harm or attack the Jews of Vienna any longer. But the
name of his party remained symptomatic: "Christian-Social," in
which the "Christian" adjective clearly meant non-Jewish and non-
Marxist.*

Hungarians, and Hungarian politicians, kept asserting loud and
clear that they were not taking their cues from Vienna. Yet the
crisis of the Magyar Liberal Party largely coincided with the crisis
of Liberalism in Vienna. The fall of the cautious liberal Kálmán
Tisza came in 1890, that of the cautious Taaffe in Vienna in 1893.
Both events marked the end of a political era. In 1894 in Hungary,
too, a Catholic People's Party came into existence. Again the terminology is telling. "People," "popular," "populist," *völkisch* had
been democratic, liberal, socialist, leftist terms for a long time, as
manifested by the vocabulary of the French Revolution. But in the
1890s this monopoly of the Left to speak in the name of the "peo-

---

*The appearance of his relatively new kind of nationalist, populist and anticapital-
ist anti-Semitism after 1895 was a phenomenon observed in many countries. It was
the common denominator of the Lueger movement, of the Dreyfus case (when
the anti-Dreyfusards were not, as is often believed, merely the last-ditch defenders
of reactionary institutions and beliefs in France), of anticapitalist anti-Semitism in
England during the Boer War and later in the Marconi affair, of the rise of Cuza's
Anti-Semitic Party in Rumania, etc. Even the occasional anti-Semitism of American
populists before 1914 was a related phenomenon.

ple" ceased to exist.* Thus the name of the Catholic People's Party
in Hungary was symptomatic. So was its language, proclaiming,
among other things, "The Fight Against Liberalism" *(Harc a szaba-
delvüség ellen)*. It was a conservative party, inasmuch as it was antiliberal—even though the word "conservative" was eschewed by almost every politician in Hungary, as in many other European
countries at the time. But it was more than merely conservative.
The party was agrarian, anticapitalist and populist. It called for the
protection of agriculture, a restriction of financial speculation, and
a tax on stock exchange transactions. It was formed by a few aristocrats, mostly from Catholic Transdanubia, and also by younger,
socially conscious Catholic priests. Unlike Lueger's party, its main
strength was not in Budapest but in the provinces, including some
of the Slovak-inhabited counties of northern Hungary and Croat
counties in the south, since the Catholic People's Party declared its
opposition not only to Liberalism but also to the suppression of the
non-Magyar nationalities by the Liberal government.† The upper
hierarchy was dubious about the political activism of some of the
lower clergy (just as Pope Leo XIII was somewhat dubious of
Lueger). But in 1894–95 they had a common cause because of the
civil marriage legislation that the Liberal government and party
proposed and that the Catholic Church opposed. With its anticapitalism the People's Party had an anti-Semitic tinge, manifested in
its newspapers and journals. It did not become a large mass party,
but it surely contributed to the erosion of the Liberals.‡ Its appearance on the political scene was but a manifestation of a new kind
of populist, democratic and socially conscious Catholicism, the
eventual chief spokesman and leader of which would be a very
intelligent "modern" priest, Ottokár Prohászka (another Magyar

*Examples: In 1914 Mussolini's new newspaper bore the name *Popolo d'Italia*.
After the war came Hitler's *Völkischer Beobachter*. In France *Le Populaire* remained
the Socialist paper till the Second World War; but even before that *L'Ami du Peuple*
(once the title of Marat's sheet) was an extreme Rightist one. Etc., etc.

†Its principal leader, Count Nándor Zichy, drew attention to discriminatory practices—for example, to the fact that the Hungarian railroad freight rates from
Budapest to the Adriatic port of Fiume cost less than the rates from Croatian
Zagreb to Fiume. (Zagreb was along the route, and five times closer to Fiume than
was Budapest.)

‡In 1897 a group of university students in Budapest sent a congratulatory telegram
to Lueger. This was symptomatic, among other things, of their myopia: Lueger's
distrust and dislike of Hungarian nationalists was not only evident but stronger
and more enduring than his opposition to Jews.

nationalist of Slovak, that is, non-Magyar origins). When, in 1905, Prohászka was made Bishop of Székesfehérvár, he made a point of eschewing the customary pomp of episcopal instaurations: he chose to walk from the railroad station to his episcopal dwelling.

And among the former Left, too, in the ranks of the Independence Party, a new populist fermentation had begun. After 1890 politicians had arisen who were concerned with the problem of the nationalities—and, at least indirectly, with the influence of Jews. Lajos Mocsáry, Miklós Bartha and Ede Egán saw that the thoughtless oppression and destitution of some of the non-Magyar nationalities would lead to disaster. They were especially appalled by the misery of the Ruthenian landless peasantry in northeastern Hungary, including their occasional exploitation by newly arrived Jewish moneylenders and tavern keepers, who were streaming into Hungary across the Carpathian mountains from Galicia. Bartha and Egán tried, and for a short time succeeded, to arouse some interest in this matter. The able Minister of Agriculture, the agrarian-minded Ignác Darányi, brought about a minimal homesteading policy for these destitute Ruthenians. The policy had few enduring effects and faded after a few years, partly because of its inadequate financing by the government, but also because these indigent people were less and less attracted to the prospects of their Magyarization. The trouble with these earnest, and often embittered, Magyar reformers lay in the unduly selective nature of their concerns. They thought that they were realistic about the immigration of Jews about whom they had, or so they thought, no illusions. Yet they had many illusions about the potential loyalty of Ruthenian or Rumanian peasants. They thought that the latter were not only more assimilable to Magyardom but that their assimilation, unlike that of most Jews, would be a positive asset for the Magyar nation. Their at the time still selective and not always extreme anti-Semitism was but part of the general crisis of European Liberalism that after 1890 appeared in the politics of Hungary, too.

At least on the surface, this was less apparent in Budapest than elsewhere in Hungary. The national election in 1901 was relatively peaceful, and largely devoid of corruption. There was little corruption in the election of 1905, too. But in that year the manifestations of the national political crisis repeated themselves in the capital. During that crisis the bitter animosities between city and country came out into the open: for instance, between City Hall, the municipality of Budapest, which was still predominantly Liberal; and the

County Headquarters, the seat of the largely agrarian County of Pest, which was not. At that time still only about 5 percent of the population of Hungary were voters. This percentage was, of course, higher in Budapest, perhaps 9 percent. Owing to their financial and educational qualifications, a large proportion of the voters in Budapest were Jewish, amounting perhaps to more than 40 percent of those entitled to vote. In Budapest, too, the breakup of nineteenth-century Liberalism, together with a polarization of politics, had begun. Until 1905 the Liberal Party carried every one of the ten districts of the capital city. In 1905, for the first time, the Liberals would lose their majority in some of the Budapest districts. In the Ninth, a district with few Jewish voters, people chose a candidate of the Independents for the first time in the political history of Budapest, after a campaign with faintly anti-Semitic undertones.

But in the strongly Jewish-inhabited Sixth District, too, the power of the Liberals was broken. Vilmos Vázsonyi, a very intelligent Jewish lawyer, had formed his "Democratic Party" and carried the election in 1905.* And Vázsonyi was but a moderate representative of that fermentation among the younger members of the Jewish middle classes of Budapest who had become dissatisfied not only with the existing government but with the entire backward political and social structure of Hungary. The sons and sometimes the daughters of Jewish bankers, lawyers and others were breaking away from the loyal, monarchist and older Liberal traditions of their parents. They were moving to the Left.

Many of them would play a role not only in the political and ideological but in the intellectual and cultural ferment of Budapest after 1900. They were a part of the generation of 1900 that is the subject of our next chapter. Before that we must make a last observation that involves the politicization of the nation around 1900, for the case of Budapest and, indeed, of Hungary was unusual. In the movement of ideas, in the history of nations, new ways of thinking and new forms of art, new fashions and novel philosophies usually—though not always—precede their political manifestations, changes in the political order. But around 1900 in Budapest the political crisis of Liberalism coincided with the recognition that new ideas, new creativities, new forms of artistic expression had to

---

*On one occasion Vázsonyi proclaimed: "I am a liberal Luegerist"—another symptomatic choice of a post-Liberal political terminology.

come. ("New Poems" was the term poet Endre Ady would use in
1906,—a turning point not only in Magyar politics but in the history of Magyar poetry, literature, painting and music.) Thus the
lamentable devolution of Hungarian politics occurred together not
only with the material flourishing of the capital city but also with
achievements of individual genius that around 1900 made Hungarian creativity rise to very high levels, and to regions unknown
before.

5

The Generation
of 1900

The concept of generations has evoked some interest among historians recently, yet few among them have written about it with the verve and insight of José Ortega y Gasset and of his exegete, the excellent Spanish historian Julián Marías. Even before them, certain Hungarian historians had been preoccupied with the problem of generations, devoting their works to it.* The most important of these is *Három Nemzedék* ("Three Generations"), the best-known work of Gyula Szekfü, probably the greatest Hungarian historian in the twentieth century. Born in 1883, he, too, belonged to the Generation of 1900—at least according to my definition of that term. This definition, by and large, accords with Szekfü's concept of what constitutes a generation, a concept that Szekfü did not define precisely, without that having harmed the value and the influence of his work. It does depend, of course, on

---

*In the Magyar language the word *nemzedék* is more emphatic than the English "generation." Example: a Hungarian term corresponding in meaning to the American Founding Fathers is "The Reform Generation" [of 1820–48].

the birth dates of certain people, but the emphasis lies on the consideration of when such a group reaches the first stage of its influence. Accordingly, my description of the Hungarian generation of 1900 concentrates on a cohort whose *formative* years occurred in or around 1900.* It will even include a few people who were born a few years later but who were still formed by the cultural atmosphere of the period, men and women born between 1875 and 1905—men and women who were very bright, very different, and some of them very successful.

They had some things in common. One was their schooling in the 1880s and 1890s, when schools in Hungary had reached high standards. Another was their definite wish to break away from a sentimental Hungarian style and rhetoric. Yet another was their unusual and new quality of quickmindedness. The wish to break out from the old habits and narrow traditions followed different paths. The aim of many of these writers, painters, composers, philosophers and scientists was to become more urban and cosmopolitan. Others, while recognizing and even being inspired by new, modern visions and expressions of art in Western Europe, were interested in neither a citified nor a cosmopolitan civilization; they chose to explore and then dip into the wells of the remnant and often hidden expressions of the microcosm of the folk culture of people in the Hungarian countryside, to gather their inspirations and create new forms of expression from such authentic and still vital sources. Others, again, remained largely untouched by the world beyond Hungary, while they wrote about the macrocosm of Hungary in profoundly new ways. An example of the first was the playwright Ferenc Molnár; of the second, the composer Béla Bartók; of the

---

*In another significant work, *Magyar századforduló* ("The Hungarian Turn of the Century"), published in 1961 and marred by the bitterness (and at least semi-Marxist) interpretation of its author, Zoltán Horváth, attention was drawn to the extraordinary talents of various Hungarians born between 1875 and 1885. The very subtitle of the book, "The History of the Second Reform Generation," is telling, but Horváth did not really employ the concept of generations. The idea of a generation, while not explicit, may also be found throughout McCagg, *Jewish Nobles and Geniuses in Modern Hungary,* and in Mary Gluck, *Georg Lukács and His Generation* (Cambridge, Mass., 1985); but in this last work—see especially her chapter "The Foundation of a Generation," dealing with people born in the decade 1885–95—her entire list (and perspective) is restricted to the circle of radical intellectuals.

third the already mentioned Gyula Krúdy, whose name is even now hardly known beyond Hungary, whereas the names of the other two have reverberated around the world. They certainly belonged to the generation of 1900 (Molnár and Krúdy were born in 1878, Bartók in 1881). Yet their characters, personalities and aspirations were very different.

Generalizations about the generation of 1900 must face another difficulty. That was the first cosmopolitan generation of Hungarians, many of whose names became known abroad. Many men and women of this generation eventually left Budapest and Hungary. For some of them, chances for a successful career in Hungary were too narrow. In other instances such a choice was the result of necessity, since their very lives may have been endangered. There were three such waves of emigration. The first, in 1919, included those who were either compromised by their public participation in the disastrous Radical or Communist regimes in 1918–19; or those who knew that they could neither complete their higher education nor pursue their chosen careers during the ensuing nationalist regime. A second, smaller wave, from 1938 to 1941, included those who feared for their lives at a time when Hungary became bound to Hitler's Third Reich; they were able to leave Budapest before the last channels of emigration closed with the entry of the United States into the war. The third and most chilling bloodletting (for that was what it was) befell Budapest and Hungary in 1944–45, involving two disparate groups of people: those who were deported or killed by German (and Hungarian) National Socialists; and those who felt sufficiently compromised by their association with National Socialism or with the Third Reich to the extent that they feared to return to Hungary from Austria or Germany, where they had repaired during the last phase of the war.*

Thus many men and women of the generation of 1900 achieved their successful (and sometimes astonishing) careers not in Hungary but abroad. Of the six Hungarian winners of the Nobel Prize,

---

*Later, during the imposition of a Communist government on Hungary, in the years 1946 to 1949, other talented people left Budapest and Hungary. Again after the 1956 Rising nearly 200,000 fled; and many others even later. But these last two waves of emigration do not concern us here, since most of these emigrés no longer belonged to the Generation of 1900 (though a few older ones among them did).

five were born between 1875 and 1905, but only one got the prize while he was living and working in Hungary; and even he (Albert Szent-Györgyi) eventually moved to the United States, where he became a fairly well-known public figure during the last thirty years of his life. Among such famous Hungarians living abroad we may find playwrights such as Ferenc Molnár* and Melchior Lengyel*; composers such as Béla Bartók, Ernst von Dohnányi and Emeric Kálmán*; conductors such as George Szell*, Georges Sebastian*, Eugene Ormandy* and Tibor Serly; violinists such as Joseph Szigeti*; movie directors and producers such as Sir Alexander Korda, Géza Bolváry, Michael Curtiz* and Joe Pasternak; journalists such as Theodor Herzl* and Arthur Koestler*; literary philosophers such as Georg Lukács*; physicists such as Eugene Wigner*, John von Neumann*, Georg Békésy*, Leo Szilárd*, Theodore von Karman* and Dennis Gabor*, chemist such as Georg de Hevesy*; physicians such as Robert Bárány; mathematicians such as Frigyes Riesz and Lipót Fejér; actors such as Paul Lukas*; actresses such as Vilma Bánky; photographers such as André Kertész*, Márton Munkácsi and Brassaï; philosophers such as Karl Kerényi and Aurel Kolnai*; architects such as Marcel Breuer and László Moholy-Nagy; psychoanalysts such as Franz Alexander*; economists such as Lord Thomas Balogh*; sociologists such as Karl Mannheim*; chemists turned philosophers such as Michael Polanyi*; and "I. T. T. Lincoln" (Trebitsch-Lincoln, one of the most adventurous mountebanks of the twentieth century).† Among these people

---

*Born in Budapest. Notice that the first names of some of these people became Germanized or Anglicized. At the same time (unlike the case of more or less illustrious immigrants to the United States from other countries) few of them changed their family name or even their spelling for the sake of easier recognition in their adopted countries. (My namesake—not relative—Paul Lukas is a rare exception.)

†Born in 1878 of a respectable Jewish family in Paks, south of Budapest, Ignác Trebitsch was, successively, a petty thief, a journalist in Budapest, a Presbyterian missionary in Hamburg, an evangelical clergyman in Montreal, a Protestant councilman in Halifax, an Anglican vicar in Kent, an associate and chief researcher of the English Quaker philanthropist and millionaire Rowntree, a Liberal member of the British House of Commons (elected in 1910; *Punch* published a drawing with the title "Paks Vobiscum"), a speculator in oil-drilling equipment in Galicia and Rumania, a subject of suits for criminal fraud, promoter of a scheme that would result in the destruction of the German High Fleet in 1914. He then offered his services to the Germans, fled to New York, was arrested on Broadway, and

some first achieved their fame in Hungary and widened their reputation abroad; others achieved their fame abroad, after which the reputation of their success reverberated in their native city and country. There were also others who, for complicated psychological reasons, ceased to consider themselves Hungarian at all (including Koestler, Alexander, Polanyi and Ormandy*).

This "brain drain" (an unattractive term) amounted to a great loss for Hungary.† Yet I wish to draw attention mainly to those people who did not emigrate: to the men and women of the generation of 1900 who, though by and large unknown abroad, became and have remained well-known, read, heard, listened to, respected and admired in Hungary. Most of these people were writers, poets and historians as a matter of course, the instrument of their talent being their native language.‡

In any event, this distinction between emigrés and stay-at-homes cannot be categorical or absolute. The achievements as well as the reputations of many of the emigrés were not wholly lost for Hungary; and what the two groups have in common is often (though not always) more important than their differences. This includes the two novel conditions of the generation of 1900. The first was the unusual variety of their talents, ranging from mathematics to poetry (and, in some cases, representing unusual combinations of genius

---

deported to Britain, where he served three years in a British prison. Repairing to Germany, he was press secretary and publicity officer of the German nationalist *Putschists* Kapp and Ehrhard in 1920, then chief military adviser to a Chinese warlord, founder of a sect of American Buddhists, etc. He died a Buddhist monk in China under Japanese occupation in 1943. (Written before the publication of his scholarly biography, Bernard Wasserstein, *The Secret Lives of Trebitsch Lincoln* [London and New Haven, 1988]).

*The latter, né Blau, was among those who "rediscovered" their Hungarian origins after the Rising in 1956 (when it became chic to be Hungarian).

†A serious researcher, Dr. József Bölöny, has been working for many years now at completing an encyclopedic list of noteworthy Hungarians abroad. A younger Hungarian historian, Tibor Frank, is writing a book about them, to be entitled *The Lost Generation*. I am indebted to these two scholars for their generous assistance in directing my attention to names that I might have overlooked. In any event, the list here is unavoidably incomplete.

‡They include, alas, novelists such as Sándor Márai and fine critics such as László Cs. Szabó, who chose exile in 1947 but continued to write in Hungarian, even though they were cut off from their native people (but perhaps with the eventual compensation of knowing that their names and writings continue to be read in their homeland).

in more than one field). The second was that, for the first time in the history of Hungary, the generation of 1900 was essentially a Budapestian one. Not all of their members were born in Budapest, but for the first time many of them were; and it was in Budapest that their scientific, literary or artistic careers began; and it was in the schools of Budapest that most of them had received their basic education.

The sources of this widespread outburst of talent were cultural, not biological. They had much to do with the atmosphere of Budapest in 1900, and certainly with the condition of its schools that by 1900 had reached standards comparable to the best ones in Europe. Their drastic improvement started under the Austrian administration in 1855, when schooling became compulsory up to the age of twelve. After these so-called Thun reforms the achievements of serious and dedicated Hungarian ministers of culture and education (József Eötvös, Ágost Trefort, Albin Csáky) were very creditable. They led, among other things, to the reduction of illiterates to a then remarkably small proportion of the population of Budapest. From 1875 to 1900 the number of schools, teachers and students in Budapest more than doubled. This numerical increase was even greater than the increase of the population at large—at a time when Budapest grew faster than any other great city in Europe. There is often—and the twentieth century provides many sorry examples of this—no direct relationship between the quality of education and the quantity of monies spent on it: but, for once, toward the end of the nineteenth century in Budapest these matters developed together.

There was a sequence in this raising of standards. It may be said that the elementary schools in Budapest reached standards comparable to those of Central and Western Europe in the 1870s, the middle schools in the 1880s and the universities in the 1890s. The most important impact was that of the middle schools, which were articulated into three kinds, the highest of them being the humanistic gymnasium—requiring, among other subjects, Latin and Greek, and attendance for eight years, usually from the ages of ten to eighteen. There were three such gymnasiums in 1876 and twelve by 1896 (the year, too, when the first gymnasium for girls was established). At the end of the eight years the passing of a final and severe examination was the requirement for admission to university studies (and the requirement, too, for most clerical or civil service positions).

Despite the sometimes extreme Magyar wish to assert the nation's independence from Austria and matters Austrian, almost the entire Hungarian educational system, including the curriculum—especially in the gymnasiums and universities—followed Austrian and German models. (That was true of many other European states, including Russia, at the time—and of American graduate schools after 1880.) One of the few important exceptions was that of the Eötvös College *(Kollégium)*, modeled largely after the Ecole Normale in Paris. It was founded in 1896, supported by the great scholar and physicist Baron Loránd Eötvös. Its first group of students included many of the exceptional talents of the Generation of 1900.*

The universities of Hungary and of Budapest, whose quality before 1850 had been, at best, indifferent and, at worst, well below those of Vienna, Prague or Berlin, grew impressively, too. Their student bodies doubled from 1892 to 1905 (the years when the first cohorts of the generation of 1900, those born between 1875 and 1888, would enter them). The number of law students increased fastest, but the number of those who acquired medical degrees in Budapest declined a little. The reason for this was that the relatively easier doctorate in law was the degree customarily required for entry to middle- or higher-grade civil service positions (and sometimes even for above-average entry positions in private businesses, such as banking). The reason for the relative decline in medical degrees was more complicated. By 1900 there were almost as many physicians per population in Budapest as in Vienna, but many of these had acquired their degrees from the then famous medical faculty at the University of Vienna, where they had qualified for entry by virtue of their Hungarian gymnasium diploma. (Some Viennese professors, such as the famous Billroth, had protested in vain against the large number of Hungarian students.) Another

---

*They included such diverse talents as the composer Zoltán Kodály, the historian Gyula Szekfü, the nationalist and populist writer Dezső Szabó, the gentle master of prose and criticism Aladár Kuncz, the art historian Tibor Gerevich, the philologist Zoltán Gombocz and others. The directors of the Eötvös, too, were exceptional men: Jenő Péterfy (see p. 154) and the quiet and dedicated Géza Bartoniek.

reason was the increased rigor of the standards of the medical faculty in Budapest after 1895. That faculty, in more than one way, would then reach the world-renowned standards of Vienna and Berlin.*

Yet—the Eötvös may be an exception—the formative years of talent developed not in the universities but in the middle schools of Budapest. This appears, among other things, from the recollections of some of the people of that period, from their autobiographies, memoirs and interviews. Many of them referred to some of their teachers in the gymnasiums with special affection, probably for two reasons. One was the relative precocity of young people at that time. Intellectually, if not physically, young men matured early: their most formative years came around the age of sixteen (that is, when they were students in the upper classes of the gymnasium). The other factor was the high standard of the curriculum, and the excellence of some of the teachers. The curriculum included six (and in some schools eight) years of Latin, three years of Greek, rigorous requirements in mathematics, reaching to the levels of integral and differential calculus, and a thorough march through the history of Magyar literature and of Hungarian (and also of Greek and Roman) history. Many of the gymnasium teach-

---

*Professors Korányi, Lenhossék, Jendrassik, Tauffer, and Grosz had by that time a European reputation. In other faculties the Islamist Goldzieher, the Finno-Ugrianist Budenz, the Asian expert and explorer Vámbéry, the physicist Eötvös, the biologist Hermann, the astronomer Konkoly-Thege, the mathematician Riesz, too, had very wide reputations abroad. But, except for Riesz, these scholars were the teachers of the generation of 1900 and not its members.

A few dates and statistics suggest the increase of educational opportunities of the generation of 1900: new building of the main university: 1873; Academy of Music (the Budapest Conservatory): 1875; National Archives: 1874; Polytechnic (Faculty of Engineering & Architecture & Public Service): 1887; Academy of Military Science *(Ludovika)*: 1883; Academy of Higher Commerce: 1891; increase of Doctors of Philosophy from 1892 to 1905 fourfold; increase of scholarly journals from 1883 to 1903 threefold; number of scholarly books published from 1890 to 1900: 6,251. By 1900 the libraries of Budapest harbored more than 2 million books. Increase of patents entered in the Hungarian Patent Office from 1881 to 1906 sevenfold. During this period there were a few extraordinary achievements by Hungarian inventors—for example, the carburetor by Csonka in 1893; the telephone transmission network of news and music by Puskás in 1893; the voltage transformers by Zipernowszky and Bláthy at the same time; and electric engines and locomotives by Kandó. Again, except for the last, these Magyar engineers and inventors were older than the generation of 1900: they were its masters.

ers were doctors of philosophy. Others were humanists and literary men of respectable stature. The level of their training and competence, not to speak of their dedication, was at least comparable to that of senior professors at the most reputable American universities now. These conditions were not altogether different from other gymnasiums in Central Europe. But the spirit of these schools in Budapest had a very palpable Hungarian verve, an element of which was the powerful Magyar nationalism of many of the teachers.

The respectful—and surely selective—memories of the generation around 1900 obscure the shortcomings of that school system. These shortcomings were, again, largely due to that Germanic system of education: an education where the unilateral emphasis was on the discipline of brainwork, and not on character. Boarding schools were few in Budapest at that time: the above-mentioned Eötvös, and a few excellent convent schools for girls. There was, for example, minimal training in physical exercise. The new gymnasiums, built by celebrated architects, sometimes with rather magnificent stairways and ceremonial rooms with coffered ceilings, and decorated with the frescoes of famous painters (Károly Lotz, for example, who painted the frescoes of the Opera, Palace of Justice and Parliament), had nothing but a small dark inner courtyard for "exercise" and an even more miserable dark gym, equipped with scarcely more than exercise bars along its walls. This was at a time when in Budapest athleticism and interest in sports grew rapidly, and when the Latin bromide of *mens sana in corpore sano* ("a sound mind in a sound body") was being drummed into the minds of the students. Another impediment to a more or less healthy development of character was the often extreme rigidity of the daily requirements. In most classes the hour began with recitation, meaning that each student had to be ready for testing and questioning each day. What this may have contributed to self-discipline and to habits of study was surely counterbalanced by the condition that these difficult and sometimes almost impossible demands also brought forth practices of all kinds of student legerdemain and cheating: that is, an early and youthful realization that cutting corners and disregarding rules, that clandestinity and prevarication were inevitable conditions of survival in a world with rigid, categorical, insensitive and often senseless rules. Students were haunted by the fear of being suddenly called on, of being inadequately prepared, and of receiving a consequent poor or failing mark at the end of the semester. Even more traumatic was their anticipation of the prospect of that severe final *matura* (or call it *baccalauréat*) examination at the age of seventeen or eighteen, when during a few hours in two days they had to account for the near-entirety of their gymnasium studies. These examinations came in early June: at times during the previous week there were student suicides. Thus the outcome of a gymnasium education, with all of its enduring positive factors, had one important negative one: there was no direct correlation between high marks and high character, and sometimes not even between one's scholastic record and one's subsequent career. (The Nobel Prize–winning biochemist Albert Szent-Györgyi once received a "C" in physics, and Béla Bartók a mere "B" in composition.)

We know much about these middle school years of the generation of 1900. Some of the best Hungarian writers of that generation wrote entire novels about the gymnasiums, about students and teachers and their relationships, fraught with the excitements, crimes, awakenings, misunderstandings and occasional tragedies.* The large number of such books was not a literary coincidence. It was a symptom of the strong and deep impressions of those middle school years in the minds and lives of sensitive writers decades after they had left their school walls behind forever.

In part, but only in part, because of the schools, Budapest in 1900 had a tremendous respect for intellectual achievement of all kinds. The emphatic pride of young people in intellectual achievement was relatively new in Hungary at the time. The novel strength of such aspirations—and of their recognition—accorded with the changing social composition and with the atmosphere of Budapest around 1900. That precocious cultural appetite came not only from the schools† but, even more, from the homes of Budapest. It came

---

*One outstanding example is Dezső Kosztolányi's *Aranysárkány* ("The Golden Kite"), about the tragedy of a sensitive gymnasium teacher. Another is the comic series of episodes in the humorist Frigyes Karinthy's *Tanár úr, kérem* ("Professor, Sir, Please!")—an enduring success, since its many thousands of readers could recognize in it the vicissitudes of their own middle school years.

†Even within the gymnasium an important cultural role was played by the volunteer intellectual societies (*Önképzőkör*, of which a stumbling translation may be "Circle of Self-Cultivation"). These were supervised by a professor, and it was there that the first literary attempts of many of the students were made. They were not published, but among the students the prestige of a creditable achievement in these amateur societies was considerable.

from the very atmosphere of the city. Great changes in reading and publishing had taken place in Hungary during the quarter-century before 1900. Before that time the literate country gentry may have read little but they read profoundly. They were the last generation in Hungary who had a fund of knowledge of Latin, a tradition that had come from the broad usage of Latin in Hungarian law—and from the fact that as late as 1840 the Hungarian Diet conducted some of its sessions in Latin. We have seen that by 1900 this class of the old Magyar gentry had become poorer; that many of them had gravitated to Budapest, where they and their sons sought and received jobs within the government bureaucracy; and that many of them were indifferent, and sometimes hostile, to the new fizz and bubble of the cultural life of the capital. But such people were a minority: by 1900 certain cultural aspirations of the capital city had affected older patricians and relative newcomers, upper and middle classes almost alike. It was a time for precocity, of dynamic mental appetites: we read in Sándor Hunyady's charming and self-depre-cating family reminiscences how at the age of fourteen he tried to talk to Ferenc Molnár about Stendhal.

In 1900 most people in Budapest read newspapers, and most of these newspapers printed a literary page of varying quality. In 1900 there were four bookshops for every one twenty-five years before. When the Pallas publishing house brought out its excellent twenty-two-volume encyclopedia in 1898 it had 22,000 subscribers, an impressive number. It meant that one of every four hundred Ma-gyar-speaking Hungarians had subscribed to it.*

Writers complained that most of their readers were writers them-selves. With some reason: the average book in Hungary sold only about 2,000 copies. But such statistics never tell us everything about the intellectual life of a place and time. They tell us little about the quality and the movements of mental life, about the perceptions and the circulation of intellectual reputations and fash-ions. In 1900 writers in Budapest earned little money: but the reputation of a writer was enormous. Men envied them and women admired them. What is indisputable about Budapest in 1900 was the respect for literature *and* for book learning, for academic and professional achievements as well as for the creativity of gifted

---

*Curiously enough, the public libraries, despite the considerable increase of their holdings, were not much frequented by the general public; and the widespread practice of lending libraries had only a modest following in Budapest.

amateurs. In this, as in so many other respects, Budapest in 1900 marks a perfect, though soon passing, balance: that of mutual respect between otherwise different people and their various aspirations. Few people could have differed more in character, temperament, background and philosophy than the old critic Pál Gyulai and the young financial aristocrat Baron Lajos Hatvany. When in 1900 Hatvany visited Gyulai, whom he admired, to show the critic two essays that he had written about Anatole France and Maupassant, Gyulai—who otherwise could be sharply critical of pretentious critical writing—advised that rich amateur: "Why don't you take time for university studies?" Gyulai knew how many aspiring young intellects graduated from the gymnasium to those coffeehouses where they found life easy, having eschewed the rigors of professional training in the universities. And so this young dilettante went off (at least for a time) to the university of Freiburg, even though the place where he was thoroughly at home was that of the *jours* and the coffeehouses of Budapest.

As late as 1926 (the golden era of the coffeehouse in Budapest lasted until about 1940) the by then ancient and conservative Jenő Rákosi recalled how "every intelligent person had spent a part of his youth in the coffeehouse . . . without that, the education of a young man would be imperfect and incomplete." In 1900 there were hosts and hostesses who more than welcomed writers at their soirées, dinners and *jours,* but the literary salon, as such, was rare in Budapest. In the 1880s many currents in the Budapestian world of letters had been generated in the salon of the Wohl sisters, but in the next decade some of the Budapest coffeehouses became centers of intellectual life.

There were nearly six hundred of them in 1900. This was, of course, the peak of the coffeehouse culture in continental Europe, certainly in cities such as Vienna and Paris, but the coffeehouses of Budapest were different. To begin with, their history was longer. Whereas the Turkish habit of coffee drinking came suddenly to Vienna and Paris at the end of the seventeenth century, in Hungary it had come more than a century before. There exists a three-volume history of the coffeehouses of Pest and Buda, covering four centuries, full of the oddest details. The author, a reputable amateur historian, Béla Bevilacqua-Borsody,* was himself a descendant

---

*He cites the Parisian social historian Guillaume de Gauthier-Villars: "To write the history of our cafés would almost amount to writing a history of France."

of venerable ancestors in the Coffeebrewers' Guild (as was the great nineteenth-century Mayor of Budapest, Károly Kammermayer).

In the history of Budapest the part played by coffee may have had more in common with the practice of Mediterranean countries than with those of Central Europe: with Italy, for example, where the most important literary journal in the eighteenth century bore the name *Il Caffè*. In the nineteenth century many literary intrigues or even political conspiracies were hatched in the coffeehouses of Europe, but I know of only one instance when a great national revolution literally started from a coffeehouse, from the Café Pilvax in Pest on the morning of March 15, 1848, Hungarian Independence Day. And when forty-six years later, in 1894, the body of Kossuth, the great national hero of that revolution, was brought back to Budapest, it was from the Café Fiume that the group of demonstrators proceeded to the Opera and to the National Theater in order to halt the performances on that day of national mourning.

During the ten years before 1900 the number of coffeehouses in Budapest grew even faster than that of restaurants and taverns. Coffeehouses were opened in new places and new districts of the capital. What they offered (or, equally important, represented) had become attractive and available to people whose social lives had previously concentrated in other kinds of public places, taverns, pubs. For entire families they could serve as respectable, and relatively inexpensive, places for relaxation. In this respect their social function resembled that of an English or Irish pub: a neighborhood meeting place for relaxation and conviviality. But the services of the coffeehouses were more extensive than those of a pub. They became even more extensive in the 1890s because of their potential profitability, including the relatively low cost of their personnel. Some of them were open for twenty-four hours a day; and some for 365 days a year.† By 1900 many coffeehouses would serve a great

---

Bevilacqua-Borsody does not say that the history of the coffeehouses of Budapest almost amounts to its cultural history, but somehow it is implicit in his book. The commemorative history of the Elizabeth (Seventh) District of Budapest, written by various authors (*Erzsébetváros,* Budapest, 1970), devotes a large portion to the history of its coffeehouses.

†It was the custom of some of the more old-fashioned coffeehouse owners (who were still proud of the title of their ancient Coffeebrewers' Guild) to serve a meal on Christmas Day (Christmas Eve having been reserved for their families) to all of their servants, including the lowliest waiter-apprentices and kitchen-helpers,

variety of dishes, every hour of the day. It was possible—indeed, often desirable—to repair to a coffeehouse for an elaborate supper. Some of these were known for their cuisine as well as for their amenities (the Hangli, for example, in a glass-enclosed kiosk along the Pest Corso). Others were famous for what they would offer during the nightlife—or, rather, dawnlife—of Budapest. At two or three in the morning they would be full of people consuming what was a Budapest specialty: not an after-theater supper but a pre-breakfast "Hangover Soup." A few coffeehouses offered music (some of them even had orchestras or gypsy bands); but unlike in the orpheums, there was no dancing in the coffeehouses of Budapest.

They were inexpensive. One could sit for hours over a cup of coffee, with a glass of cold water frequently replenished by a boy-waiter, and avail oneself of a variety of local and foreign newspapers and journals hanging on bamboo racks. One could send or receive messages and letters from the coffeehouse. Free paper, pen and ink were available there. In this way the Budapest coffeehouse was more of a club than a pub. This was of particular value in a city where in 1900 private clubs were, by and large, few; and where none of those of the upper classes—the National Casino of the aristocracy, the Country Casino of the gentry, or even the Leopold-stadt Casino of the upper bourgeoisie—were places for intellectual congregation.* At a particular table—their reservation was sac-rosanct—this or that group of journalists, playwrights, or sculptors and painters would congregate, usually presided over by one or two leading figures. Many writers and journalists found the atmosphere of their Budapest coffeehouse so congenial that they repaired there for work, rather than for relaxation (or at least for a combination of both). Entire newspaper articles, at times entire

---

and to those of their habitual guests who were lonely bachelors or widowers and for whom their customary coffeehouse was a second home.

*The first clubs of writers, journalists, artists and actors, the Otthon (Home) and the Fészek (The Nest), were established in 1899 and 1901, respectively, in the lower-middle-class streets of the Elizabeth District. An important source of their upkeep was the cut that the management got from their gaming tables and gaming rooms. (Gambling in coffeehouses was forbidden.) Unlike their colleagues in Western Europe, many Magyar writers and artists had a strong (and often disas-trous) penchant for gambling and the turf. Here, again, their inclinations and passions corresponded with those of the Magyar aristocracy, and especially of the gentry.

short stories, chapters of a novel and a large part of the theater criticism were composed at the tables of the noisy, crowded cof-feehouses of Budapest. In those frequented by journalists and writ-ers the headwaiters (some of whom were celebrated for their knowledge of literature) kept sheaves of long white sheets of paper (called "dogs' tongues") available to any writer who chose to com-pose his article or essay there. These headwaiters were also the sources of tips of the turf, of useful gossip, and—more useful to writers—of extension of credit as well as of occasional loans of petty cash.

By 1900 many of the coffeehouses of the early nineteenth cen-tury—the Crown, the Turkish Emperor, the Coffee Fountain, the White Ship and the once elegant The Seven Elector Princes—had disappeared. They gave way to more spacious establishments whose furniture and décor, including large gilt mirrors and giant chande-liers, were luxurious—for example, the Café New-York, opened in the semipalatial building of the same name in 1894. It says some-thing of the importance of coffeehouses in Budapest that the Café New-York was designed by the same famous architect (Alajos Hauszmann) who was in charge of the reconstruction of the royal palace. (Ten years before Hauszmann had designed and built a then famous coffee- and teahouse, the Kiosk on Elizabeth Square.) Half a mile from the New-York* there were at least five famous coffee-houses along a four-block stretch of Andrássy Avenue alone, fre-quented by writers and artists: the Japan (mostly architects, sculp-tors and painters), the Hall of Arts (painters), the Opera, the Dreschler and the Abbazia, whose clientele was a steady mix of

---

*In 1900, and for many years thereafter, the spaces in the New-York were occu-pied by specific groups: writers and journalists, other visitors (The Deep End); and other alcoves along the galleries were habitually reserved for particular groups of intellectuals and artists. Aspiring young actresses and young women of light virtue were to be found around the tables of yet another portion along the galleries. But the New-York was not really a place for pickups. To the contrary: it would attract a few aristocrats and many members of the bourgeoisie, together with foreigners of cultural interests. Many a contract for a play or movie was negotiated, and even signed, at its tables. When in the 1920s tourism to Budapest revived, and when the fame of Hungarian actresses, actors and writers had spread to far Hollywood, movie magnates such as Zukor, Fox, Goldwyn and Louis B. Mayer visited the New-York (the first two were of Hungarian origin). During the Stalinist years the New-York was renamed Café Hungaria; but everyone in Budapest still calls it New-York. The main interest of most foreign visitors now is its Art-Nouveau décor.

bourgeois and journalists. (A small group of painters who had two tables reserved in the Royal were the "royalists," of course.) Other recognizable congregations included the Sódli on the Museum Ring (older writers and some of the university professors), and the Lloyd (stockbrokers and people from the Bourse). Some people, in 1900 and later, would, on occasion, talk contemptuously about "this coffeehouse culture" of Budapest. Yet in some of the remaining coffeehouses—or, rather, on the walls of the houses where some of these once stood—successive governments of Budapest, including the present one, found it proper to install plaques commemorating those remarkable Hungarian writers, poets and artists who had sat there many decades ago, in very different times.

That coffeehouse culture was connected with the press, perhaps more than anywhere else in Europe at the time. The years around 1900 were the golden age of newspapers, for two reasons. With the increase of literacy and of the population, there was an ever-widening reservoir of potential newspaper readers to be tapped; while at the same time—before the newsmagazine, radio and newsreel—newspapers still kept their near-monopoly on the communication of information and opinions (and also of criticism). The profits of the owners of the Budapest newspapers allowed for the hiring of more and more aspiring journalists. For the first time even a fledgling young reporter could exist on a salary, while his "profession" was attractive enough to suggest various kinds of promise. More important was the chance of serious writers to earn some money from the publication of some of their short pieces or from their occasional theater or music criticism in the papers.

This overlapping of journalism and literature led to a certain contamination of earlier standards. The catering to an ever increasing circle of readers led to conditions where this widening of appeal meant a growing shallowness of content. Here, too, the years around 1900 represented a turning point. The older liberal newspapers *(Pesti Napló, Pesti Hirlap, Budapesti Napló, Budapesti Hirlap)*, some of which had very respectable histories (in the 1860s *Pesti Napló* had played an important role in the formation of public opinion in favor of the Compromise of 1867), were beginning to lose their influence, though for some years they remained profitable. In 1896, for the first time, a cheap penny newspaper *(Esti Ujság)* made its appearance on the Budapest boulevards. In the same year the municipal authorities permitted the hawking of newspapers by quick-footed newsboys, adding yet more strident sounds to the crowded and noisy streets of Pest. The crudely edited newspapers of this newer kind (called boulevard press), filled with scandals and pictures, did not yet have much impact on the formation of public opinion, but they represented a new kind of urban provinciality. This was significant because around that time the older Budapestian quality of the more serious newspapers had begun to diminish. They had become national political organs. In 1900 only one of every twenty Hungarians was an inhabitant of Budapest; yet, on the average, one of every two Magyar-language newspapers, literary journals and scholarly or other periodicals was printed there. There were twenty-two daily newspapers in Budapest in 1900.* Only one serious German-language newspaper, the *Neues Pester Journal,* was left. Together with the earlier-mentioned unhealthy fixation of the national interest on the parliamentary theatrics of Budapest, this concentration was, by and large, unhealthy. This large number of daily papers (more than in Vienna) had become increasingly political, the organs of different political parties and groups. Nor were the standards of even the best Budapest newspapers quite up to the standards of the great classic newspapers of the great Western capital cities of their time. The freedom of the press in the Dual Monarchy allowed for this excessive preoccupation with (and for their often excessive rhetoric about) national politics. They employed correspondents abroad only on occasion; they printed remarkably little foreign news. In sum, they were ethnocentric—almost, if not quite, as Hungarocentric as the politicians in the new big Parliament.

For the sake of an enlightened public opinion these conditions were damaging. They were less damaging for their service to literature. By this I do not only mean Hungarian literature: the more traditional papers gave respectable space not only to Hungarian writers but also to short stories and essays by such modern foreign authors as Knut Hamsun, Hermann Sudermann, Jack London,

---

*One-half of the printing shops of the country were in Budapest, too—in 1900 more than half of them in that Seventh (Elizabeth) District, around that portion of the Ring where most newspaper offices, cafés and the earlier mentioned clubs of writers and journalists were to be found. It was in 1900, too, that the first Linotype machines were put into service by at least two of the Budapest dailies (less than eleven years after their invention). In 1900 the first photogravure picture weekly *(Tolnai Világlapja)* appeared.

Emile Zola, Anatole France and "Gyp" (the Comtesse de Martel).

A more important contribution to literature was that of the literary (and semiliterary) journals. The oldest and most respectable among them was the *Budapesti Szemle* (traditionally in a blue and yellow cover, resembling that of the old *Edinburgh Review*) in which already in the 1880s readers could find serious literary criticism by the superb critics Jenő Péterfy and Frigyes Riedl, as well as historical essays by the first-rate historian Dávid Angyal. At that time another literary review, the more lighthearted *Magyar Salon,* appeared but it was short-lived. In 1890 began the publication of the weekly *A Hét,* directed by the Hungarian Jewish poet József Kiss. It was supported, too, by the fine critic and patron of the arts Zsigmond Justh, who had been at home in the salons of Paris and whose promising career was cut short by his early death. In 1895 the publishing house Singer and Wolfner launched another literary-cultural periodical, *Uj Idők* ("New [or Modern] Times"); yet its tone was less modern, less iconoclastic, less "Pestian" and more sentimental and more family-oriented than *A Hét.* * In 1900 *A Hét* was undoubtedly the principal literary medium in Hungary. It was a powerful instrument representing the voice of a modern Budapest. That voice was at times uneven and harsh, often unduly political in its contents and inclinations, but it attracted a substantial readership as well as the ambitions of an amazing number of amateur writers. As in the advertisements of many of the daily newspapers, we may find pungent traces of the seamier life of Budapest at the time (I am referring to the fairly outspoken allusions of its personal advertisements, offering erotic opportunities) in the letters to the editors of *A Hét.* The outspokenness of the editorial answers reflect the strength, breadth and sometimes unrefined energy of that appetite for literature—or, at least, for literary fame—that was so prevalent in Budapest in 1900.†

---

*Another semiliterary weekly, *Fővárosi Lapok,* was yet another competitor, with ample space for literature and fashions (among other things, it published the first short writings of Gyula Krúdy, newly arrived and still largely unknown in Budapest, barely twenty years old in 1899). In 1900 there appeared another spate of literary periodicals, *Magyar Kritika, Uj Magyar Szemle* and *Jelenkor* (the latter edited by the fine writer Zoltán Ambrus, wishing to create a Magyar equivalent of the *Revue des deux mondes* in Budapest). The last three were short-lived.

†Two such editorial answers from *A Hét* in 1900: "Your poems are unacceptable." Or: "We are not encouraging anyone to write poetry."

In the development of Hungarian literature 1900 was a time of transition between generations. The three outstanding poets of a Magyar *fin-de-siècle,* Gyula Reviczky, János Vajda and Jenő Komjáthy had died, in 1889, 1897 and 1895, respectively. The grand old man of the nineteenth-century Hungarian novel, Mór Jókai, had become senile (and supposedly in the clutches of an ambitious young girl whom he had married in his dotage). The inimitable Kálmán Mikszáth was also getting old—and bitter. One of his last novels, *Különös Házasság,* (English translation, "Strange Marriage," was published in 1900. In it Mikszáth's charming mix of humor and sarcasm, of his avuncular, though ironic, indulgence in describing the virtues and vices of the Magyar country gentry, no longer balanced perfectly: both the style and the themes of Mikszáth belonged to a century now past. He died in 1910. The greatest of Magyar critics, Pál Gyulai, was very old, too; he would linger on till 1909 and write little after 1900. Every one of these men except Reviczky had been born well before 1850. They had been living witnesses to the drama of the national War of Independence. All of them had been born in the Hungarian provinces. Most of them came to live in Budapest later. There they would witness the transformation of the city into a metropolis and the focus of a different, modern Hungarian literature.

The difference between them and the generation of 1900 was more than that of old age and youth. But before the generation of 1900 would come into its own there was another generation of writers in between. In 1900 most men of this literary generation were in their late thirties, which meant that they were, by and large, in charge of the literary life of Budapest. The writer, critic and playwright Zoltán Ambrus (who, as we have seen, attempted to found a Magyar *Revue des deux mondes* in 1900) was born in 1861. Four outstanding writers of this generation were born in 1861: Géza Gárdonyi, Zsigmond Justh, Sándor Bródy and Ferenc Herczeg. All of them were born in the provinces. They were very different. Gárdonyi was a modest and reserved writer, with a deep interest in the psychology of the people of the Hungarian villages. Justh was a gifted and sophisticated descendant of an old and relatively well-off gentry family, a man of great refinement who was well known (and, what is rare, well liked) by *tout Paris* and yet thoroughly dedicated to the cultivation of specifically Magyar forms of literature; he died tragically young. Bródy was the first Hungarian Jewish novelist, a writer of remarkable talent: a handsome man, bohemian and gambler, whose easygoing character was complemented by his frequent concern with themes reflecting the tragic social injustices of his time (his serious novel of this kind, *Erzsébet dajka* ["Elizabeth, the Nurse"], appeared in 1901). Herczeg was a young novelist when he became the editor of the journal *Uj Idők* in 1895. People saw him as a "conservative" writer, appealing mostly to the Gentile middle classes and to the gentry; yet his plays, dealing mostly with men and women of his class, would help in raising the level of the prose of the Magyar theater to modern European standards.

Among the 1900 generation of Hungarian writers the chronological coincidence of their ages is startling. Endre Ady was born in 1877; Ferenc Molnár and Gyula Krúdy in 1878; Zsigmond Móricz and Dezső Szabó in 1879; Margit Kaffka in 1880; Gyula Juhász and Mihály Babits in 1883; Ernő Szép in 1884; Dezső Kosztolányi and Georg Lukács in 1885; Árpád Tóth in 1886; Frigyes Karinthy in 1887. This meant that their formative years took place around 1900. The first three were already published writers by that time. Between 1900 and 1910 these founders of modern Magyar literature came into their own. All of these men and women, in their different ways, represented a breaking away from the older literary traditions. Yet their importance lies not in the novelty of their modernism but in the quality of their language. They brought to Hungarian literature not only new themes, but new qualities of sensitivity that were equal (and in some instances, perhaps, unsurpassed) in Europe and in the world at the time. That their names are unknown beyond Hungary is the inevitable consequence of their writing in the lonely, unrelated language of a small country. In the long run, this melancholy condition does not affect their accomplishments. The contrary is true, especially in our time when it appears that while "science," with its symbols and at least some of its applications, has become more and more international, literature not only remains but becomes more and more deeply national—*national,* not *nationalistic*—because of its inevitable dependence on language, which is, after all, the greatest and deepest asset of a nation, of its knowledge and of its memories on which the entire quality of its understanding of its present depends.

Three originally Hungarian writers of the generation of 1900 whose names are still known outside Hungary are Ferenc Molnár, Georg Lukács and Arthur Koestler. All three of them were born in Budapest. Our problem is that their international reputations reduced (and, in the case of Koestler, eventually eliminated) their Hungarianness, by which I mean not race, nationality or citizenship, but their writing in Hungarian for Hungarians. Molnár was a precocious talent whose first play in Budapest was produced (and in a theater with high literary standards) in 1900, when he was twenty-two. A few years later he wrote the novel *Pál-utcai fiúk* (an American edition, "The Paul Street Boys," was published in 1927). Its theme is the bravery, tragedy and death of a little boy among two groups of his schoolmates who are playing at war in a working-class neighborhood of Budapest (in the Ninth District). The book is both realistic and sentimental in the best sense of these words, one of those very rare instances of juvenile literature whose appeal to young people and to adults is not only parallel but equal. Rereading it after many years, I was astounded to find how it reflects those particularly Magyar values of its time (it takes place in 1889): for in those proletarian surroundings the values and the behavior of these working-class and lower-middle-class boys, swarming on the dusty, empty lots of Budapest, incarnate their respect for self-sacrifice, bravery and honor, reflecting the standards of an older Hungary. That Molnár could represent this, in a modern book, in modern Budapestian language, shows his talent as a writer. It also shows how well he understood the mental and spiritual climate of Magyar Budapest at the time. But for him this would not last long. He found his talent writing light comedy for the stage. Like Pirandello (a more serious playwright), Molnár became a master of surprise and legerdemain on the stage. His plays were full of persiflage. He was a man of great wit (an early exemplar of a specific Pestian humor) and a *viveur.* The repute of his plays *(The Swan, The Guardsman, The Devil, The Play's the Thing, Liliom)* spread from the Vígszinház, the Comedy Theatre of Budapest, to Vienna, Berlin, Paris, New York and Hollywood. He spent less and less time in Hungary, even before the shadow of Hitler's Reich began to spread over his native country. Like so many other well-known Central European refugees, Molnár sailed from France to New York in 1940. Because of his savings and his American royalties (the play and the movie *Carousel,* made from his *Liliom,* were very successful),* he led a comfortable but lonely existence in the Plaza Hotel, where he died in 1952. He left behind a sad diary of these last years: the bitter ruminations of an old man, full of self-pity and loneliness, whose wit and appetite for life were gone forever.

The place of Georg Lukács in the history of Hungarian letters and learning is more complicated and controversial. In many ways he was a typical member of the generation of 1900. In one important sense he was not. The son of a respectable and honorable liberal Jewish banker, he was among those intellectuals who early in their lives (in his case, soon after 1900) broke not only with the liberal (and loyally monarchist) civic tradition of his parents but with the standards and manners of the Budapest bourgeoisie. (The "intellectual," overlapping and yet distinct in meaning from a writer or a poet, was a relatively new phenomenon in Budapest at the time.) Lukács became a radical and, later, a Marxist and Communist literary philosopher and critic. A philosopher and critic: but not much of a writer. Throughout his entire life (he died in 1971) he wrote Hungarian badly.† He was essentially a German thinker and writer, preferring to live in Germany long before circumstances, and his association with the Communist regime of Béla Kún in 1919 (in which he was the Commissar of Culture) made him leave Hungary. His style, rhetoric and the structure of his thought were Weimar-German. One of the figures in Thomas Mann's *The Magic Mountain* was supposedly modeled after him. When Hitler came to power Georg Lukács fled to Moscow, from where he returned to Budapest with the small but then all-powerful group of Hungarian Communists in 1945, at the age of sixty. Thereafter he would serve the ideological needs of a Stalinist regime, at least until the national Rising in 1956. His politics at that time should be of no interest to us, except to note that he was rediscovered (or, rather, discovered) by American and other Western intellectuals after 1956, in his capacity as one of the very few remaining cosmopolitan and well-educated Marxist scholars, and probably also be-

---

*Between 1913 and 1948 more than a dozen of his plays were performed on Broadway; some of these were adapted by P. G. Wodehouse, Gilbert Miller and Edna St. Vincent Millay.

†Georg Lukács is no relation of mine. *Nomen est omen:* his international name is telling. Unlike the cosmopolitan Molnár, who kept his Magyar first name even abroad, Lukács is known outside Hungary by the *German* version of his first name, Georg.

cause of the revived retrospective respect and interest paid to Weimar culture in the 1960s and 1970s. Yet even then, during his last twenty years in Hungary, his influence (except for a small conventicle of "revisionist" Marxist students) was limited, not only because of his political past but mainly because of the wearisome heaviness of his Hungarian writing style.

The third Hungarian writer known worldwide is Arthur Koestler. I include him in the generation of 1900 at the tail end (he was born in 1905). His childhood and early youth surely belong there. He was the son of an unsuccessful Jewish businessman, skating on thin ice. He left Budapest only in the early 1920s. He was brought up in a cultural climate that was dominated by the Generation of 1900 until 1919. Unlike Molnár and Lukács, Koestler wrote about his youth in his various autobiographies. These were written in his middle age, in his anti-Communist period, which in this instance is telling because even then he wrote indulgently, nostalgically and, to say the least, incorrectly: ("[those] idyllic days of 1919") about the intellectual freedom and excitement during the short-lived Communist regime in Budapest. After leaving Budapest in 1921 (though returning for a few visits), Koestler lived in Vienna, Palestine, Berlin, Moscow,* Paris and London. As in the case of Georg Lukács, Arthur Koestler was greatly influenced by Weimar Germany and certain German thinkers. He was a brilliant journalist and linguist with a restless and fertile mind, on occasion a writer with more than conventional philosophical interests, who did not forget Hungarian but who neither wrote Hungarian nor chose to identify himself with Hungarian letters or with Hungarian causes. What he inherited from his early youth in Budapest were his quickmindedness, his often astonishing versatility, and his appetite for the pleasures of life (including many pretty women)—a temperament that was certainly more Budapestian than German.

And now I must turn to those great unknowns abroad. If space were a measure of their importance, then each of them would deserve more detailed descriptions than those I have given to the

---

*It may be uncharitable but not untruthful to suggest that his short stay in Moscow (and his consequent break with Communism) may not have been due only to ideological disillusionments. There were many reasons why to the hedonist Koestler life in the drab and dreary Moscow of the 1930s would not appeal.

three Budapest-born writers who acquired their fame abroad. I cannot do this here. All I can give here is a summary, a necessarily inadequate description of those Magyar writers and poets who, in my scheme, belonged to the generation of 1900, in order to give a modicum of reality to what, to American readers, would otherwise be nothing but a skeleton, an academic list of exotic names. Yet I must add that a sure measure of their accomplishments does exist, after all. This is the fact that their writing has not only remained respected, but that they are avidly read (and frequently republished) in a very different Hungary now, more than fifty years after the death of most of them. There are two reasons for this. One of them is the continued timeliness of their language, which is modern *not* because of its novelty. To the contrary, it is laced less with the twentieth-century argot of Budapest than it is laden with sometimes very old Magyar words; but the tones, sounds and therefore meaning of their prose and verse speak to readers as directly today as eighty or more years before, devoid as these are of the phraseology and of the circumlocutions of the more ceremonial older Magyar prose or of the sentimentalities of the older Magyar poetry. That is the source of their enduring readability and enjoyment. It shows that no matter what their subjects, none of these writers were period pieces. They have survived the limitations of their lives and of their times, which, after all is said, is the perennial mark and measure of great art.

A very great Hungarian writer (and surely one of the greatest prose writers of Europe) in the twentieth century is Krúdy. I translated a few of his paragraphs in Chapter 1, descriptive passages of Budapest around 1900. Very few of Krúdy's writings have been translated into foreign languages; only one of his books exists in English. He is translatable only with the greatest of difficulty—in essence, hardly translatable at all. One reason for this is the alluvial soil of his imagination and memory, whereby his writing is full of rich and unique allusions to Magyar things, places and times, evoking meanings to people at the bottom of whose minds and hearts those words already lie (for words are not symbols of *things,* they are symbols of *meanings*). Another reason is the lyrical tone of his prose, a slow cello-like music rising and falling, in accord with the rhythm of the Hungarian language that, again, is so different from other European languages. It is thus that Krúdy's long paragraphs end on a soft, falling note. His descriptions are often magical, and nearly always inimitable. I wrote once that his novels are four-dimensional paintings whose beauty is manifested not only through shades and forms but through the fourth dimension of human reality—time itself—as the thin stream of the story at once bursts into a magnificent fountain, the water splashing and coursing in rainbow colors. He was not so much like Proust, who loved high society and yet condemned it, as like Monet, who painted beautiful gardens because he loved them. Like Proust (whom he surely never read), Krúdy was re-searching times, scenes and people lost. His earliest writings were suffused with nostalgia for an older, better Hungary. He traced the still visible path of sunken memories: the still living fragrances, colors, shapes, clouds of the past. He did not need the taste of the *madeleine;* his delicacies were always fresh and ready, stored in his mind. The way he wrote at the age of twenty-five reveals something astonishing to anyone who is interested not only in writing but in the mysterious alchemy of the human heart: he knew everything about old age during the physical splendor of his youth; he knew everything about autumn in the spring of his life. Throughout his life he was fascinated with dreams. He knew something that the psychiatrists of this century do not know, which is that in our dreams we really do not think differently, we merely remember differently. He was not only a Hungarian Proust, he was a Homer, not of certain places but of certain times, a Magyar-writing Homer of the great subterranean development near the end of the Modern Age—that of historical consciousness. Except by a few Hungarian writers, Krúdy was not deeply appreciated during his lifetime, mostly because of the fantastic volume of his output. That was an inseparable condition of his fantastic life and character. As Szerb wrote, he was running after money but wrote master-pieces instead. Like Balzac, he was always short of money; he wrote twelve, sixteen sheets every morning, with an old-fashioned steel pen, in violet ink. Unlike Balzac, he never corrected anything, not even proofs. He seldom read what he wrote. No one has, even remotely, written like Krúdy in Hungarian. He defies categoriza-tion. He was neither a "populist" nor an "urbanist" writer, the two categories that, in the twentieth century, often divide Hungarian writing into two groups, sometimes unnecessarily or lamentably so. He wrote about the lights and the shadows of certain streets in Budapest and about the dreamy mists in the copses of faraway valleys and remote counties of Hungary with the same kind of imagination and intuition, with the same kind of lyrical mastery, in the same way.

Another great writer of the generation of 1900 was Mihály Babits. Unlike Krúdy and other people of that precocious generation, Babits wrote slowly. When his first volume of poems appeared he was almost thirty years old. He was for a while an assistant professor in a gymnasium, deeply conversant with Greek and Latin literature; he would later produce an exquisite Hungarian translation of Dante. This reserved and modest man was a classicist and a modernist, a Hungarian and a European, a Catholic and a humanist. "Apart from the artistic worth of his works," Szerb wrote, "he was a cultural fact, the new synthesis of the Hungarian and the European spirit and intellect." (Babits also wrote an extraordinary history of European literature, *Az európai irodalom története.*) Babits's poetry is deep and yet easy to grasp; his metaphors, similes and other figures of speech consist of startling phrases and sentences rather than of pungent words. Babits was one of the great Catholic writers of this century, here and there reminiscent of Julien Green or François Mauriac. The philosophical unity of Babits's writing is such that, had he been born in France, he might have been recognized as *the* great Catholic humanist poet of this century, while his morality and decency are neither puritanical nor even Jansenist. He began writing novels in his early middle age. They are more somber than his poems. In these novels Babits wrote, on occasion, about schizophrenia and other vagaries of the human soul. His novels also deal, here and there, with the ugly and sometimes deadly conflicts between a still unfinished and incomplete Hungarian urbanity and the thick-blooded enmities and suspicions of small-town people. At any rate, there was a unity in the life of this good, great and lonely man who remained faithful to his Catholic humanism and liberality of spirit in difficult times, often at great risk to his reputation and career.

The other great urban—and urbane—writer, with affinities to the French spirit, was Dezső Kosztolányi. Like Babits, Kosztolányi was a poet and novelist and a fine translator of European literature, a man with philosophical inclinations. It is almost impossible to compare the two—who was the better poet—because they are so similar, and yet different at the same time; Kosztolányi was, however, the better novelist of the two. It may be said that whereas Babits was concerned mostly with thoughts and beliefs, Kosztolányi was involved with language and sentiments. His poetry is impressionist or symbolist, more finespun than Babits's; or, in other words, more existential and perhaps less essential (in the philosophical sense of that adjective). Kosztolányi turned to the writing of novels relatively late in his life. At least three of his novels, *Pacsirta, Aranysár-kány* (see p. 146 *n.*) and *Édes Anna* are masterpieces, not only because of their language but because of their portraits of a society —more precisely, of its then prevailing sentiments. In one respect, he was not unlike Krúdy in that his novels and some of his essays do not resemble those of any other European writer of his time. With a mixture of reluctance and relief, I am trying to avoid transla-tions of passages in this chapter, but I will cite at least one throwa-way remark by Kosztolányi in order to show, and not merely to suggest, the acuity of his mind. "I know," he once wrote, "that *knife* is also *culter, couteau, Messer, coltello, navaja.* Someone might even be able to convince me that I am wrong. But no one can convince me that *knife* does not mean *knife*"—a remark that is worth an entire library of lucubrations by semanticists, semioticists, linguists and structuralists.

It is remarkable how such Magyar writers from the provinces* could assimilate and adopt the highest standards of Western Euro-pean (particularly French and English) literature naturally and ef-fortlessly, not only responding to modern styles but exemplifying esthetic and humane values through their own sensitivity. They were, thus, true representatives of a generation that had not only come of age, but of the fact of how truly and authentically Hun-garian culture—with all of its particular and sometimes exotic char-acteristics—belonged to the West.

*Margit Kaffka was the first modern woman among Hungarian writers, with a fine and precise prose, full of an intelligent and restrained melancholy—another of those Hungarian talents who had come to Budapest from the provinces, and who combined the self-imposed solitude of a writer with the occupation of a dedicated professor in a middle school. Alas, she died young. Árpád Tóth was a fine poet who became very knowledgeable of European literature. Some of his translations were unusually masterly. He was a lonely and pessimistic man, as was Gyula Juhász, one of the Magyar *poètes maudits.* His life was punctuated by suffering, including a severe inherited illness that eventually led to insanity. Attila József was born in 1905 and did not begin to write until the interwar period. A poet of great seriousness, József came from a proletarian family and background, Left-oriented at a time when that was not only unpopular but relatively rare. Unaffected by insanity but in the throes of despair (despite his then growing literary reputation), he threw himself under a train in 1937.

What an extraordinary harvest of death was that for this generation in the twilight years from 1933 to 1941, from the rise of Hitler to the time when Hungary would be sucked into the Second World War! Krúdy, Kosztolányi, Juhász, József, Karinthy, Babits all died between 1933 and 1941. None of them had reached the age of sixty.

The West . . . the Danube enters traditional Hungary at the westernmost village of Dévény. In 1906 two of the most famous —perhaps the most famous—lines of the most famous poem of the most famous poet of twentieth-century Hungary read: "Shall I break through below Dévény/With new songs for new times?" This was the epigraphic poem—an unusual poem, without a title, printed on the first page of a book of poems by Endre Ady, entitled simply and starkly *Új versek* ("New Poems").

I know of no instance in the history of world literature—or in the history of any country—where such a volume of poems, where such a poet had a comparable impact: not Pushkin, not Byron, not Lamartine, not Whitman. In Hungary in 1906 this volume produced a veritable explosion. That impact alone (which, of course, is not necessarily a hallmark of the enduring value of a poem) is testimony to the extraordinary importance of literature in Hungary at the time. Ady was a historical and political, as well as a literary phenomenon. (Again there was a Hungarian tradition to this, in a country where the declamation of a single poem by its poet, Petőfi, on the steps of the National Museum in 1848 made not only a romantic scene on the first day of the Revolution, but later became, together with the mysterious death of this poet on a battlefield, the principal symbol of that epoch; and where, in 1956, the chain of emotional events leading to the Rising began with a public meeting in the club of writers and poets.) Endre Ady was for a time the protagonist of the generation of 1900. His function was not merely symbolic but connected with the flow of greater events; and the fact that the explosion of "New Poems" came at the time of that multiple turning point in 1906 is very telling.

More than eighty years later it is telling, too, but in a different way. There is something that is dated in Ady's poetry and prosody, and in his view of the world. The artist, as Ezra Pound once put it, is the antenna of the race, meaning a sensitive receiver and transmitter of certain signals. Ady *was* such an antenna of the Magyar race, by putting crystallizing thoughts and rising sentiments into often magical words and phrases, but these thoughts *had been* already crystallizing and those sentiments had *not* been altogether unspoken. He was a catalyst—and a public and visible one—rather than a forerunner, the flash of the lightning rather than the antenna. The antenna senses the coming of a storm, whereas the lightning connects with the thunder, at a time when the storm is breaking, when it is nearly over us.

Yet Ady was a great poet—and, in some ways, a revolutionary and a seer—with all of the genius and with the inevitable shortcomings of radical revolutionary seers. He was born in 1877 of a very old Magyar Calvinist family of Transylvanian gentry. There was little literary promise in his early writings. His first volume of poems was published in 1899. His introduction to an urbane and literary atmosphere came not in Budapest but in the Transylvanian city of Nagyvárad.* There came the turning point of his life: a violent and passionate love affair with "Madame Leda," an older woman, the wife of a businessman. Ady went with Leda to Paris, where he met few Frenchmen: but Paris helped to open his eyes. Suddenly, in 1906, the language and the vision of this previously mediocre poet and publicist exploded. New words, new similes, new metaphors, new rhymes and new meters erupted out of him. Their sound was deeply, harshly, rhythmically, bitterly Magyar. Their appeal to all kinds of people, including intellectuals who otherwise paid little attention to poetry, was phenomenal. "This is *our* poet, boys!" exclaimed, somewhat vulgarly, the sociologist Oszkár Jászi. Zsigmond Móricz would remember: "No one will ever be able to measure his impact on the entire youth of our time . . . Ady was himself the focus of passions that were burning in the minds of masses; his poetry became thus the searchlight and the flamethrower . . . and where his words fell the seeds of new powers were cast in the souls of men."

He was a presence: a handsome man, with a large head, his dark locks hanging over his forehead, visible night after night in the Three Ravens. He drank heavily. He suffered from a slowly advancing syphilis. After nine or ten years of fever and fame he grew calmer. He married a young woman from another Transylvanian gentry family. He died less than four years later, in January 1919, ravaged by his illness, unable to speak, in a dark room in a dark

---

*In some ways Nagyvárad was a Little Budapest. From there (I wrote once): "Magyar (and sometimes Magyar-Jewish) geniuses took wings to fly to the greater world of Budapest and Paris. It was then, in the coffeehouses of Kolozsvár and Nagyvárad that the Baudelaireans and the folklorists argued and drank into the night, a Transylvanian night in which the coffeehouse smoke instantly wafted away in the clean dark air in the narrow streets, between the uneven rows of the yellow-stuccoed one-story provincial houses with their earthy odors and sometimes erotic promises and the lone swaying electric tram-car lighting up the cobblestones at the far end" ("In Deepest Transylvania," *The New Republic*, February 3, 1982).

apartment in a dark house in a dark street of a dark Budapest in the dark time of a short-lived and badly confused Hungarian radical republican revolutionary regime whose ideas he had symbolized and for which he was, to some extent, responsible. Sad and early as his death came (he was only forty-one years old), Ady died none too soon. He had almost outlived his time. At least the political ideas of that generation whose bard and spokesman he had been were then being tried, and very soon found wanting. But the important matter for us—and the lasting value of his work—is not his Hungarian politics; it is his Hungarian vision.

He was deeply Hungarian, revolting against the ceremonial remnants of a feudal order. Yet this Magyar Calvinist from the eastern marchland of the Hungarian plains flailed away not so much at the Austrian and other foreign baroque incrustations of Hungarian life but against what he saw as the semi-Oriental backwardness of the country and of much of its gentry. This is why his loneliness in Paris had no real effect on his purpose: to bring a corrupt and antiquated Hungary up to the "West." He was contemptuous of anything that was backward, "Oriental," bureaucratic, conservative. He hated the Premier, Count István Tisza, another Calvinist, who came from the very same part of Hungary as Ady; he saw in Tisza a rigid, unimaginative, haughty demigod.* Ady was a revolutionary, not only in his political and social ideas, and in the style and rhythm of his poetry, but also in the way he wrote about so many topics, including carnal love. Before the generation of 1900 Hungarian love poetry was archaically modest. János Arany, the greatest Hungarian poet of the nineteenth century, never wrote a love poem. Ady's eroticism was a profound and bitter one: in one of his famous poems love was the biting, fighting rutting of hawks on a bed of fallen leaves *(héjanász az avaron)*. The depths of this anticlerical Calvinist and sometimes self-proclaimed agnostic should appear from one of his religious poems. I am compelled to translate here a stanza from one of his most shattering poems about God Himself:

> *A bourdon bell was his greatcoat*
> *Torn and with red letters mended.*
> *Frayed and worn stood this ancient Lord,*

---

*Their hatred was mutual. In one instance, Tisza called Ady "a leaf-bug on the tree of Magyar culture." (Yet in 1904 Ady had requested a subsidy from Tisza for his journey to Paris.)

He clapped and beat against the fog,
He rang. He rang the bell for Advent. *

He chastised his people and country, and loved them. He thought that erotic love was the highest experience of life, yet he was drawn to, even obsessed with Death, which is so often present in his poems. His political propositions were often radical and therefore myopic, dictated by his hatreds; but his visions about a coming war were startling. In sum, he was that very Magyar type of great poet who is, by nature, a great, pessimistic visionary. "Dreams," he once wrote, "have made great nations great. A dog can be awake and sober. Dreams drive men, nations, societies, humanity." Some of his writings bear the mark of period pieces— of course of a very important period—but his genius, probably more than that of anyone else in the generation of 1900, is marked by the universality of his appeal: by the fact that he has been admired and followed by all kinds of people, from all sides of that, alas, so often murderously divided Hungarian ideological spectrum, from Left and Right alike, till the present day.

The odd thing is that Ady, who was obsessed with the "Oriental" backwardness of Hungary, was less European than the calmer, Catholic Babits. We can see this now. No one saw it at the time. The Ady explosion in 1906 led straight to the appearance of a new literary journal, with its first issue on January 1, 1908. Its name was symptomatic: *Nyugat* ("The West"). Its aims and standards were resolutely higher than that of *A Hét;* its contributors were more than a literary group; in its pages appeared the writings of almost all of the first-rate talents of that time—at least for a while, for a new division was beginning to appear, about that orientation of Hungary to the "West." The descriptive analysis of that rift may be beyond the province of this book, but we may not eschew it altogether. While the West meant urbanity, cosmopolitanism, refinement to many people, to others these things meant (and still mean) decadence: not only esthetic or moral decadence but a decadence of Hungarianness.

For the generation of 1900 included, too, the first great pioneers

---

* *"A Sion-hegy alatt."* Of the last two lines the French translation by the poet Jean Rousselot may be better:

> *"Il battait et frappait le brouillard*
> *Il carillonait les matines."*

of Magyar populist literature. Both Zsigmond Móricz and Dezső Szabó were born in 1879. They had other things in common. They were Magyar Protestants. They were bitterly contemptuous of the half-feudal social order of their nation, of a "gentlemanly" Hungary. They also came into their own relatively late but not because of their want of quickmindedness: Szabó had the necessary rapidity that is an inevitable ingredient of a sharp and sarcastic mind: in Móricz's case because of the deliberateness (rather than reserve) of Magyar peasants. Yet both writers, too, with all of their indifference, and occasional hostility to cosmopolitanism, were discovered by the urbanists in Budapest. Both began to appear in print only a few years after 1900. They belong to the generation of 1900 not merely because of chronological calculation. They were the first Hungarian writers who wrote about the psychic depths of their peasant race. The virtues of the "people" of Hungary had been eulogized without cease throughout the nineteenth century, but that poetic apotheosis was almost always sentimental and, therefore, insubstantial. The imagination and the language of Móricz and Szabó were drawn to the tragedy of the peasantry: they emphasized not only the corrupt limitations of the social order but the bitter virility of peasant blood. Here their similarity ended. Móricz was the greater writer of the two, in spite of his intemperate portrayal of a dark sexuality that in its nakedness was reminiscent of some of the Russian writers. The elemental force of his language was authentic; and though, like many Magyar Protestants, he was drawn to the East, he was also calmly at home among the Hungarian and Budapest "Westerners" who could appreciate the breadth of his talents. Oddly enough, Szabó, whose feverish prose exalted the racial qualities of Magyar stock, knew and understood peasants less than did Móricz (whose father was a peasant, whereas Szabó came from an old Magyar middle-class family). Moreover, Szabó, unlike Móricz, was essentially an essayist and publicist: his continued reputation among Hungarians rests as much, if not more, on his political and social writings as on his novels. For Szabó's apotheosis of the Magyar folk, his populism, was essentially a reaction and, therefore, largely negative—the outcome of his negation and hatred for everything that was Habsburg, German,* "gentlemanly," capitalist and Jewish. He hated more than he loved. His hatreds were not

*He admired France and the French spirit, yet he was, in every sense, an enemy of refinement: another contradiction in the inclinations of this complicated man.

opportunistic—hence the near-Swiftian characteristics of some of his writings. He was the first intellectual anti-Semite among Hungarian writers, whose first important novel, full of such inclinations and their expression, appeared only when he was forty, during the Kún Communist dictatorship, when this was not only inopportune but dangerous. His sharp and shrill anti-Semitism had appeared earlier, indeed, relatively soon after 1900, whereby he gained a certain kind of popularity among some people. But, with all of his personal failings—there were many, for this forever combative writer was also inordinately vain—it would be entirely wrong to consider Szabó as a forerunner of Hitlerism. With all of his thumping emphasis on blood and race, in his later writings he was full of warnings against pan-Germanism and against a Magyar alliance with Hitler's Reich; he would also warn, on occasion, against the obsession of anti-Semitism that, as he sometimes (though, alas, only sometimes) proclaimed, was a dead end.

We shall soon see that after 1900 a small but significant rift opened between Jewish and non-Jewish Hungarians, and between "Jewish-Budapestian" and "national-Hungarian" culture and literature. This break would eventually widen into a chasm, with tragic consequences. But that was not yet true of the generation of 1900. Aware as some of them were of that opening chasm, none of the earlier mentioned great writers and poets of the generation of 1900 (and none of its leading painters, architects, composers or sculptors) were anti-Semitic, except for Dezső Szabó (who was, at any rate, *sui generis,* fighting a war against all comers throughout his life). Another evidence that the culture of Budapest, and of Hungary, had not yet divided into two parts, a non-Jewish and a Jewish one at the time, consists of the presence of at least two Jewish Hungarian writers of lasting popularity. Ernő Szép was a novelist and playwright of great sensitivity and verbal talents. (Only a few years ago the great Catholic poet János Pilinszky ranked him among the finest writers of modern Hungary.) To the generation of 1900 belongs, too, Jenő Heltai, even though he was born in 1871; he matured relatively late, his first writings appeared shortly after 1900.* He combined the creativeness of a novelist, short-story

---

*This was also true of Dezső Szomory, born in 1869. His late appearance in print was due to the fact that he had repaired to Paris in 1890 in order to escape his compulsory military service. This somewhat neurotic and dandified odd bird wrote at least one fine play, *II. József* ("Joseph the Second"), and some unusual prose,

writer, poet of light verse and serious playwright. Szép and Heltai were relatively minor talents whose accomplishments have, however, stood the test of time because of their sensitive portraiture of not only the habits and fashions but also of the desires and the aspirations of men and women around the turn of the century and after. Like Molnár, Szép and Heltai had a lighter touch than some of the other writers; but, unlike Molnár, they remained not only deeply steeped but also anchored in the world of their native country, treasuring its language and many of its traditions even during their undeserved vicissitudes and humiliations. To them I must also add the name of Frigyes Karinthy, a critic, essayist and humorist, the great, lasting and popular success of whose parodies of writers, mostly Hungarians, suggests how vivid and widespread was not only the production but also the consumption of Hungarian literature in the early twentieth century by an entire generation of people in Hungary to whom the names of these many writers were household words, and who were well enough acquainted with some of their writings to recognize and relish their parodies.

If the Impossible we could not really reach / Still our aim was sacred: splendid things to write" (Ady). In ancient Magyar there had been something sacred, or at least mystically spacious, about the verb *ír,* "to write": it could also mean "to draw" or "to paint." We have seen that close relationship between the literature and the national history of Hungary, between what poets and writers were doing and saying and what was said, and sometimes even done, in national politics. But when it comes to painting, such effective or causal relationships cannot exist because of the uniqueness of each canvas, the direct effects of which cannot be compared to the sometimes resounding effects of language in a poem, pamphlet or play. This is obvious. Less obvious but very remarkable is the fact that the break between the visions of the older and the newer generation in 1900 was even more definite in Hungarian painting than in Hungarian literature. We have seen that in Hungarian literature the generation of 1860 represented a kind of bridge between the old and the new. With two outstanding exceptions (László Paál and

---

in which his self-indulgent employment of impressionist language would be interspersed with specific, *boulevardier* turns of phrase, consciously and willfully so.

Pál Szinyei-Merse),* there was nothing like that in the development of Hungarian painting. The break between the older, sentimental and romantic—and mostly German-trained—school of painters, represented by Mihály Munkácsy, Gyula Benczúr, Bertalan Székely and Károly Lotz and the modern Magyar painters coming into their own around 1900 was definite, and comparable to the break between the Salon painters and the Impressionists in Paris thirty years earlier.

It is pleasant to record that this abandonment of older practices and of a largely exhausted (and therefore less and less authentic) tradition took place, for once, without excessive bitterness and quarrels. Among all of the talents in the generation of 1900 the characters of the Magyar painters appear especially attractive. Few of them gave way to the always, to some extent, self-indulgent poses of a rebellious bohemianism. Remarkably few of them showed an interest in politics; it is even more remarkable how few of them were attracted to radical and revolutionary ideologies.† Many of them were reserved Hungarian gentlemen. Most of them had come from families of the older, cultured Magyar gentry of the provinces. János Vaszary's brother Kolos eventually became the Cardinal-Primate of Hungary.

All of them were serious craftsmen: Simon Hollósy, Károly Ferenczy, János Vaszary, József Rippl-Rónai, Béla Iványi-Grünwald, Adolf Fényes, Lajos Gulácsy, Tivadar Csontváry (Kosztka), László Mednyánszky; this list of that new generation of Hungarian painters is, of course, incomplete. That unusual coincidence in the birth dates of Hungarian writers of the generation of 1900 does not quite apply to them. Nor do the labels of Impressionism, Post-Impressionism, Expressionism. It is neither within my ability nor within the scope of this book to describe their work in detail, but I must give at least a minimum description about them. They were very individual. Even the more-or-less "impressionist" among them— Hollósy, Ferenczy, Iványi-Grünwald, for example—do not really resemble their French counterparts; if anything, their styles of painting are reminiscent, here and there, of Thomas Eakins, Mary Cassatt, Childe Hassam and Maurice Prendergast, those fine Ameri-

---

*See Chapter 1, p. 9.
†One of the most startling drawings of Csontváry, perhaps the most radical stylist among them, shows the old Franz Josef bowed over his desk. Its date is 1915.

can painters of the early twentieth century (of whom these Magyars were probably unaware). The German or Austrian influence was wholly absent among them, except in some of the paintings of Gulácsy, somewhat akin to the style of Klimt. The most modern-Gallic among them was Rippl-Rónai, who was a friend of Bonnard, Gauguin, Vuillard and Maillol; he painted a startling portrait of the latter in 1899. (That was ten years after Rippl-Rónai had studied for a short time with Munkácsy in Paris, but he left Munkácsy soon.) The most unusual painter among them was Tivadar Kosztka, the only one among them who adopted a pseudonym, Csontváry. The son of an upper-gentry family, Csontváry worked for a while as an apothecary, then had a sudden illumination at the age of thirty-seven. He said that he would become the greatest plein-air painter of the world. Yet he was not a grandiloquent but a secretive and withdrawn man. His canvases resemble nothing else in the history of painting. The largest one of them, "Baalbek," measures more than three hundred square feet. His colors are astonishing. His themes are themes from the Bible, from the Gospels, an electric power station of a Serbian town at night, a moonlight ride in Athens, Baalbek in Lebanon, etc. His colleagues did not think much of him, partly because of his eccentricities. He died of starvation in 1919. When his belongings were to be auctioned off, a young man bought a few of his large canvases at the last minute, outbidding a team of drovers who wanted to buy them to use as tarpaulins for their horse carts. A museum in the town of Pécs has now been devoted exclusively to Csontváry's works. As with the best writers of the generation of 1900, a mark of the achievement of these painters is their slowly rising—rising, and not merely lasting—reputation during the last sixty or seventy years. Unlike most of the works of the generation of painters who preceded them, few of their canvases are period pieces.

What did they have in common? By and large all of these Hungarian painters were fine colorists. Their colors are richer than their textures. Most of them excelled in landscape painting, often in large vistas under masses of clouds. The melancholy is not in their themes or even in their settings but in their nuancings, mostly of light. Their universal impulse was to move from atelier painting to plein-air, but that was generally true of the best painting of Europe and America in their time. The unusual feature of their lives was their withdrawal to the Hungarian countryside around 1900, a movement whose direction was the exact opposite of the majority of Hungarian writers and other artists (and also of painters in other European countries, who were drawn to the magnet of their capital cities as in Vienna). In 1895 Simon Hollósy departed from Munich with a group of his young colleagues and students, including a few Swedes and Englishmen, to the small eastern Hungarian village of Nagybánya. Eventually about fifty painters gathered there to live. Two other painters' colonies, in Gödöllő and Szolnok, followed their example, in 1899 and 1901, respectively. There was no bohemianism in these choices. The very amenities of Nagybánya, Szolnok and Gödöllő had nothing resembling Provincetown or Schwabing or the Place du Tertre or even Pont-Aven. They were workshops, in the honest meaning of that often inflated word. These colonies did not last long, but this did not matter. What mattered was the serious purpose of these craftsmen: to draw inspiration from new visions of nature, color and light that went beyond the yearning for the open freedom of plein-air. Nor was their withdrawal to the Hungarian countryside a move from cosmopolitanism to nationalism. In some ways the contrary was true, for every one of these painters had eschewed the nationalist and sentimentally historical themes of their predecessors. Yet there *was* something deeply Hungarian in their vision of nature—somewhat in the way in which a Monet (even more than a Manet or a Cézanne) is a *French* painter and not merely a painter of *France.* *

At first their public appreciation was slow, but then the reversal of their reputations came swiftly. In 1900 an exhibition of Rippl-Rónai evoked indifference at best and acrid, dismissive critiques at worst; in 1906 another exhibition of Rippl-Rónai was successful in every sense of the word. In the same month of January 1908, when the appearance of *Nyugat* marked a new era in the intellectual

---

*Of this generation only two Hungarian painters became well known abroad. One was the portrait painter Philip de László in London, whose vogue and repute around 1900 led to commissions even from the royal family. The other was the facile and talented Marcel Vértes (Vertès), at best a minor Dufy, who was fairly successful in Paris in the 1930s and New York in the 1940s. He does not measure up to the other Hungarian painters of the period. It may be significant that Vértes drew a few shrill, self-serving revolutionary political posters in 1918, the vulgarity of which leaves a bad taste in one's mouth. The third Hungarian visual artist of renown was the abstract designer László Moholy-Nagy, associated with the Bauhaus school. Most of his life was spent in Germany and the United States.

history of Hungary, some of the modern painters staged an exhibit, having formed a group with the name of "Ours" (MIÉNK, an acronym of "Magyar Impressionists and Naturalists' Circle"). By that time the serious private collecting of modern art in Budapest had begun.

In 1900 the national and modernist striving existed among Hungarian architects and sculptors, too. The quality of their achievements does not compare with those of the painters. The recognition that eclectic architecture had reached a dead end was pronounced in the writings and exemplified in many of the buildings of Ödön Lechner (who, however, did not belong to the generation of 1900: he was born in 1845 and died in 1914). Lechner, and a few other Hungarian architects of the time (the younger Béla Lajta, Károly Kós and Dénes Györgyi did belong to the generation of 1900) wanted more originality and no longer Hungarian variants of Austrian and German city buildings. They were also aware that, unlike in literature or music, the historical conditions that had so tragically circumscribed Magyar independence for centuries had not allowed for the development of authentic Magyar forms and traditions in architecture, except perhaps in Transylvania. In any event, Lechner, who was also influenced by those British architects who incorporated Indian forms and designs in their monumental public buildings in India, remained famous for at least three of his extremely secessionist ("secessionist," rather than Art-Nouveau) buildings in Budapest: the Postal Savings Bank, the Geological Institute and the Museum of Industrial Arts. I made a passing reference to them in Chapter 2. Their ornamentation is surely excessive, with strange, twisted ornaments on their roofs and parapets.* Some people called the Postal Savings building "the palace of the Gypsy Baron." But there are three features in Lechner's work that deserve our attention even now. One is his ability to incorporate ceramic (that is, nonporous) and authentically Hungarian-made and designed tilework in the façades of his buildings in the smoke-laden city. Another is his remarkable attention to his interiors. Perhaps the finest, and most enduring, of his achievements is the entrance hall of the Geological Institute. And we must pay respect to Lechner's originality: in several instances his designs and his ornamentation preceded those of the now-celebrated and world-famous Catalan,

---

*"What are these ornaments for?" someone once asked Lechner. "Who will see them?" "The birds will see them," Lechner answered.

Gaudí, with whose style Lechner had more in common than with the Viennese or Bruxellois or Parisian Art-Nouveau architects of the period.*

"Architecture in general is frozen music" is a famous Germanic bon mot open to question: for is music, then, melted architecture? Not at all. Historians, including art historians, ought to direct their attention not on *why* in different fields of creative art certain styles correspond, but on *how* and *when* certain sensitive people are able to express their authentic desire to create something that is not only "new" but a reaction against still prevalent and popular styles and forms that, to them, are deadening because of their falseness. That the road to truth leads through a graveyard of untruths is an adage applicable to art as much as it is to philosophy. It is surely applicable to the best minds of the generation of 1900 in Hungary, and perhaps evident in no field as much as in music. Here we come to the two Magyar geniuses whose fame eventually became world-wide: Béla Bartók and Zoltán Kodály. Bartók was born in 1881, Kodály in 1882.† Both of them were precocious talents. Bartók began to compose at the age of nine. Unlike Kodály, he was an excellent pianist. He gave his first public concert at the age of eleven, playing a Beethoven sonata as well as his own composition. In 1902 Kodály met Bartók. Both were dissatisfied with the state of Magyar musical culture, even though by that time the quality and the availability of musical training, especially in the Academy of Music (as well as in the Opera) of Budapest, had reached high standards. But it was not operatic music that interested Bartók and Kodály. They understood how musical culture in Hungary was hemmed in by second-rate epigones attempting to emulate Liszt and Wagner on the one hand, while popular Magyar music was represented by the confections of gypsy bands. In 1902 Bartók had not yet broken with Viennese influences. He admired Richard Strauss, both *Heldenleben* and *Zarathustra;* indeed, his first symphony, *Kossuth,* was marked by the strong influence of Strauss. But then came a change. Sometime in 1904 Bartók and Kodály, together with a serious student of Magyar folk music, Béla Vikár,

---

*Kós, Lajta and Györgyi would have had more in common with twentieth-century British and Scandinavian designs, but most of their building came after 1910.
†The third famous Hungarian composer of the generation of 1900 was Ernő (Ernst) von Dohnányi, less modern than Bartók and Kodály and, by and large, anchored within the German musical tradition.

began touring the far reaches of Hungary, collecting folk songs, with the help of a phonograph. They would proceed from village to village, usually calling on the local teacher, who would then lead them to people known for their songs. Bartók and Kodály were now convinced that the old Magyar folk music had little to do with the popular "folkish" tunes; and that it was radically, and fascinatingly, different in its tonal and harmonic structure. In 1906 Kodály wrote and published his dissertation on the structure of Magyar folk songs; he produced his first symphonic poem *Nyári Este* ("Summer Evening")*; Bartók's *First Suite* was performed successfully, and he received his appointment to the Chair of Piano in the Academy of Music. By that time both Bartók and Kodály had discovered the exquisite and revolutionary new harmonic structures of Debussy. Their divorce from the nineteenth-century German symphonic and tonal tradition was complete.

Thus by 1906 in the development of Hungarian music, painting, prose and poetry a new generation achieved a virtual revolution, breaking with many existing traditions and forms, turning to the Hungarianness of words, colors and sounds for inspiration. Two elements may explain this extraordinary coincidence. One of them was the role that Budapest fulfilled: a central focus, or at least the central source of information, formal and informal, of what was happening in Magyar art. The painters may have been working in Nagybánya; Bartók and Kodály may have been tramping through the villages in the far valleys of Transylvania; but they returned to Budapest and it was in Budapest that their discussions, exhibits and performances took place. The other element in these multiple coincidences was that for the first time in the history of Hungary there existed a considerable and identifiable public in Budapest whose interest in the reception and the consumption of art was both evident and propitious. Less than a generation earlier there had been no opera, no symphony orchestra, few serious bookshops, few serious art dealers in Pest and none in Buda. By 1900 all of this had changed. The bourgeoisie of Budapest, like that of most other European capitals, was desirous to receive and avid to adulate not only the frequently published literary celebrities, but also actors, actresses, musicians, composers, singers, painters and sculptors of

*He revised it in 1929, dedicating it to Toscanini.

many kinds. In the four years before 1900 alone three new full-time theaters were built in Budapest. By 1904 there were 16,000 seats in its theaters, about one for every sixty-four inhabitants. The theatrical culture of Budapest was reaching its peak. Here is the program of the four leading theaters on an ordinary weekday picked at random, March 22, 1900. Opera: Wagner's *Flying Dutchman.* National Theater: Grillparzer's *Medea.* The People's Theater (Népszinház): Offenbach's *Belle Hélène.* The Comedy Theatre (Vígszinház): a comedy by Feydeau. It is a list of offerings equal to that of any great city of the world in 1900.

The jewel-like Opera of Budapest opened its doors in 1884. (During the previous eleven years the Opera performed in the National Theater.) Three of its first directors came from abroad: Gustav Mahler, Arthur Nikisch, Hans Richter. (The last two were born in Hungary.) Mahler had been recognized and supported by no less an important personage than Count Albert Apponyi, a rising power in national politics; there came, however, a disagreeable quarrel which led to his replacement. What had improved greatly in the years before 1900 was the repertory of the Opera and the standards of its singers. A knowledgeable and sophisticated operagoing public had come to exist in Budapest. Twenty-five years later this public came to be known in Europe as one of the most critical and demanding.

There was another new development. The golden era of the Budapest operetta was about to begin. As in New York, where, sometime after 1900, the American musical comedy, with the ballads of its songwriters, became a uniquely American form of art, dominating American popular music for a half-century, new, sophisticated and different from the English, French, Italian, German and Viennese operettas of the period, something of the same happened with the operetta in Budapest. The change began in 1900. On the one hand, the nineteenth-century Hungarian tradition of the Magyar light theater, the folk play *(népszinmű),* was about to disappear. On the other hand, the composers and musicians of light music had risen from the disreputable orpheums of late nineteenth-century Budapest, to appear increasingly in regular theaters offering their stage to the Budapest operettas. (The still extant Fővárosi Operettszínház, the Budapest Operetta Theater, was still an orpheum in 1900.) There was a promising symbiosis of producers and consumers: the taste of the public was changing, it was ready to receive and to respond enthusiastically to a new kind of light music.

Two of this generation of operetta composers soon became world-famous: the Hungarian-Austrian Franz Lehár (who, like Liszt, could be claimed on occasion by Austrians by virtue of his family origins); and Imre (Emeric) Kálmán.* Yet the composers who were less well known abroad—Béla Zerkovitz, Pál Ábrahám, Viktor Jacobi, Miklós Brodszky, Pongrác Kacsóh and Albert Szirmay—produced operetta music whose sophistication and harmonic structure were as good, if not better, than Lehár's (Jacobi's *Sybill* is an example). The producers and owners of the Broadway theaters became aware of them. (The young Viktor Jacobi died in New York in 1921. Albert Szirmay would teach arrangement and instrumentation to the young George Gershwin in New York.)

Many of these composers and musicians, as indeed many of the playwrights, actors and actresses, were habitués of the Café New-York, from where the careers of quite a few of them eventually led to New York City and to Hollywood. (The young Ormandy, for instance, lived in an apartment in the building of the New-York.) And there was yet another similarity between Budapest and New York: the beginning of the movie industry, which in Budapest around 1900 progressed faster than in other European cities. It is interesting to record that while the American word "movie" first appeared in 1908, the Hungarian word *mozi* (meaning not a film but a moving-picture theater) was coined by the respectable Hungarian writer Jenő Heltai in 1907. The inventors of the movie were the French Lumière brothers in 1895, and the first movie performance in Budapest took place in April 1896, less than a few months after the first public showing of a film by the Lumières in a café on the boulevard des Capucines in Paris; in Budapest this happened in the café of the newly opened Hotel Royal on the Elizabeth Ring. The first regular movie theater in Budapest opened in the Elizabeth District, too, in November 1899. Its entrepreneurs were the owners of a small café. It occurred to them that the perfect man to crank the projector should be one of their strong-armed employees who was in charge of grinding the coffee beans. Eventually the career of such world-famous movie producers and directors as Alexander Korda and Michael Curtiz† began in that noisy, rapid-fire atmo-

---

*The best-known examples of their operettas: Lehár: *Merry Widow, Land of Smiles.*
Kálmán: *Countess Maritza, Princess Chardas.*
†The director of *Casablanca,* one of the most famous American films ever made, in 1942, was the Hungarian Michael Curtiz (né Kertész), surrounded as he was by a slew of Hungarian scriptwriters in Hollywood, many of whose first names

sphere of the Elizabeth Ring, in the smoky hurly-burly and the sometimes tawdry glitter of the New-York Café.

It was this quick, superficial, moneymaking boulevard "culture" of Pest, confected and exemplified by representatives within a new generation, which soon after 1900 led to a rupture that now, almost ninety years and three generations later, is still unhealed. The rupture would come between the cosmopolitan and the nationalist, between the urbanist and the populist, between the Jewish and the non-Jewish representatives of the generation of 1900, and between the "Budapestian" and the "real Magyar" spirit. This distinction between Budapest and "Hungary" is the subject of our next chapter, and it was coming to a head less than twenty years after 1900. It was pronounced by a no less important figure than Admiral Horthy, the head of the new "national" Hungary when he entered Budapest in November 1919, riding a white stallion. This was a few months after a short-lived Communist government in Budapest had fallen. Horthy's speech included a few words about "Budapest, the guilty city." In the Hungarian language the adjective *bűnös* means both "guilty" and "sinful."

It was at that very time—the winter of 1919–20, when the state of Hungary had fallen to abysmal depths, two-thirds of it having been dismembered among its neighbors—that the Magyar historian Gyula Szekfü was inspired to conceive and compose his great and shattering historical retrospective that I mentioned at the beginning of this chapter, entitled *Három Nemzedék* ("Three Generations"). The thesis of the book is the decline of the quality of three generations of Hungarians; and that this decline contributed, if not led, eventually to the national tragedies that then existed. Throughout his life Szekfü was a lonely scholar and writer, willing to risk unpopularity as he attempted to revisit and correct sentimental legends of his nation's history.* In "Three Generations," too, he

---

were László. It is a curious oddity that the hero of this movie is a Czech "underground" leader by the name of Victor Laszlo: Laszlo is neither a first name nor a family name in Czech. (Readers interested in a further discussion of this strange business—and in an acid criticism of this, to my mind, imbecile movie—may read my *"Casablanca* Revisited" in *Four Quarters,* Winter, 1987.)

*In his first book, *A száműzött Rákóczi* ("Rákóczi in Exile," 1913), Szekfü pointed out some of the shortcomings of that national and legendary hero. All kinds of critics attacked Szekfü for this, sometimes in a vulgar manner.

would not shy away from telling some unpleasant truths. Much of the book, including its excellent style, is still worth reading, and its intelligent method is still worth studying. But it bears many marks of the dark time when Szekfü wrote it. Of the "third" generation —not exactly corresponding to my chronological definition of the generation of 1900 but, still, of the generation that had achieved its influence around 1900—Szekfü had not much good to say. More significant, for our purposes, was Szekfü's dismissal of the culture of Budapest that he regarded as self-serving and shallow. He described the very architecture of the city as false, brummagem, gimcrack, a paste of mortar and other cheap materials. And there were Szekfü's severe strictures against Jews. While he wrote approvingly about the more traditional, older Jewish inhabitants of Hungary, he developed and illustrated statistically his thesis, according to which the thoughtless permission of large-scale Jewish immigration into Hungary during the nineteenth century was a national disaster. He had little good to say about the contribution of the entrepreneurial spirit to the prosperity of the country. He excoriated the "Jewish influence" in Hungarian letters, art, science and, of course, in the commerce of ideas. Without naming names, he even gave little credit to Hungarian historianship of the period around 1900 (whose principal representatives were three first-class historians of Jewish origin—Dávid Angyal, Henrik Marczali and Vilmos Fraknói—all converts, the last a Catholic bishop and Secretary-General of the Hungarian Academy of Sciences).* Szekfü wrote that in the Hungary of 1900 historical science, too, was "pallid," carrying the symptoms of the national malady of the period—that is, not brave enough to resist and to contradict the harmful national legends and illusions.

"Three Generations" was, obviously, inspired by its circumstances. It was published at a time when a new, nationalist, antiliberal, anti-Marxist and anti-Communist regime came to rule over a dismembered Hungary and a Budapest disturbed and exhausted after its revolutionary fevers of 1918–19. Some of the members of the generation of 1900 had fled into exile; others were temporarily silenced or disavowed because of their association with the Left. Yet this did not last long. It was not only that in the 1920s the Budapestian spirit revived; that Hungarian culture could again achieve and assimilate high standards, especially in literature, music

*None of them belonged to the generation of 1900. They were born earlier.

and the theater. It is, too, that by 1933 Szekfü had begun to change his mind. He wrote a new edition of "Three Generations," including a sequel "And What Follows After" *(Három nemzedék és ami utána következik),* a strong and somber critique of the narrow spirit and pompous pretensions of the ruling "Christian" upper-middle class—that is, of a generation after 1900. Szekfü, who throughout his life emphasized the necessity of his nation's Western orientation, and the inevitable necessity of its Habsburg and German-Roman connections, was among the first in Hungary to raise a warning against the tremendous danger of the Third Reich at a time when Hitler had not yet consolidated his power. Eventually this great conservative historian would become an often savagely attacked spokesman of the need to resist the pressures and temptations of a German alliance and of Hungarian versions of National Socialism. From a critic of the Budapest Jews he became one of their defenders at a time when this was not only unpopular but a dangerous task that he took upon himself. But this was not only Szekfü's reaction to the existing political situation. He was no longer inclined to emphasize the shortcomings of the generation of 1900. He realized that what came after them was worse.

Other Magyar patriotic conservatives, too, in the 1930s experienced a similar change of their minds and of their perspectives. In their nationalist youth they had reacted strongly, and sometimes extremely, against the then seemingly outdated and corrupt practices of late nineteenth-century Liberalism and of the "Budapestian" spirit. Now, in the face of what they saw as the often vulgar and destructive ideology of the newer nationalists, they took their stand to oppose them, becoming the often lonely defenders of an older Hungarian tradition of an urbane as well as democratic liberality.* They were preoccupied with the present and the future of Hungary, but their perspective of the past had changed, too. They saw that many of the cultural achievements of 1900 were worthy of respect, indeed.

---

*This included their Anglophilia before and during the Second World War, when the division among the people of Hungary (and perhaps especially in Budapest) corresponded to a great extent to that between Germanophiles and Anglophiles. This division corresponded, too, to differences of class and of culture, since it went deeper than political preferences; it was a division between people who saw in Germany and England the respective incarnations of two different civilizations.

6

Seeds of Troubles

I n the fall of 1899 the building boom in Budapest suddenly faded. Construction costs had risen while the demand for new buildings fell. But there was no financial panic. Building in Budapest was not about to stop. After a year or so construction became widespread again, though at a slower pace than before. It would, by and large, continue thus until the outbreak of the Great War in 1914.

What people (including financiers) did not, and could not, know then was that this real-estate decline was part of something different from the economic fluctuations that they had known in the nineteenth century. Sometime in 1899 a general inflationary trend had begun. During the next fifteen years, until 1914, prices in Budapest rose by 40 or 45 percent, especially rents. A rise in salaries and wages followed, but not enough to keep up with this constant increase in the cost of living. Only those in the free professions and occupations, people not dependent on fixed salaries, were largely unaffected by it. The relative equilibrium of the last decade of the nineteenth century was gradually disappearing in the material, financial and economic spheres of life, just as in the political, intellectual and spiritual spheres.

Thirty years before 1900 most people in Budapest had welcomed the liberalization of enterprise because of its broadening advantages, and because of the abolition of antiquated restrictions imposed by guilds, municipalities, remnant customs and the government. By 1900 more and more people were inclined to think that economic liberalism, capitalism and freedom of enterprise profited some people but not others; that the profits of a minority were accumulating at the expense of a majority. Count Pál Sennyey, perhaps the finest conservative mind of a passing generation, who in the 1870s had found no difficulty combining his (then fairly unpopular) loyally monarchist and Catholic convictions with his support for commercial freedom, changed his mind ten years later: he said that he had to revise his views on the latter. In 1901 the Catholic People's Party proposed in the Parliament a severe tax on stock exchange transactions; it failed to pass but only narrowly. The very words "free enterprise" began to acquire an ambiguous tinge: a mental association with dubious practices by unscrupulous people. "Free competition is a fraud," Dezső Szabó wrote.

"The liberal ideas," wrote the acute Győző (Victor) Concha in a brilliant book entitled *The Gentry,* "have lost their appeal." We have seen in Chapter 3 that "the gentry," this imprecise but telling term of a Magyar class, played a very important part in the history, politics and society of Hungary and in the Hungarian Parliament in the nineteenth century, well beyond its numerical proportion. We have also seen that, unlike their counterparts in England, the economic and financial conditions of the Magyar gentry were deteriorating. Most of their traditional estates were not very efficient. After 1899 agricultural prices began to rise, too, but at a slower rate than industrial prices and than living costs in Budapest. In the very year 1900 an unusually large number of estates were sold. We have also seen that—again, unlike in England—many of the Magyar gentry no longer preferred living in the country and had moved to the capital; that few of them were interested in business, commerce or finance there; that they instead sought—and received—positions within the government. In sum, the formerly liberal and antistatist country gentry became the mainstay of the national, and increasingly nationalist, governmental bureaucracy.

After 1900 that bureaucracy became inflated and rigid. In 1906 the judicious and conservative Lóránt Hegedüs wrote, in a critique of the Hungarian fiscal and taxation system, of "the irresistible, and unhealthy, desire of our society to make the state into an ever bigger Leviathan. This is a grave illness, because it does not allow for a lessening of governmental expenditures and duties; to the contrary, it wishes to accomplish everything with the help of the mythical personality of the State. . . . In reality, [our] society desires to nationalize itself."

The consequences—and the sources—of this tendency were deeper than merely economic. It was not only that the Magyar gentry had become, at least relatively speaking, poorer. They felt —and not without reason—that their principal role in the preceding century, that of constituting the leading political and cultural class of the nation, was diminishing rapidly. With notable exceptions in mind, we may essay this generalization: by 1900 this once liberal and patriotic class was becoming conservative and nationalistic. Goethe once wrote that there are no manners that do not have a moral foundation. The gentry were losing or, rather, changing, their manners. During the nineteenth century many Hungarian thinkers and writers such as Mikszáth, who themselves had come from the gentry, had chastised their pretensions and manners.* Now, instead of the unquestioned and unquestionable authority the gentry had had in their county places, they were asserting their authority in their bureaucratic capacities as officials of the state, exercising their power and, at times, their arrogance in Budapest. Their sympathetic and concerned observer, Concha, wrote, they "could not really find their place in the new conditions of national

---

*Beginning with Széchenyi and other conservatives such as Kemény (see pp. 116, 190). A history of Hungarian manners is yet to be written. I mean their history, rather than their sociology, for these manners changed. The Hungarian habit of kissing the hands of women, for example, came down from Vienna only in the nineteenth century. Before that the custom was to kiss the hands of older men. The habit of clicking heels (around 1900 this was not only a habit of army officers in uniform) had come from Austria and Prussia. The habit of dueling was still frequent in 1900 (in Budapest there were special fencing schools, *salles d'escrime,* serving that purpose; they offered quick instruction to men facing a duel who were unaccustomed to the art of swordplay. Mikszáth wrote: "A Member of Parliament is easily identifiable: he is occupied with a dueling affair, involving either himself or an important friend.") The gentry's habit of lavish hospitality, of exaggeration, of spendthrift behavior in public—that is, the custom of making an impression of wealth, power and charm beyond reason—often rested on unsure foundations.

life." Yet even in Budapest the habits of the gentry had a very definite function. In 1900, and well afterward (indeed, in some ways, until the very end of World War II), their chivalrous masculine courtesy and authoritarian behavior were widely imitated. Even in Budapest they had not lost their image as the principal representatives of Magyardom. They were being challenged, here and there, but who would take their place? Their style and rhetoric were still widespread, and often dominant.

Their greatest shortcoming was the shortsighted exuberance of their nationalism. This is important, because in 1900 the nationalism professed by the gentry was identical with what would pass for Hungarian nationalism at large. It was a time when nationalism and national consciousness—the powerful and profound existence of which Marxist and other "scientific" and materialistic thinkers have entirely overlooked—had begun to affect entire peoples. It had become stronger than religion, and stronger than class consciousness. During most of the nineteenth century in Hungary patriotism and liberalism were allied causes and movements. But by 1900 modern nationalism had begun to replace the older patriotism. A typical example of this occurred in Austria, where the new nationalists had become pan-Germans: that is, they wanted to unite with the "folk," or race, of Germans beyond the borders of Austria—if necessary, at the cost of the dissolution of the Habsburg Empire itself. (As Hitler would remember in *Mein Kampf* about his youth: "I was a nationalist; but I was not a patriot.") After 1900 in Hungary, too, nationalism was becoming less patriotic and more racial. At worst, it became corrupt and selfish.* In 1904 an article by the

---

*Two illustrations of the questionable essence of Hungarian nationalism of some of the upper classes around 1900:

In one of Mikszáth's most famous novels *(A Noszty-fiú esete a Tóth Marival)* the young Noszty, a charming and irresponsible scion of the gentry whom his father had pushed as social secretary on a, to some extent, *nouveau riche* county governor (of Slovak ancestry), advises the official about his inaugural banquet. At the wine merchant, Noszty orders 500 bottles of champagne: 50 bottles of French and 450 bottles of Hungarian champagne. "Naturally," he says to the merchant, "you will change the labels." "Of course, sir." The new county governor sees the light; he sees what his accomplished secretary means: pasting French labels on the Hungarian bottles. Not at all. Noszty instructs the wine merchant to paste Hungarian labels on the 50 bottles of *French* champagne. "This way," he says, "everyone will be impressed with your patriotism. We will put the fifty French bottles aside. They are for us, at the head table."

In 1906 a national campaign for economic independence from Austria led to

historian Dávid Angyal in *Budapesti Szemle* attempted a distinction between a "patriot" and a "chauvinist" (it is perhaps significant that he did not use the word "nationalist"): the former loves his country and is anxious to defend it; the latter wants to exalt and extend its power without cease.* In 1905 Endre Ady wrote an article, "The Twilight of Nationalism." "The world is full of signs. We are living through the final fading, the twilight, of nationalism." He could not have been more wrong.†

Many years later the conservative Count Kunó Klebelsberg remembered how, before 1914, "we carried on with politics as if we had lived on an island in the middle of the Pacific Ocean. Very few people could see beyond Vienna. There was a great deal of incredible naïveté in our judgment of foreign affairs. . . ." The trouble with Hungarian nationalism was its negative character. To be a nationalist you had to be anti-Austrian. When in 1904 the moderate Socialist Ernő Garami supported a joint customs arrangement with Austria he was violently attacked not only by the chauvinist Independents but by their conservative Catholic People's Party opponents—not only to assert that the Catholic Party was nationalist, too, but because Garami was Budapestian, Socialist and Jewish. As Chesterton once wrote, it is hate rather than love that unites people—or, at least, brings them together.

This kind of nationalism, rather than economic or financial conditions, included increasing criticism of Budapest—the assertion of ineradicable differences between the capital city and the rest of Hungary, even by politicians and writers who made their living in the capital. "Agrarian" spokesmen would denounce "corrupt, antinational, destructive, decadent" Budapest. As late as 1893 the con-

---

the so-called Tulip Movement. Men and women wore a small red cloth tulip on their lapels to demonstrate their dedication to Hungarian manufactures. It was then found that the tulips had been ordered and made in Bohemia, one of the Austrian provinces.

*Anticipating George Orwell's classic essay, written during World War II, distinguishing a nationalist from a patriot. (An American problem is latent within the linguistic usage confusing the two: by a "superpatriot" we really mean a supernationalist.)

†Yet later the visionary capacity of Ady asserted itself. In 1913, in an article entitled "Eagle and Rooster on the Red Flag," he suggested that among Socialists, too, Germans are Germans and French, French above all—an accurate prediction of the failure of "international" socialism in 1914.

servative Count Manó Andrássy proposed that the ancient seat of the Cardinal-Primate of Hungary be moved from Esztergom to Budapest. (This was not done, but a vicariate in Budapest was established.) Very soon afterward it became evident that among Catholics Budapest—or what they regarded as "the spirit of Budapest"—was no longer popular. In 1880 the poet Gyula Reviczky would merely accuse Budapest of a "satisfied stagnation." Twenty-four years later Miklós Bartha and Dezső Szabó would describe the capital as a fever-ridden "Sodom." No one had written, or thought, of Budapest in such terms before.

Around 1900 the rift opening between Budapest and the country corresponded, to a considerable extent, to the rift opening between Jews and non-Jews. The latter was more significant and struck deeper.

As late as the 1880s many of the gentry welcomed the increasing presence of Jews and their Magyarization. By 1900 some of them became, if not hostile, irritated by the presence of the Jews, especially in Budapest. Except politically, they could no longer be patronizing toward them; to the contrary, they thought that many Jews had become unduly powerful, and not only in financial life.

This requires explanation. At that time Jews amounted to more than 20 percent of the population of Budapest and to about 40 percent of its voters. Their financial, commercial, professional, and now increasingly cultural and intellectual influence there was even larger than these numbers indicate.* But this "problem" was not a matter of statistics. It was a reaction; but not a traditionalist or an old-fashioned one. Anti-Semitism in Budapest after 1900 was a *modern* phenomenon. Non-Jewish and Jewish Hungarian writers, thinkers and public figures assailed, and dismissed, expressions and manifestations of anti-Semitism after 1900 as the products of "darkest reaction." (Americans, too, are accustomed to believe that reli-

---

*After 1900 the proportion of the Jewish population in Budapest (and also in Hungary at large) no longer increased. On the other hand, 36 percent of journalists in Budapest were Jewish in 1890; 42 percent in 1910. For the first time, Jewish ownership of land in the country also grew, to 7 percent in 1904; and 70 to 75 percent of the lessees of large estates were also Jewish—a relatively new practice around that time.

gious and racial prejudices are reactionary remnants of the past, unfitted—not only morally but practically—to the twentieth century.) There is some truth in these views but not enough. The break in the extraordinary symbiosis of Hungarian Jews and non-Jewish Hungarians in Budapest in 1900 and after was the result of new ideas, rather than of old ones. The chief attackers of the Jewish presence and influence were populist and democratic rather than reactionary and aristocratic. Most of them had started out as liberals and egalitarians, and turned toward a new kind of radicalism afterward.* Their anti-Semitism had a greater influence among the young than among the old.

In some ways—but only in some—this corresponded to a general historical phenomenon. From about 1875 to 1900 the development of anti-Semitism in Hungary had certain parallels with that in Austria, Germany and France. But there were significant differences. The 1867 law guaranteeing civic and legal equality to Jews in Hungary had been unique in Central (and Eastern) Europe at the time. In 1883 a notorious trial divided Hungary almost as the Dreyfus case would divide France more than a decade later. Jews in an eastern Hungarian village were accused of murdering a young Christian peasant girl; there were anti-Jewish riots in Budapest (a Jewish student was killed by working-class apprentices), but, unlike in Paris, respectable opinion, including most of the aristocracy and the gentry, rejected anti-Semitism. The Prime Minister was emphatic in defending Jews. The elder Count Gyula Andrássy, going beyond Bismarck, who had once remarked that a few drops of Jewish blood might be beneficial to Prussia, said that he wished there were more Jews in Hungary, not fewer. In the election of 1884 a small Anti-Semitic Party appeared in Hungary (at the same time such a party appeared in Germany), and won a few seats, but in a few years this party had disappeared from the Parliament.

---

*The chief torchbearers of Hungarian anti-Semitism, Győző Istóczy and Gyula Verhovay, had become obsessed with this issue *after* they had started their political careers on the Left: the first was originally a Liberal deputy, the second an Independent. The Independent Party expelled Verhovay and a few other anti-Semitic members from its ranks in 1882 (the same year Verhovay was slightly wounded in a duel to which he had challenged an aristocrat of the National Casino). It is perhaps significant that Istóczy declared his retirement from politics in 1895 (he did not quite keep to it; see p. 207) when the new, less extreme, yet often outspokenly anti-Semitic People's Party had come into existence.

By 1900 they were forgotten. The anti-Semitic wave of the 1880s was a thing of the past. The optimism of the period was adopted and shared by the Jewish people of Budapest. The fear of persecution, that deeply pessimistic essence of the Jewish spirit, must have been there still, but it was diffused and weak. In few, if any, cities of the world had Jews prospered as freely and as much as in Budapest toward the end of the nineteenth century. Because of the Hungarian cultural assimilation of so many Jews, the very atmosphere of Budapest was different from that of Berlin, Vienna, Prague or Cracow. There were sixteen Jewish Members of Parliament and two dozen Jewish professors in the universities. In 1900 it seemed that the compound of the older Hungarian and the newer Jewish aspirations had fused into something inseparable and lasting.

The semblance of that symbiosis in 1900 was more than a Liberal optical illusion. The evidence for it exists in the historical retrospect of sensitive and philosophical writers such as the Catholic Mihály Babits, who in his novel *Halálfiai* in 1927 described two young men, "Imre" and "Rosenberg," full of naïveté and optimism at the turn of the century, when "these two descendants of Eastern races, the Jew and the Magyar, grasped each other's hands enthusiastically, professing their devotion to their common culture and their faith in the future with shining eyes."* We find many examples in the memoirs of that period of such delicate and, in retrospect, heart-rendingly naïve friendships: of idealistic and hesitant young Magyars freshly arrived in Budapest from the country, avid for culture and intellectual life; of a sudden blossoming of their friendship with and admiration for the quicker-thinking, more cosmopolitan, more worldly young Jewish men of their age. Such friendships were many in that period. They were perhaps unique in Europe, for elsewhere the meeting of non-Jewish and Jewish intellectuals at that time took different forms. We must note, too, the then not infrequent marriages of *deeply* Magyar geniuses to Budapestian Jewish wives: the cases of Krúdy and Kodály, for example. When in

---

*That this relationship of Jews and non-Jews was an essential issue appears again in two other novels by Babits. His *Kártyavár* (1915; 1923) includes the breakdown of honest relationships between prominent Jews and non-Jews in a suburb of Budapest about 1905; in *Timár Virgil fia* (1922) the theme is the relationship between a shy, celibate Catholic religious teacher and his favorite student, essentially his adopted son, a half-Jewish boy who eventually becomes an intellectual in Budapest.

the 1930s Antal Szerb, the great critic and historian of Hungarian literature (himself of Jewish origin), wrote about the, alas, "often unbridgeable" differences between the Magyar and the Jewish spirit, he also wrote that 1900 was the time when these different tones had not only seemed to form but that they made a harmonious accord, complementing each other to a great and mutual advantage.

This accord would not last. Early in the nineteenth century some of the greatest liberal Hungarian statesmen, writers and thinkers—Széchenyi, Kisfaludy, Vörösmarty, Kemény—expressed their concern with the unlimited immigration of a Jewish proletariat from Poland and Russia into Hungary. Their warnings were not expressions of anti-Semitism, and not only because that term did not yet exist. They were not hostile to the older Jewish settlers and inhabitants of the nation; and they desired the Magyarization of Jews. Their distinction between newcomers and older inhabitants was sometimes expressed by the Magyarized Jews themselves; for example by Mór Wahrmann, the city councilman who had been the parliamentary architect of the unification of Pest with Buda and Óbuda in 1872; he warned against the unlimited immigration from the East. But then came a change. By 1900 these distinctions (except perhaps in the minds, and occasionally in the expressions, of some of the older, patrician Jewish inhabitants) were fading. The tendency and the expressions of anti-Semitism were beginning to be directed mainly at the assimilated Jews of Hungary, and principally against those in Budapest—against evidences of their prosperity, power, influence and tone.

Again I must insist that this involved not only a crisis of Liberalism but a transformation of nationalism. One of the reasons (and it was an important one) why the older Magyar Liberals and Independents had welcomed the Magyarization of Jews had been Hungarian nationalism. There were not enough Magyars to populate large portions of the Hungarian kingdom; and the fact that Hungarian Jews, almost without exception, chose to identify themselves with the Magyar language and with the Hungarian cause was an evident benefit to the latter. Even after 1900 some of the older Liberals wrote that this assimilated Jewish presence was a national asset, strengthening the Hungarian cause. But very soon after 1900 this idea began to lose its appeal. In 1901 the book of the earlier mentioned Miklós Bartha—a populist, democrat and radical—was a significant event. *Kazárföldön* ("In the Land of the Khazars") was

a feverish exposé of the exploitation of the poor Ruthenian peasantry in northeastern Hungary by the Jewish shopkeepers, tavern-
owners and moneylenders newly arrived from Galicia.* In this
book Bartha still made a distinction between the older Jewish people of Hungary and this new flood of "Khazars"—"a verminous
pest," in his words. But that occasional distinction was faint and
pale in the context of the often savage tone of his writing. Bartha
denied the assimilability of most Jews. He termed that a thoughtless
and corrupt Liberal illusion. He preferred the Ruthenian and
Rumanian peasantry who, he thought, would and could become
good and loyal Hungarians, were it not for the machinations of the
Jews and of the Liberal government condoning the latter.† The
government and the Liberals disavowed Bartha, who was, of
course, attacked by the Jewish press in Budapest. Soon his anti-
Semitism became more and more indiscriminate. It became directed, more and more, against "Jewish" Budapest, against the
influence of assimilated Jews in its politics and culture. He came to
regard the existence of Jews as *the* principal problem and danger
to his nation.

Sometime between 1900 and 1905 the people in Budapest, both
Jewish and non-Jewish, began to recognize, or at least sense, un-
easily, that the problem was no longer only the extent of Jewish
immigration but also the acceptance of Jewish assimilation—in

---

*See Chapter 4, p. 134. In the same year Bartha's friend and hero, Ede Egán, was
shot, an event in which many people preferred to see evidence of a Jewish conspiracy. *Kazárföldön* was reprinted by anti-Semitic publishers in Hungary several times
after 1920 (and in 1970 by a small Hungarian-American group in New Jersey).
It may be significant that the thesis adopted, by Bartha, among others, according
to which most Jews coming from the East were the descendants of an Oriental
tribe, the "Khazars," was the subject of Arthur Koestler's last book. It may suggest
the persistence of some of the memories of his youth in Budapest.
†In 1902 Ady wrote: "Yes, [people] now defend the Ruthenians, because their
defense can be made into an attack against the Jews." In 1913 he expressed his
bitter disillusionment with the Transylvanian Rumanian poet Octavian Goga, a
spokesman of Rumanian anti-Semitism, a former friend of his: "I do not wish to
analyse that beautifully flowering anti-Semitism of Rumanians: but their hatred of
Jews seems truly Byzantine to me. My faith includes the necessity and decency
of a dose of philosemitism . . . the belief that the Lord brought about one, and
perhaps only one, people to the benefit of Magyardom: the Jews. They are an
anti-toxin in our confused, dreamy bloodstream, against our dark eastern [tenden-
cies]. . . ."

other words, not only the questionable Magyarization of the incom-
ing Jews but the actual Hungarianness of the already established
ones. Now this happened at a time when the assimilation of Hungarian Jews, especially in Budapest, seemed to run at full tide. But
history is never of one piece since, among other things, it contains
the element of momentum: the massive continuation of movements
that, on a deeper level, are losing their essential dynamism. After
1900 the increase of the Jewish population of Budapest slowed
down; its proportion remained stationary, if not declining; yet at
the same time its influence, acceptance and acculturation still grew.
More than half of the ennobled Jewish families received their titles
after 1900, most of them in 1905 and after, when the old Liberal
political order was breaking up.* Yet in the social life of Budapest
some subtle, and some not so subtle, changes were taking place as
early as 1900. Certain clubs that in the past had admitted distinguished Hungarian Jewish members now closed their doors to such
men. (In the 1870s Miksa Falk, a prominent Hungarian journalist
and public figure—he had been the tutor and friend of the Empress
Elizabeth—the son of converted parents, refused Franz Josef's offer
of a noble title: but as late as 1898 he became a member of the
gentry Country Casino.) The rowing clubs, with their floating
docks and clubhouses along the Buda shore of the Danube, now
divided into those with non-Jewish and Jewish memberships. Even
along the promenading parallel Váci and Crown Prince streets of
the Inner City there developed a subtle distinction: one was the
daily *corso* of a distinctly non-Jewish, the other of a more-or-less
Jewish public. Some of the Jews in Budapest analyzed this. In some
of their writings the acidity of their criticism was directed at those
Hungarian Jewish families of an upper stratum who, in these writers' words, were aping Gentile Magyar gentry habits. There are
evidences of this in some of the early feuilletons of Ferenc Molnár.
In 1902 a comedy by the non-Jewish (but not at all anti-Semitic)

---

*In 1910 the Jewish Samu Hazai became Minister of War, in 1912 the formerly
Jewish János Teleszky became Minister of Finance, and in 1913 for a short time
the Jewish Ferenc Heltai was Mayor of Budapest.

   And it is surely significant that in James Joyce's *Ulysses* the prototype of *modern*
man, whose life and mind he attempts to describe in their entirety on a June day
in Dublin in 1904 (where hardly any Hungarian Jews lived at the time), was a
Hungarian Jew. (Yet Bloom's original Hungarian name, Virág, was not necessarily a Jewish surname in Hungary; and, as it appears from odd little details in
Finnegans Wake, Joyce knew less Hungarian than he thought he did.)

Zoltán Ambrus was devoted to the ironic description of the fortunes and misfortunes of a newly elevated Jewish baronial family. In 1904 the non-Jewish Ferenc Herczeg wrote that "all of Hungary is still Liberal; but no one likes Jews. Jews themselves don't. . . . A Jewish convert may seem to be accepted as a Christian among Christians, among Jews not at all." (The book was one of Herczeg's few commercial failures.) Some of the Hungarian Jewish writers and intellectuals now began to question the Hungarian nationalism of the generation that had preceded them*—perhaps logically, at the time when in the Parliament the extremely nationalistic Independents were still designated as "the extreme Left." Now, some people thought, another, non-nationalist Left was needed. They were both right and wrong.

They were wrong because of what I suggested earlier: their attribution of anti-Semitism and of the new nationalism to the remnant forces of old-fashioned "clerical reaction." Yet among the Catholic clergy it was the young priests, and not the older hierarchy, who embraced a new kind of nationalist populism and social-mindedness, including an ideology opposed to cosmopolitanism, capitalism, Jewish influences and "corrupt Budapest." The rising spokesman of a modern and social-minded Catholicism in Hungary, Ottokár Prohászka (we have seen how he would eschew the customary pomp during his episcopal installation in 1905), shared these inclinations. Prohászka and others saw such recognitions as a necessary ideological response to new conditions not the continuation of something old. There was a need for an "awakening"—a word that the anti-Semitic leaders Istóczy and Verhovay had used, the first as early as in 1881, without much of an echo at that time. In 1899 Prohászka would speak of a "Christian awakening" *(ke-*

---

*In this respect there was a limited parallel between the Jewish identification with nationalism in Austria and in Hungary. In 1882 at their Linz meeting, Austrian Liberal Jews, Socialists and Pan-Germans were allied in promoting the *German* national culture of Austria at the expense of other nationalities within the Austro-Hungarian Empire. Within a few years it became evident that the new nationalists (as distinct from the older patriots) in Austria were not only anti-Czech or anti-Magyar but also, if not more, anti-Jewish. Until the end of World War II a "nationalist" in Austria meant someone who was not only anti-Jewish but also pro-German—that is, wishing to unite with Germany, if necessary at the cost of the very independence of his own country. This usage was less absurd in Hungary, where, however, during World War II the political adjective "nationalist" often (though not always) suggested someone who was pro-German.

resztény ébredés) in Hungary.* By that time such sentiments appealed to a considerable portion of university students in Budapest (who were otherwise not very religious in their personal lives). The proportion of Jewish students in the university had risen. In many instances the friendly association of non-Jewish and Jewish students went on. In other instances it did not. For the first time anti-Semitism was more rampant among the younger than among the older generation. In 1900 someone found that in one of the halls of the university the cross had been broken off from the Hungarian coat of arms. Students accused a Jewish student of this. Unpleasant demonstrations ensued, only to be calmed by the government. Yet, as is their wont, most intellectuals—and not only Jews among them —overlooked the evidence contrary to their ideas. They failed to recognize what this meant: that the growing movement of hearts and minds was from the "Left" to the "Right" rather than the other way around; from an old liberalism to a new awakened nationalism; from tolerance to intolerance. They should have remembered the warnings of the old monarchist and conservative Franz Grillparzer, the Austrian playwright and poet, in 1849: that "progress" may mean the progress *von Humanität durch Nationalität zur Bestialität* (from humanism through nationalism to bestiality).

We must recognize that the element of envy for the accumulations of Jewish wealth and its evidences was an ever present and important element in this "awakening." But it was not the only element in the developing rift between Jewish and non-Jewish Hungarians. That rift filled with an uneasy anxiety the minds of otherwise unexceptionable, liberal Catholic thinkers and writers such as Concha, a respectful admirer of Tocqueville, Montalembert and French liberal Catholicism. In his book about the gentry he advocated the abolition of "antagonism" between the Country and Leopoldstadt casinos, the first representing the gentry, the other the largely Jewish upper class of Budapest. He called for an "amalgamation" of their "now rigidly and absolutely heterogeneous" composition and tendencies. This will take time, he wrote; it would take "a more general diffusion of the Hungarian Christian and national

---

*Not only the origins but the subsequent usage of that word were ominous. After 1919 "Awakening Magyars" were a powerful anti-Semitic group (as in Germany, the idea of a national "awakening" [*Deutschland Erwache*] was a Nazi or Nazi-type slogan during the rise of Hitler).

Gyula Krúdy.

The young Kodály.

The young Bartók.

Ferenc Herczeg.

Mihály Babits and Endre Ady.

Ferenc Molnár.

József Kiss.

Sándor Bródy.

Simon Hollósy.

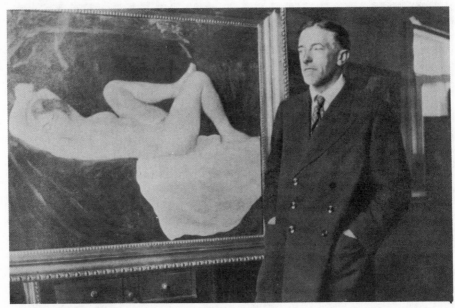

Károly Ferenczy.

*Kálmán Széll, Prime Minister
of Hungary in 1900.*

"Thaw" (*1895*)
Pál Szinyei-Merse

"Black-hatted Woman" (1899)
János Vaszary

"Black-veiled Woman" (1899)
József Rippl-Rónai

Poster of the Spring 1899 exhibition
János Vaszary

"Woman Painting" (1903)
Károly Ferenczy

"Christmas" (1903)
József Rippl-Rónai

"At the Trough" (1902)
Béla Iványi-Grünwald

"Sunny Morning" (1905)
Károly Ferenczy

"Landscape at a Hilltop" (1901)
Károly Ferenczy

"The Well of the Virgin Mary in Nazareth" (1907)
Tivadar Csontváry

"Roman Bridge in Mostar" (1903)
Tivadar Csontváry

Entrance hall of the Geological Institute: Ödön Lechner.

Perhaps the first electric locomotive ever built, by Kálmán Kandó.

A motor car of the Budapest subway, the first in Europe.
This equipment remained in service for over fifty years.

ideals, ending with the final assimilation of the Jewish element within the body of the nation." Then he added:

> If this will not happen, that is, if the Jewish elite insists on its leading role and on its blind following of internationalist and anti-Christian slogans—and lately some of them have started along that route—then, in view of the impossibility of a coexistence among two leading classes in a nation, we must expect a bitter and open struggle for the supremacy of the national and Christian idea. . . . But we must hope that the Jewish element will recoil from such a fatal struggle that would be the consequence of its presumptions to direct our society . . . because the Jewish element still has a serious task to fulfill— which is to infuse into the Magyar nation certain qualities and virtues that Jews among us possess and that the Hungarian nation still lacks. That should be sufficient for its ambitions.*

Concha may have exaggerated the extent, and the new direction, of Jewish tendencies and influences. But we must recognize, too— and this is not easy to write after the Judaeophobic and anti-Semitic horrors practiced by totalitarian governments and populations during the Second World War—that such tendencies did exist, and that sometimes their expression was tactless. We have seen that in the 1890s the principal literary journal in Hungary was the Budapestian *A Hét,* directed and edited by a Hungarian Jewish poet, József Kiss, a man of considerable repute; and that its foundation had been welcomed by all kinds of Hungarian Gentile writers. Yet in an article in 1893 in *A Hét* someone wrote that "Jews have forever been the sowers of human civilization; and the coming century, too, is being prepared by Jews." That at least some of the Pest intellectuals made their own contributions to the lamentable coming of a rift should appear from another article in *A Hét* in 1900: "The Danube," it said, "flows along *the edge* [my italics] of Budapest; because Buda is not really one half of the capital city but merely a

---

*In 1917, in answering an important questionnaire (an *enquête*) of *Huszadik Század* (see pp. 198–199) with the significant title "Does a Jewish Question Still Exist?" Concha was one of the few who said that, alas, it did; and that 1900 was a turning point, after which "a younger portion of Hungarian Jews took a direction entirely opposite from the rest. . . ."

place for excursions. . . ." It was yet another expression of the animosity—or, at least, the half-contemptuous dismissal—of anything that was old-fashioned, Catholic and conservative, by some of the Pest intellectuals.

"Awakening" anti-Semitism notwithstanding, in 1900 there were few people who thought, especially in Budapest, that the main problem of the nation concerned Jews. There were few older Hungarians left who thought that assimilation, though desirable, was impossible. Most non-Jews, like Concha, thought that assimilation, though still incomplete, was desirable and possible. But there were already others who thought that assimilation, even when it *seemed* possible, was in reality both impossible and undesirable. The latter were still few in number. But theirs was a new kind of anti-Semitic perspective, according to which the principal problem in Budapest and Hungary was the relationship of a "hard" minority to a "soft" majority, with the former attempting to impose—and succeeding in imposing—its desires, values and standards on the latter. What was —and still is—wrong with this view is the attribution of conspiracy behind it. In reality, that "hard" minority was not that hard, and the "soft" majority not that soft. As a matter of fact, the many members of that minority no longer thought of themselves as a minority. They thought that they had become full-fledged members of the majority (or, at least, hardly distinguishable from them). Conversely, many people of the "soft" majority, surely in Budapest, had adopted some of the values and standards, and some of the language and tone, of that minority without that minority having foisted those upon them.

Very soon after 1900 the rift between Budapest and the rest of Hungary developed into a sharpening conflict between Left and Right. The clashes of this conflict would now come in the intellectual arena of Budapest, even more than in the national Parliament.

In the university, too, a conflict, unlike that of the year before, began in 1901 not in the corridors but in its classrooms, not because of what a Jewish student was supposed to have done but because of what a professor was saying. Gyula Pikler, a professor of law, was a Spencerian positivist who was accused of teaching a denial of Christianity. Demands for his suspension traveled from university groups to the Parliament. Two years later a similar crisis occurred.

Another professor of law, Bódog Somló, also an enthusiastic advocate of Spencerian philosophy, was attacked for his teaching. This time some of the members of the faculty arrayed themselves against their colleagues. These two tempests in the university teapot and the earlier mentioned affair of the cross in 1900 died down, mostly because the Minister of Religion and Education, Baron Gyula Wlassics, declined to give heed to the protestors and interfere with academic freedom. Among the university students thereafter these agitations ceased.

Pikler and Somló were among the founding members of the Society of Social Science *(Társadalomtudományi Társaság)* in 1900, the story of which is significant, among other reasons, because of its chronology. It is perhaps the most evident example of the developing conflict of ideas, and of the growing bitterness and division between two kinds of intellectually committed men in Budapest: from their collegial harmony in 1900 to their quarrelsome disagreement in 1906, from their enthusiastic dedication to an enlightened mentality in 1900 to the irreconcilable division in their ideas of "progress" in 1906, from their universally accepted liberalism in 1900 to the hostile radicalization of the dominant group in 1906 —yet another intellectual revolution marked by the boundaries of those years.

There was something naïve about the founding of this society when we compare it to the intellectual history of Western Europe at the time. Before the constitution of the society its members sent a telegram to Herbert Spencer ("the great visionary," Oszkár Jászi wrote), assuring him of their intellectual homage and asking for his approbation. (Spencer answered in September 1899, congratulating the society for its founding.) Yet by 1900 the Spencerian ideology of society and of human nature was no longer in vogue in Western Europe. The reputations of very different thinkers, such as Henri Bergson and William James, had risen. On the other hand, it was true that a "scientific"* study of society in Hungary did not yet exist. Surely in the minds of many serious intellectuals and academicians there was a definite need for it. Thus the society met, duly constituted, in 1900. Its first president was Ágost Pulszky, a venerable liberal and humanist whose family had a deep and his-

---

*Again we must note a linguistic condition: in the Magyar language the word "science" *(tudomány)* is not in the least restricted to the natural sciences; and "scientist" and "scholar" are the same word *(tudós)*.

toric association with Hungarian liberalism and humanism through much of the nineteenth century. Many of the principal founding members had been Pulszky's students. The list of the members and officials of the society is an illustration of the unity of high culture and learning in Budapest in 1900. It was a kind of Liberal Areopagus. It contained Christians and Jews in perhaps equal numbers; the official positions of the vice-presidents and their secretaries were shared by Professors Pikler and Somló (who were Jewish) and Gratz and Hegedüs (who were not). In 1901 Pulszky died. The next president was Count Gyula Andrássy, the scion of one of the most distinguished and historical families of Hungary, a patriot, monarchist and aristocratic liberal (though no longer associated with the Liberal Party after 1905). During the Pikler and Somló affairs, in 1901 and 1903, respectively, the members of the society, Christians and Jews, relative conservatives and liberals alike, supported the two beleaguered professors.

From its founding in 1900 the society sponsored its own periodical, entitled *Huszadik Század* ("The Twentieth Century"). Its editor was Oszkár Jászi.* It developed into a serious organ, ranging well beyond "scientific" sociology.† Jászi and his colleagues were prone to take the bit between their teeth with their "progressive" dedication, galloping into politics, philosophy, and literary criticism, sometimes on a fairly high level. Yet there was a fatal flaw of presumption—at times amounting to arrogance—in the minds of Jászi and his friends. In the very first issue of *Huszadik Század,* in an article entitled "Scientific Journalism," Jászi wrote that "the

---

*Jászi was a very typical member of the generation of 1900. He moved from a Spencerian liberalism into more radical waters, and played an important role in the short-lived radical republican government of Károlyi after the collapse of 1918. Sincerely concerned with the problems of non-Magyar nationalities, he tried to save the unity of Hungary by adopting the idea and the slogan of an "Eastern Switzerland," but his political advocacies and tactics in 1918 were devoid of reality. Untainted by an association with the ensuing Communist government, he nevertheless had to go into exile in 1919, first to Vienna, and then to a professorship of political science at Oberlin College in the United States. After 1919 his radicalism evolved into a more moderate liberalism; but the estrangement of this otherwise intelligent man from the realities of his native country was complete.
†Ady wrote that it was "the most important and most modern science"—at a time when nine out of ten students in Hungary had no idea what it was. Ady wrote in 1905: "A new humane and luminous world is driven ever higher by the eternal law of causality: by the only truth, that of natural science."

pages of [this journal] will remain closed to one, and only one, tendency. Every explicit or implicit, courageous or cowardly expression of a reactionary world view will be proscribed . . . [in spite of] our strong belief in freedom of speech . . . reactionary political theory cannot, by definition, be political theory." The Somló affair, too, arose from the report of the address Somló had given at the society in 1903—among other things, his exaltation of "the *profound* [*sic*] words of Zola: 'Science alone is revolutionary.' The antiquated character of this kind of positivism in 1903 should be evident to us. To many members of the society it was not. In any event, the influence of the society and of its journal was growing. By 1906 the Jászi group were trying to establish a kind of free university for the untutored masses. Their director was Jászi, whose phraseology in his opening speech is again telling: "We must create a new ethic, a new morality, in the place of the collapsed morality of religion or metaphysics. A new morality whose fundaments are: science, human solidarity, and freedom of research. . . ." Evidently the society, or at least the dominant group to which Jászi belonged, was now ready for the political propagandizing of the working classes (as had been the case with their advocacy of universal suffrage during the political crisis in 1905). Now they thought—even more, they seemed convinced—that *they* had become the flag-bearers of Hungarian culture and progress. Few of them were, as yet, Marxists. Yet they were no longer Liberals; they had become radicals.

Apart from the shortcomings of their "progressive" ideology, there were fundamental flaws in what these often young progressives and radicals were thinking, saying and doing. What evidence there is indicates that the working people of Hungary, including the proletariat of Budapest, remained indifferent to their cultural efforts.* Much more important, and significant, was that they had alienated their relatively conservative and liberal colleagues. In 1906 the Society of Social Science split. The former had attempted to correct, or at least to modify, the direction of the society and of its journal, which had become increasingly political and assertive, even shrill on occasion; but their cautious admonitions were in vain.

---

*Almost—if not quite—like the Russian peasants to the agitations of the young *narodniki* in the 1870s. But the parallel is incomplete: the Russian peasantry were illiterate and superstitious, and the Budapest proletarians were not.

In the history of Budapest the break in the ranks of this society was not an important event, though a significant one: but it *was* an important event in the history of Hungarian intellect.* As in national politics and in the Parliament, the once humane, and far from ignoble, unity of Hungarian liberalism was broken. Gratz, Concha and other conservative liberals were driven out of the society. Andrássy resigned. And—I took the trouble to look up the minutes of the agitated meeting of the society (on August 17, 1906, *after* these members had already departed)—the manners and the rhetoric of the society during that meeting were appalling. Its members, who had often with reason criticized and assailed the loud and raucous, unrestrained and unmannerly "Oriental" rhetoric and behavior of so many people in the Hungarian Parliament, now manifested the same habits during their own meeting of a society dedicated to intellectual freedom and the "Westernization" of Hungary: screaming abuse, shouting down their few remaining opponents, and taking self-satisfaction and evident pleasure from the acrid violence of their words. And while that Parliament was, after all, a representative assembly of Hungary at large, in 1906 and after the membership of the society was representative only of a certain portion of the intelligentsia of Budapest—mostly Jewish, and increasingly radical.†

So here, too, the tragic rift between Hungary and Budapest, between Christians and Jews, between the older liberals and the newer radicals, had come: a devolution from their harmonious symbiosis to their bitter divisions in less than six years. That division was not complete: there remained Christians and Jews and old-fashioned liberals on both sides (it must be recorded that the brav-

---

*The concentration on political history has obscured the meaning of this event—in many ways even relatively recently, when this group and *Huszadik Század* have been receiving more attention among historians in Hungary and abroad than heretofore. The excellent Gusztáv Gratz, who was not only a principal founder and official of the society but also a principal historian of that entire period of 1867–1920, hardly mentioned it in his history, published in 1934—perhaps also because this noble and humane man, an old-fashioned conservative liberal, opponent of the radical Right before World War II, may have thought then that to criticize his Jewish radical opponents of 1906 was *vieux jeu,* and that it would only serve the cause of nationalists and anti-Semites.

†Jászi wrote in 1906: "It is not only the factories that are filled with the heavy, dark, unsanitary air of the capitalist spirit. So are the groves of the Muses."

est and most reasonable opponent of the radical majority during that meeting was the Jewish Pál Wolfner); but the seeds of troubles had not only been sown, they were sprouting. Less than two years later a younger group of radical intellectuals founded the Galileo Circle (its first president was Karl Polanyi). Alas, the history of that Galileo Circle became a part not only of Hungarian intellectual but also of Hungarian political history, with a direct connection of some of his members to the short-lived Communist regime and its Red Terror in 1919.*

"Men of letters," wrote the Scottish poet Alexander Smith in *Dreamthorp* (1863), "forerun science like the morning stars the dawn." We have seen how the Catholic and humanist Babits wrote about the glowing friendship and accord of aspiring young non-Jewish and Jewish Hungarian intellectuals around 1900 in *Halálfiai,* which is not a historical novel but a portrait of youthful lives and aspirations at the time; and what he wrote of the time around 1906 is telling again. His protagonist, Imre, Babits wrote, "now stood alone on the battlefield; alone, like a lamb who had lost his way between two flocks, looking around haltingly, shyly, not knowing where he belonged."

We have seen that in 1900 *A Hét* was the principal literary journal in Hungary. Every aspiring poet, writer or critic wished to appear in its pages. Its editor, the Jewish poet József Kiss, and the principal Hungarian chauvinist, the German-born Jenő Rákosi, were the closest of friends. Yet in 1900 a society of more-or-less conservative Hungarian literary men, the Kisfaludy, refused to elect Kiss to membership. Soon afterward the often still unspoken conflict between the culture of Budapest and that of the rest of Hungary began to be expressed in the literary journals of Budapest itself, including undertones directed at the Jewish "problem." In 1902 Ferenc Herczeg, the favorite conservative author of the gentry, wrote a criticism of a play by the Jewish Sándor Bródy. Herczeg liked the play, but he wanted to draw attention to its "desperately sad allegory. That allegory is characteristic of the relationship of Budapest and the Hungarian provinces; or, if you wish, to the relationship of the intelligentsia and the peasantry. *Voilà* the city. It is the capital city of the country; yet it has not grown with the flesh of the nation . . . we could not fuse it with our veins. . . ."

*See Chapter 7, pp. 209–13.

In 1904 Herczeg returned to this theme at the meeting of the other conservative literary society, the Petőfi:

> Budapest, while Magyar in its language and in its sentiments, contains many foreign elements in its chemistry; and the literature of Budapest, even though its purposes are confidently national, contains many unconsciously alien elements. Our language is smoother and more flexible than that of the old writers, at times even more folkish, but somehow less Magyar; our perspective may be wider but it is by no means deeper. We speak and feel Hungarian, but our mental pace and our morals are less and less Hungarian. On the horizon of literature the ruling constellation is the social question; yet we are better acquainted with the disturbing questions from French, German, Scandinavian literature than with those affecting the future of the Magyar nation.

Herczeg had a thoughtful and intelligent response from the cultured Jewish critic Ignotus. (The title of this response was excellent: *Védvám a művészetben*, "Protectionism in Art.")

> What is the purpose of this distinction between Magyar and non-Magyar literature; of this making Hungarianness into a literary yardstick—against the literature of the present, when men who write Hungarian live on Hungarian soil and could not be anything else even if they wanted to? . . . What kind of esthetic justification baptizes "morality" as Magyar and "immorality" as foreign? . . . This kind of iconoclasm . . . wants to exclude the city of Budapest from the sphere of Hungarian literature under the pretext of protecting the nation. . . .

A response to both Herczeg and Ignotus (and to the outspoken anti-Semitic Bartha, who called Budapest Sodom) was written by the old Liberal Mihály Réz: "this attempt to boycott Budapest is wrong . . . I will not go that far . . . I will not deny the glorious progress of the last fifty years . . . only say that this has been the result of the last fifty years, while the nation is one thousand years old . . . I will not exclude those people in our capital who are foreign in origin and in their religion, while I must state that the culture of some of them is still foreign. . . ." Perhaps significantly, this, too, was printed in Kiss's *A Hét.*

S eeds of Troubles" is the title I gave to this chapter: but semina-
tion is one thing and fructification another. Historians often err
by their retrospective attribution of causalities—that is, not only in
seeing the past from the perspective of the present, something that
no one can avoid, but proceeding from the assumption that some
things that happened earlier inevitably led to some things later, the
post hoc ergo propter hoc fallacy. It is better and wiser to pay heed to
Jesus' early parable of the sower and his seeds: that "whilst he
sowed, some fell by the wayside, and the birds of the air came and
ate it up," and that "some fell upon stony ground," while others
were "scorched, and without roots withered away," and that "some
fell among thorns; and the thorns grew up and choked it, and it
yielded no fruit." The historian of sinful human nature ought to
know that this is true of all sowers and all seeds, good and bad; of
seeds of promise as well as seeds of trouble. And this applies to our
subject and our theme. The seeds of trouble were there, and many
of them had begun to sprout, but their fruition was not inevitable;
they did not inevitably lead to later tragedies.

Not even to the deepening of rifts that, in the history of Budapest, had opened visibly after 1900. By 1906 they were there; but
many of them, in many ways, ceased to deepen, or even matter very
much. The basic rift—that between Budapest and the country—
began to lose its meaning. Politically and socially the nation was
divided; but after 1906 the positing of Budapest versus Hungary
was losing its appeal. Both the magnetism and the effulgence of
Budapest had grown too strong for that. The language, habits,
fashions and manners of Budapest were becoming nationwide.
Fewer and fewer people would posit the contrast between "cosmopolitan"—that is, partly alien and unpatriotic—Budapest and the
"truly" Hungarian rest of the country. That idea would revive in
1919–20 but without enduring effects.

On an emotional level, the rift between "Christians"—more precisely, non-Jews—and Jews may have been deeper; but after 1906
that, too, seemed to lose some of its meaning. For one thing, the
years from 1906 to 1914 were years of an increasing prosperity
that, in many ways, not only masked but was more effective than
the steady upward crawl of inflation. Hence the sometimes appar-

ent economic and financial disparities between the wealth of Jewish and non-Jewish people in Budapest lost some of their edge. What happened after 1906 was something like a growing and fairly peaceful coexistence between the now ever older and ever more assimilated Jewish bourgeoisie and the non-Jewish middle, or lower-upper, classes of the capital; and even between many of their cultural and ideological representatives. This kind of coexistence would last until the great national catastrophes of 1918–19. In these ways that sunny-afternoon atmosphere of the last years before the Great War in 1914—those "Edwardian" years, so often described by English writers and English reminiscences since, if sometimes ruefully, as the last years of Liberal England—may be applicable to Budapest and to Hungary, too, more so than to Vienna or Berlin. There were plenty of tensions, including new ones, but it is remarkable how some of the earlier bitterness faded. And in this respect it is remarkable, too, how some of the early critics of Jewish influence, men such as Herczeg or Gratz or Szekfü, eventually became brave critics and opponents of anti-Semitism when that ideology had risen to become semiofficial, widespread and popular.* Within the Catholic Church, Bishop Prohászka, literally the *bête noire* of Radicals and of some Jews, became a proponent of something like Christian Democracy (or at least of a Hungarian version of the moderate German Catholic Center Party). And there were still many of the lower clergy, including certain younger Jesuits, who kept speaking and writing against Jewish cultural and "spiritual" influences (though, again, it was some of these, including Jesuits in Hungary, whose record in protecting and saving Jews during World War II deserves our respect).

It is at this point that I must devote a few lines to the Catholicism of Budapest at the time. A few lines, but not more: for, even though the great majority of the people of Budapest were baptized Roman Catholics, evidences of their religiosity were not very apparent around 1900 and after. There were some signs of the "awakening"

---

*Conversely, we must remark that some of the Jewish intellectuals of that radical and "progressive" generation would become convinced conservatives (and a few of them Catholic converts) after 1920. Among such emigrés of 1919, Béla Menczer and Aurél Kolnai (the latter a friend of G. K. Chesterton, his best man at his church marriage in 1933) stand out. (The work of the perhaps better known Michael Polanyi, whose *Personal Knowledge,* published in 1939, marks the transformation of a radical and "scientific" positivist and determinist into something of a humanistic scientist, is a mixed bag.)

that Prohászka had called for in 1899: as elsewhere in Europe, the beginnings of a neo-Catholic intellectuality were there; for one thing, the membership and the volume of publications of a Catholic publishing society *(Szent-István Társulat)* grew fifteenfold in twenty years. Yet in absolute numbers that volume and its subsequent influence were still small. As some writers observed, the "Christian" gentry, for example, were not very religious in their habits. Most of its men seldom went to Mass; their wives and children were the regular churchgoers and believers. Here, too, the politicization of those times had baneful influences. Around 1900 the "Christian" adjective became popular; yet we have seen that its connotation was merely negative, meaning non-Jewish, noncosmopolitan, non-Marxist. We have also seen how the Catholic People's Party, beginning in 1894, was both anti-Liberal and—at times subtly, at times outspokenly—anti-Jewish. Its often commendable social advocacies pale in retrospect against the evidences of the often strident and demagogic tone of some of the Catholic press, including the daily *Alkotmány.* And yet, again, it was from the ranks of that Catholic party that some of the finest spokesmen and thinkers of a humane Catholicism grew to national prominence after 1919: prelates and nuns such as Sándor Giesswein, Sándor Ernszt, Miklós Griger, Margit Schlachta, defenders of Jews and, in the case of Schlachta, their truly heroic protector before and during the Second World War.

The rift that would not heal in Budapest and Hungary was that between the Left and the Right. It began to include new elements: the radicalization of the erstwhile Independence Party, and the slowly growing presence of Socialists, involving the already mentioned radicalization of some of the Budapest intellectuals and workers, too; but the development of those political elements no longer belongs to our story. In any event, the tornado of 1914 would roar over that rift, burying it—at least temporarily. In a symbolic coincidence, the entire sky burst open above Budapest on July 23 of that year, a veritable tornado without precedent in the natural history of the city either before or after. Winds of more than one hundred miles an hour destroyed scores of buildings, tore away the roofs of the Basilica in Pest and of the Coronation Church in Buda, damaged the great Chain Bridge itself, and brought deaths and many injuries. Two days later Austria-Hungary broke relations with Serbia. A war had come—from the assassination of the heir to the throne, the Archduke Franz Ferdinand, who was an embittered opponent of Hungary, and perhaps especially of Budapest—a war with Serbia (and soon with Russia, France and Great Britain) with whom Hungary had no quarrel; but no matter. A storm of national enthusiasm swept along the boulevards of Budapest. On that chilly, dank, rainy afternoon and evening of July 25, 1914, instant demonstrations broke out, including every class of people in Budapest, without a single gesture of opposition by radicals, socialists or pacifists—by and large the same phenomenon that would occur in Vienna, Berlin, St. Petersburg, Paris and London—a storm of emotion and relief, unifying classes and people, burying their daily cares in an enormous tidal wave of a nationalist madness.

Because of this there is one other matter that deserves our attention. What happened in Budapest from 1900 to 1914 were, after all, tendencies and phenomena not wholly separate from the rest of the world. But the crisis of Liberalism around 1900, the failure of Socialism and pacifism before and in 1914, the growing social problems, and the general decline of the order and of the appeal of the ideas of the nineteenth century were not simply the "inevitable" results of changing material and economic conditions across Europe. Ideas matter only when they are incarnated by human beings; and—about this Proudhon was a deeper seer than Marx—people respond less to ideals of social contract than to realities (perhaps, we should add, to their impressions of the realities) of power. In 1900, and surely in 1914, the greatest power in Europe was Germany. Despite the increasing desire, and the increased achievement, of Hungarian independence from Austria, and despite the great differences in the Hungarian and German temperament and character, for the first time in Hungary's history the respect for German power brought with it a strong influence of German culture and of its forms. That the Hungarian educational system followed, by and large, German and Austrian models is not a sufficient explanation for this. Nor did the government of Wilhelmian Germany practice, as yet, a diplomacy of cultural propaganda. That a large proportion of the population of Budapest still knew German had something to do with that influence that had become a new element in history, accompanying the relations of governments and states: the influence that the image of the civilization and of the culture of a nation (and a nation is, after all, a cultural prototype) has on another nation.

In the early twentieth century in Budapest that influence was evident among people of the Right as well as of the Left. During the nineteenth century the Magyar Liberals had been pro-English; the nationalists and Independents had been traditionally pro-French, sympathizing with France throughout and after its defeat in the Franco-Prussian War. In the 1880s, however, the anti-Semites got some of their inspiration and guidance from the German example, as indeed Istóczy and Verhovay said; and in 1899 Istóczy exalted Germany as "the most powerful nation in the world." The nationalists and anti-Semites among the Independents were among the first Hungarians to become anti-British. They cheered on the Boers, while the old Liberals still maintained their admiration and respect for Britain. Among the new "conservative" Catholics, too, their "Christian Socialist" ideas were often translations of Austrian and pro-German nationalist and anti-Semitic propositions into Hungarian terms, as indeed the Catholic People's Party was a Hungarian version of a Christian *Volkspartei*. The new French Catholicism of a Péguy or a Bloy was unknown except to a few Catholic intellectuals. By 1900 admiration for Germany was strong especially among the students of the Budapest Polytechnic University and also among many of its professors. Literature and the arts were still strongly Francophile ("that wondrous, great, holy city of Paris," Ady wrote). But the Leftists and radicals of the Budapest intelligentsia, too, were bound to German forms of thought. It showed in their terminology and in their writing. When the young Georg Lukács's first book of essays, *Lélek és forma* ("Spirit and Form"), was published in Budapest in 1910, Babits reviewed it in *Nyugat*. Babits wrote that the very prose and the ideas of Lukács were "wholly German . . . employing a modern, affected German terminology" that Babits confessed he did not like.* A translation of "Spirit and Form" was published only a year later in Germany—a rare achievement for a Hungarian intellectual—and it received respectful reviews by German intellectuals. Thus it was not surprising—though it is odd, in retrospect—that shortly after the outbreak of the War of 1914 Béla Balázs, a typical and far from insensitive esthete of the Jewish radical Budapest intelligentsia,

---

*It says something about Lukács, rather than Babits, that he attributed the latter's criticism to anti-Semitism. A recent Hungarian-American historian (Gluck, p. 93) wrote that Babits's mention of the Germanic element was an "irrelevant comment." It was not.

published an essay entitled *Párizs vagy Weimar* ("Paris or Weimar"), that is, France or Germany: which was the true representative of European culture? and that Balázs came down on the side of the latter.

It was 1914: and at the five o'clock *thés dansants* (a relatively new custom) in the new, large and luxurious hotels on the Pest side of the Danube the *jeunesse* (and sometimes not only the *jeunesse*) *dorée* of Budapest was already dancing to the rhythms of the maxixe, the cakewalk, the boston, the ragtime and the tango. But the massive sight of Germany blocked other, more substantial views from the West for many people: a cultural and national tragedy that would come again, in far more powerful and sinister forms, twenty or more years later.

Since Then

For a while after July 1914 Budapest seemed unharmed by the war. The nationalist enthusiasms quickened the heart-beat of the city. But sometime during the first winter of the war something unexpected began to appear in the streets of Budapest, something that clutched at the hearts of people, no matter how quickly they would turn their heads away from the sight of maimed or blind soldiers back from the front. Less visible at first but more and more evident was the destitution of tens of thousands of the wives and children of the working classes whose husbands and fathers were at the front. The governmental support of their welfare was insufficient. A few of the great industrialists of Budapest established public kitchens for them. Still, by and large, the people of Budapest suffered less from the privations of the war than the people of most other European capitals. So far as the supply of food went, Hungary was better off than Austria. There were workers' protests and strikes, here and there. There was a measure of popular impatience with profiteers who made out well from the war. But the tensions that began to appear were less social than political.

This is not a political history of Budapest, let alone of Hungary; but it is impossible to avoid politics as we approach the end of the war, those tragic developments and events whose effects and memories would darken the minds of more than one generation, lingering on for decades. One gets the impression that sometime in late 1917 those shafts of sunshine that illuminated, if only temporarily, the streets and the squares and even the spirit of the city during the first years of the war had disappeared; that the climate of this summery city had given way to a darkening, rain-laden and heavy; that the clocks had moved from an early afternoon to a late hour. And there was more to this than a kind of metaphorical imagery conjured up by an impressionistic historian. We know that the conventicles of those groups of people who worked at the coming upheaval gathered in dark apartments in dark houses in the dark streets of Pest, in the afternoons and evenings. Whether we contemplate the meetings of the radical intellectuals of the Galileo Circle (ordered dissolved by an otherwise liberal government in early 1918 because of its subversive propaganda), or the rooms where the poet and prophet Ady lay dying, or those of the dark-paneled Hotel Astoria where a "National Council" would proclaim the Hungarian October Revolution, the scene is marked by darkness. That revolution took place on a late October day spattered by rain, under torn, racing clouds, in a soiled air. In the surviving photographs the asters worn by the demonstrating soldiers (it was called the Aster Revolution) have no sparkle, even though they may be glimpsed, here and there.

What had happened was this: Austria-Hungary lost the war. The governments of Tisza and Wekerle knew, by and large, what that meant. Their opposition did not. During the war that opposition began to coalesce with the radical intelligentsia, and around the figure of Count Mihály Károlyi, arguing more and more loudly that Hungary had no interests in this war, because Hungary had no quarrel with the Western democracies. That those Western democracies had little interest and no sympathy for Hungary—indeed, that their leaders had already committed themselves to all kinds of territorial promises to Rumania, Yugoslavia and Czechoslovakia at the cost of Hungary—had not entered Károlyi's head, nor that of any of his followers. The end of the Austro-Hungarian Dual Monarchy meant the end of Hungary's territorial integrity; yet Károlyi and his friends rejoiced in the former, without recognizing the latter. During the last days of October 1918 the Austro-Hungarian Empire began to break apart. During that rapid sequence of events the definite one was the proclamation of the Hungarian National Council on October 31, from that Hotel Astoria on that day of the asters. There was a tragic footnote to that gloomy day: armed men broke into the Hermine Avenue villa of Károlyi's old parliamentary opponent, Tisza. They murdered him, for no purpose or reason (Tisza had resigned more than a year earlier). Károlyi made (or thought he made) a fine gesture by sending a very large wreath to the Tisza household next day. The family threw it on the garbage heap.

So much for asters and wreaths. A few days later Károlyi and his government delegation traveled to Belgrade to pay their respects and assure the French General Franchet d'Esperey, commander of the Entente forces in the Balkans, of Hungary's love for and loyalty to the Entente. The general treated these Hungarians with contempt. Károlyi was dismayed. He now transferred his hopes: he said that Hungary must trust the ideals of President Wilson. That did him, or Hungary, little good. Within a month Czechoslovak armed bands and Rumanian and Yugoslav armed groups spread over ever larger portions of the Hungarian Kingdom, unvexed and unopposed by Hungarian arms, since the Hungarian army units, in accord with Károlyi's original intentions, had virtually dissolved. It began to dawn on people that a wholesale amputation of Hungary was in the making. When in March 1919 Károlyi learned from a note of a French officer that the Rumanians, Czechoslovaks and Yugoslavs would be allowed to advance to demarcation lines deep within the body of Hungary proper his willpower collapsed. He resigned. He declared that he now turned "to the proletariat of the world for justice and assistance." He turned over the "government" to a small but vocal group of Hungarian Communists led by Béla Kún, who proclaimed that Hungary could now count on the aid of the Communist Soviet Union, another mirage.

What followed now were 132 days of a Hungarian—or, perhaps more precisely, Budapestian—Communist regime. They were marked by imbecility, inefficiency and terror. The ordinances, regulations and reforms of that regime were senseless at worst and disregarded at best. Its money was worthless. It brought hunger to Budapest in the summer of 1919. Its belief in Lenin's aid—at a time when Lenin was menaced by civil war on many fronts—defies reason. At the same time Kún and his colleagues, hoping for their diplomatic recognition, were not above a bit of fawning on the Entente. The authority of that "government" over the Hungarian countryside was often nonexistent. Their terrorist brigades who attempted to enforce it knew that. At the end of July 1919 a Rumanian army began to move toward Budapest. It was still more than fifty miles from the capital when Kún and some of his crowd fled to Vienna. Three days later Rumanian troops shambled and shuffled down the streets of an unbelieving Budapest. By that time a Hungarian counterrevolutionary group had rallied in Szeged, wherefrom a Hungarian national army, led by a former admiral of the Austro-Hungarian navy, Miklós Horthy, advanced slowly toward Budapest. The Rumanians left. On a wet November morning Horthy's troops marched into Buda. Sitting on a white horse, Horthy received a welcoming delegation. His speech contained this phrase about Budapest: "the guilty city."

By that time a new kind of terror, an anti-Communist one, was riding rampant across the Hungarian countryside. Men and women associated with the Communists were beaten and hanged in the villages. A wave of anti-Semitism had risen, too. Béla Kún was Jewish; thirty-two of the forty-five Commissars of the Hungarian Communist Republic had been Jewish; consequently, many people associated that regime with Jews (even though most Hungarian Jews had not allied themselves with the Communists). The new government felt compelled to proclaim its "Christian and national" ideology.

On a bright sunny day, June 4, 1920, street life in Budapest came to a standstill. Shops were closed. The trolley cars stopped. Black flags flew. The church bells rang. That morning, in a Paris suburb, the peace treaty with a dismembered Hungary was signed. That dismemberment was without precedent in European history, save perhaps for the second partition of Poland. Two-thirds of the kingdom of Hungary were turned over to successor states: Rumania, Czechoslovakia, Yugoslavia (a small slice even to Austria). It was a day of national mourning.

So Budapest had become the capital of an amputated country, a city of nearly 1 million people in a nation of 7 million.

Since 1914 its population had not really increased. During the war and the ensuing years of chaos and revolution, many people left the capital and other people arrived, mostly refugee families from the lands and towns turned over to the new neighboring states, people who often had to be lodged in railroad cars along the outer sidings of the great stations, where they lived for long months or even a year. Budapest was a city of dust-laden misery and fear.

T hen things began to improve. Hungary and Hungarians tend to be unsuccessful after their most astonishing triumphs, but they have an instinctive genius for recovery after their worst disasters. A semblance of peace began to spread over the capital and country. That it was not—it could not be—a return to the halcyon years before 1914 was reflected by the novel usage of a phrase, *békében,* "in peacetime," employed by an entire generation or two, including my parents and grandparents. It did not mean the return of peace in the absence of war. It meant the years before 1914. Yet most of the twenties and some of the thirties were more than a mere armistice between the two world wars. People in Budapest breathed freer. The air had become lighter. Here and there the city began to sparkle anew. These are not mere figures of speech. They suggest developments on many different levels. A fine statesman, Count István Bethlen, was Regent Horthy's Prime Minister in a period of "consolidation." Financial stability and a measure of industrial prosperity returned. The high standards of education and of publishing climbed to their earlier, prewar standards, even surpassing them in some instances. The years 1921 to 1935 could be (and sometimes are) called the Silver Age of modern Hungarian letters. In the late twenties there was a kind of silvery elegance in the theaters and the drawing rooms and in the appearance of fashionable women in the streets, hotel halls, shops and foyers of Budapest, with a dash of panache that evoked the attention and admiration of foreign visitors. That elegance was more than a dressing-up, of well-cut lamé; it shone, here and there, through the letters, journals and books of that period, through the light smart operetta music and perhaps, too, in the façades of the new private villas designed and built by Budapest architects. On any evening, leaning on the southern parapets of the Margaret Bridge, one saw that incomparable vista of the great bend of the Danube surrounded by its grand setting of baroque curve and sparkle, the latter enhanced by the myriad electric lights of the buildings and on the hills and by the then still few, slowly moving white sheaves of the automobile headlights on the great bridges farther downstream. That trademark of Budapest, the long garland of electric bulbs lighting up the entire noble outline of the Chain Bridge, was yet to come. But tourism, for the first time, had become an important element in the life of the city, especially in the summers. After about 1926 Budapest began to attract tens of thousands of foreign visitors. They included such different people as the Prince of Wales and the King of Italy; or H. L. Mencken and Evelyn Waugh.* "With the Danube," Jules Romains wrote, "Budapest forms one of the most beautiful cityscapes that exist along a river, probably the most beautiful one in Europe." "This town is really astounding," wrote Mencken to his wife in 1930. "It is by far the most beautiful that I have ever seen. I came expecting to see a somewhat dingy copy of Vienna but it makes Vienna look like a village. There is something thoroughly *royal* about it. . . . The Danube is under my window, and across the river, on a range of hills, lies a long series of truly superb palaces." He stayed at the same hotel, the Hungaria, where Blowitz had contemplated that scene thirty-six years before. Yet Mencken also wrote that "Budapest is magnificent, but it looks like an empty ballroom. Hungary lost 2/3 of its territory and people by the war, and is barely able to exist. There are traffic cops, every street corner, magnificently turned out in trench coats and swords, but there is no traffic to regulate. . . ."

That was, perhaps, an exaggeration. (Mencken was there in January 1930; there was not much automobile traffic in Budapest in midwinter then.) True, Hungary was hurt badly by the worldwide Depression, especially in its agriculture. But Budapest was affected less than the rest of the country; and after 1933 the general economic conditions began to improve. Groups of modern buildings were beginning to rise, here and there. The sunny, the athletic, the muscular side of the character of Budapest was much in evidence in the 1930s. But another matter became more and more evident, a matter largely invisible to foreign visitors, a matter not apparent in pictures. That was the rising presence of the German Third Reich in the minds of the people of Budapest, in the minds of its admirers and of its adversaries, of its potential followers and of its potential victims.

---

*They included, too, visiting artists who came because of the high standards of the theaters and orchestras and, most important, of the audiences of Budapest: Arturo Toscanini, Bruno Walter, Victor de Sabata, Sir Thomas Beecham, Ottorino Respighi, Enrico Caruso, Feodor Chaliapin, Beniamino Gigli, Arthur Rubinstein, Vladimir Horowitz, Amelita Galli-Curci, etc., etc.

That presence descended like a sudden shadow in 1938, on a Friday evening in March when Austria surrendered to Hitler. Now the Third Reich, giant and triumphant, had arrived at the western edge of Hungary, a mere one hundred miles west of Budapest. Some people saw in that event the unfolding of a wave of the future, carrying tides of good fortune for Hungary and for themselves: for the rise of Germany meant the decline of the European order, or disorder, imposed upon the defeated nations after World War I. And that rise of a new Germany meant something else, too: a new alternative to both Capitalism and Communism, whose unpopularity was still vivid in so many minds. In May 1939 elections were held in Hungary, the results of which were telling. Almost every fourth vote in Budapest was cast for the National Socialist parties whose emblem, the arrow cross, was a Hungarian version of the swastika. A considerable portion of those votes came from the working class, the very class whom the radicals of a previous generation had extolled as the proletarian vanguard of a new humanism. In 1939 the bravest and the most determined opponents of Hitler in Budapest and Hungary were old-fashioned men and women, with old-fashioned convictions of decency and honor, often the very same people whom radicals a generation before had dismissed as "reactionaries"—the epithet flung at them by National Socialists in 1939 (and by Communists in 1945 and after). That there were Hungarians who, at the risk of considerable unpopularity, said that what National Socialism stood for represented a great and profound danger to everything that was good and decent and honest in the traditions of their people and of their country ought to command our respect even now. They prevailed, at least in some ways and for a time, even though they would fail at the end of the coming war.

For almost five years Budapest was spared the horrors of the Second World War. In many ways—though, of course, not all —Budapest and Hungary remained islands of relative peace in the midst of Hitler's Europe. Eventually, Hungary had to enter into formal alliances with Germany and declare war on the Soviet Union, Britain and the United States; but the Regent and important officials in the government were not convinced either of the justice or of the inevitability of a German victory.

All of that is a complicated story; and, I repeat, this is not a political history of Budapest or of Hungary at large. What this historian (and those were his most impressionable years of his youth) wishes to convey is a sketch of a portrait of Budapest during the Second World War. There were somber elements in that portrait. They include the presence of German uniforms, on occasion; the rabid tone of the many Germanophile newspapers, journals and pamphlets; and the slowly spreading knowledge that the presence of death had come into the midst of more and more families whose sons or husbands or fathers had died or disappeared in faraway Russia. Yet until the last year of the war there were fewer of these than during the First World War; and the sight of blinded or maimed veterans on the streets of Budapest was rare. There was food rationing, but shortages were few. There was censorship, but Conservative, Liberal and even Social Democratic newspapers existed. Members of those parties would, on occasion, speak out in the Parliament. Some of the newspapers and journals hardly disguised the anti-Nazi opinions of their editors and contributors. In 1942 and 1943 books were published and plays were staged in Budapest whose themes and tones were the very opposites of Hitlerian ideology. A duality in the lives of the Jewish population of Budapest existed, too. On the one hand, the government and the Parliament had passed legislation restricting their freedoms shortly before the war, mostly (though not exclusively) because the treatment accorded to Jews was *the* litmus test in the eyes of Berlin at the time. On the other hand, the lives of the majority of Jews in Hungary were still relatively safe, more so than in almost any other German-occupied or -allied state in Europe.

All of this would soon come to an end. But the people of Budapest did not know this. Except for one odd occasion, not a single bomb fell on Budapest during more than four and a half years of the Second World War. There was the hope that the war would end soon, and that Budapest was about to survive it, largely intact. It was at that time when some people (including myself) began to think of Budapest as an old city. We had begun to savor those sights and those occasions that reminded us of noble things, of the times of the nineteenth and eighteenth centuries. There was more to this than nostalgia or an antiquarian snobbism. In that newly found loyalty to an old past there was the pleasure of finding its living presence in some of the buildings and in some of the interiors of Budapest; in some of the written words and memories of some of its urbane authors; in some of the customs and habits and phrases of older people, evidences of the patrician decency of a past that was still alive. In the winter of 1943–44 there was something in the atmosphere of Budapest that stimulated a silent, inward crystallization of the meaning of its past—surely in the mind and in the memory of the present writer.

I n the early morning hours of March 19, 1944, a Sunday, in a few apartments and houses of Budapest the ring of the telephone suddenly broke the dark silence. Knowledgeable people were calling their friends. The news was bad. The Germans were occupying Budapest.

Hitler had had enough: enough of the tergiversations of the Hungarian government; enough evidence that principal men in that government were trying to establish contacts with the Allies; enough, too, of the still extant presence of hundreds of thousands of Jews in the middle of Europe, in a country close to Vienna, in a land that the Russian armies were approaching. Hitler forced Horthy to appoint a thoroughly pro-German government. What remained of the independence of Hungary was largely gone. Not a shot was fired. German tanks appeared in the streets of Budapest. The Gestapo arrived. Soon the bombing of Budapest began.

So war had come to Budapest, physically, in the spring of 1944. There had been a tacit agreement between the Hungarian regime and the British and American air forces operating from southern Italy, to the effect that their planes would cross over Hungary largely unvexed and that Hungary would not be bombed. Now that was over. Beginning in early April British and American planes would drop bombs on the industrial ring and on the railyards of Budapest. Their damages were not decisive. The city of Budapest, with its famous buildings and bridges, was still largely intact during the beautiful and murderous summer of 1944.

Far from intact were the hopes and fears of the people of Budapest. The Jews among them were ordered to sew a large yellow star on their clothes. They were subject to other humiliations and curfews. Certain houses in each district of Budapest were marked with a yellow star: the Jews of Budapest were forced to move into these. From them they would be corralled and then packed into freight trains on their way to Auschwitz. The deportation of the five hundred thousand Jews from the country and the country towns had gone according to schedule; it was about completed. Late in June the Regent, prodded by his conscience and by serious foreign warnings, shook off his apathy. A regiment would move into Budapest, opposing the forces in charge of the deportations. That did not prove to be necessary; and the Jews of Budapest were—temporarily —saved.

In the late summer of 1944 Hitler's empire seemed to be collapsing. The Germans left one capital city of Europe after another: Rome, Paris, Brussels, Bucharest, Sofia, Helsinki, Athens, Belgrade. It seemed that the hour for Budapest was coming fast. The Russian armies had entered the Hungarian plains. At night, when the noise and clatter of the city had died down, people in Budapest could hear the faint rumble of artillery from the east. The atmosphere of the city had changed again. Knowledgeable people in the city, eloquent as usual, buzzed with gossip or at least with conjecture. They knew or pretended to know that the Regent and his remodeled government had sent secret armistice delegations to the Allies and to Stalin. The Germans knew it, too; and they were better prepared. On October 15 Horthy's armistice declaration was read on the Hungarian Radio. A few hours later Budapest was in German and Arrow-Cross hands. A few German Tiger tanks clattered up the stony streets of Castle Hill. There was an exchange of fire with a Hungarian elite troop. That resistance may have been symbolic; it was hardly effective. The Germans and the Arrow-Cross leaders crowded into the courtyards of the royal palace, in one of the bathrooms of which Horthy felt constrained to sign his abdication. The new government was an Arrow-Cross one, comprising men whose characters and whose intelligence were lower even than those of the Nazis in Germany: an unlearned rabble, including criminals.

The results of this successful coup were a reign of terror in Budapest, the destruction of Budapest, and a kind of Hungarian civil war. The main objects of terror were the remaining Jewish people in Budapest. A volunteer guardian of these people appeared in the person of the Swedish Wallenberg. (His protection could not function everywhere: Arrow-Cross bands would on occasion corral and drive Jews to the Danube quays, murdering them then and there.)

Winter had come; and the Russian armies moved closer to Budapest. Within the city chaotic conditions began to prevail. Thousands of Hungarian soldiers, officers and civilians went into hiding, unwilling to follow the orders and the directives of the Arrow-Cross government. By the time the Russian siege of Budapest began, the Arrow-Cross cabinet had left the city. It had ordered the civil officials and the military and the employees of important industries to go with them westward, retreating toward Germany. The Arrow-Cross leaders still believed in the ultimate victory of the Germans. Most Hungarians no longer did; and many of them no longer obeyed that "government"'s orders. This is what I meant by a Hungarian civil war. Fighting among people in Budapest was relatively rare, but Hungarians, and their allegiances, were divided between those who looked forward to the defeat of Germany and those who did not.*

On Christmas Eve the siege of Budapest began. Budapest was, after Stalingrad and before Berlin, the only large city in the tremendous German-Russian war where the two largest armies of the world would grapple in house-to-house fighting. The Russian command may have wanted to avoid that, but the Germans and their Hungarian allies chose to maintain their presence in the encircled city with a relatively large body of troops.

It took the Russian armies three weeks to conquer the Pest side, and another month to put an end to German and Hungarian resistance in Buda. In many districts the fighting spread from house to house. There were instances when Russian and German soldiers were shooting it out across dank and dark cellars, faintly lit by a candle or two, along the walls of which frightened people lay, covering their ears and eyes. The remnant German trucks and tanks were systematically pulled back from district to district, from street to street. Even more damaging than Russian artillery were the thousands of small tactical bombs of Russian fighter-bombers, flying low over the rooftops, since antiaircraft artillery had ceased to function. The Russian infantry would advance after these bombs

---

*The greatest modern Hungarian poet, the deeply Catholic János Pilinszky, saw the horrors of the end of the war, in Germany, as a young man. Thirty years later he said: "I live with my memories, those memories of the last war. Something very important had happened to us. Suddenly we felt that we left an irreparable atrocity behind us. And even if ahead of us there were a beautiful future, a lovely future, it would become a moral desert if we failed to feel a responsibility for what had happened then. With those poor people, with those awful, humiliated, scandalized poor people. . . ."

seemed to have burned out or destroyed the lines of German trucks and tanks assembled in the narrow streets—burning out and destroying, as a matter of course, many of the surrounding houses in the process. The Inner City of Pest was taken by the Russians on the morning of January 18, 1945. On their way to Buda the Germans blew up every one of the great bridges across the Danube. The battle for the inner core of Buda, mostly Castle Hill, was even more vicious. It fell on February 12, after a desperate—and failed—attempt by the defenders to break out to the west during the preceding night.

Coming out of the cellars, the people of Budapest found their city destroyed. The bridges, and many of the famous buildings, were in ruins. The royal palace had gone up in flames. Seven of every ten buildings were badly damaged; only twenty-six of every hundred buildings remained relatively intact. Nearly all of the windows in Budapest were broken, and that winter of 1945 was unusually cold. Electricity, gas, the telephone were nonexistent. Only the municipal waterworks kept functioning (a Russian commander had chosen to spare them). The streets were strewn with rubble, burnt-out vehicles, long coils of broken wires, and here and there the bodies of the dead, mostly civilians. The war was over; the sufferings of the people were not. The behavior of the Soviet soldiery was indescribable. Immediately behind the fighting patrols appeared a flood of soldiers in the streets, some of them caracoling on horseback, others wildly careening in their new American-made Jeeps, descending on civilians and breaking into houses. They robbed people of their coats, gloves, boots and especially wristwatches at gunpoint. Thousands of men were corralled by Soviet soldiers on the streets and marched off to cages full of prisoners of war; some of them would never return, others only after years of captivity deep within Russia. The Soviet command announced the capture of 110,000 German and Hungarian prisoners. In reality, there were not that many; the remainder were made up of civilians in the streets when and where Russians pleased to take them. Tens of thousands of women were raped in the dark cellars, where drunken Soviet soldiers, often Mongols, appeared night after night. Even after the fighting had ceased Russians, on occasion, set houses and apartments on fire, or destroyed their contents without any reason. For more than a year after the siege it was extremely dangerous to walk the streets after dark.

In 1945 the three capital cities of Europe that had suffered the greatest destruction were Budapest, Warsaw and Berlin. And for the next fifteen years or so the prospects of Budapest were perhaps the darkest of the three. Four years after the war, in the Western (and greater) portion of Berlin, a stunning, nearly miraculous, recovery and rebuilding began. From the ashes of Warsaw the Old City rose again in ten years. But in Budapest the rebuilding and the recovery were much slower. The last of the great bridges spanning the Danube stood anew only in 1963. For some years all that was accomplished was the clearing of some of the rubble. The restoration of the gutted and burned great buildings had hardly begun. Except for a new sports stadium, the capital investments of the new regime did nothing for the city. An atmosphere of fearsome decay stood silent in the Budapest streets, hemmed in by the pockmarked walls of apartment houses built in another time, ever dingier and more broken-down. The once fine vista of palatial buildings and hotels along the Danube quays was gone. That line of buildings was broken by rubble-strewn lots. The sunlit face of the self-confident young matron that Budapest had once been was now disfigured by toothless gaps.

All this corresponded to greater events. After two transitory years of a restricted and incomplete parliamentary democracy the dictatorship of the Communist Party was nailed down. After the twilight came the night. Aware, like Stalin, of the unpopularity of Communism, the new rulers of Hungary thought that they had to eliminate, through police terror, every possible vestige of any alternative. The latter, they thought, were still incarnated in the presence of the remaining bourgeois people in Budapest. Before 1949, when the iron curtain was erected along the western borders of Hungary, a numerically small but historically and socially significant exodus had taken place: many of the remaining democratic politicians, and a considerable segment of the upper-middle class, the surviving *haute bourgeoisie,* had fled the city to the West. In 1950 and 1951, at the height of the "cold war" between the Soviet Union and the United States, at the doors of innumerable Budapest apartments the bell would buzz at dawn. The police came, with orders of deportation for many of the remaining bourgeois families.

In 1953 Stalin died. There were changes in Hungary too. The deportees were permitted to return. By 1956 the political atmosphere had become lighter. A great revolution was around the corner, though no one knew it at the time. Tocqueville once observed that the lives of peoples do not follow the laws of nature; that revolt is likely to occur not when oppression is strongest but when it has begun to weaken. Thus it was that the Hungarian Rising began in Budapest on October 23, 1956. During the next electrifying days the hate for a senseless and corrupt Communist and Soviet tyranny united an entire people. They actually succeeded in driving Soviet tanks out of Budapest, except around the building of the Communist Party headquarters, where in the cellars the leaders of the Party cowered in fear. But then the Soviet leadership, stunned and confused at first, made an inevitable decision. Hungary was slipping out of the Soviet orbit. This they could not tolerate, since it could mean the collapse of their entire Eastern European empire. In the cold night of November 3–4 the Soviet armed forces came back. Their cannon pounded Budapest again. Here and there street fighting went on for days. Houses were burned and gutted once more, and pockmarked by artillery shells and machine-gun fire. A new government was installed, while the people of Budapest thrashed in fury and despair. A hundred thousand of them now rose at night, now not in response to the police ringing at their doors but with the purpose of escaping toward a decent life and freedom. Having packed a few belongings in small suitcases and rucksacks, they trudged downstairs in the cold dawn darkness to begin their trek toward the Austrian border that was still open. They were leaving their native city without regret. The grimy walls of the houses and the rime-covered pavements, stony and silent, saw them go.

There were at least two matters in the 1956 story that should demand our attention. That Hungarian Revolution began, and continued, essentially as the Rising of Budapest. It was from there that the nation received its inspiration. We have seen that, early in the twentieth century, many people in Hungary (and in Budapest itself) thought and spoke about the unsavory contrast between the unhealthy and cosmopolitan atmosphere of Budapest and the healthy national life elsewhere in the country, and that in 1919 the epithet "guilty city" was applied to Budapest, albeit briefly, by the nationalists. Now, in 1956, it was Budapest that spilled its patriotic gore and glory for the nation and the world to see.

The other matter—which no one saw, or could see at the time —was that, despite its suppression by the Soviet army, the revolution was not a total failure, after all. Except in some tragic, and politically dictated, instances, there was no real return to the police tyranny of the years before 1956. The new government (and, presumably, the Russians themselves) did not wish to see that. János Kádár, the new leader of Hungary, said a few years after the Revolution: "Those who are not against us are with us." He, and his government, wished to encourage a new kind of national unity, within the constraining limits of Hungary's political situation, but at the same time allowing a sense of increasing individual and cultural freedoms. What he, and the Hungarian people, have achieved was a measure of increasing prosperity and privacy. What he, his party and the government have not achieved was the kind of national unity he wanted, since newer problems and recurring divisions kept appearing, though often below the surface events, in the lives and minds of Hungarians.

Our task in this book concerns, however, the story of Budapest. And there great changes began to appear a few years after 1956. In the early 1960s portions of the city began to shed their appearance of grimy despair. The rebuilding of some of the historical buildings of the city had finally begun. The last of the great destroyed bridges, the Elizabeth, rose above the Danube, regaining (perhaps symbolically) its old name, that of the Habsburg Queen-Empress who had loved Hungary and Hungarians. Much of this was encouraged by Kádár's government, because of their wish to establish some kind of unity through respect and attention (and expenditures) paid to monuments of the national past. But the inevitable element in these reconstructions was the sentiments and the creative ambitions of those people in Budapest—historians, archeologists, architects, planners and designers—whose love for and pride in the history of the city had grown anew, and whose energies now had an outlet, sanctioned by the authorities, for the purposes of rebuilding. By the 1970s much of this rebuilding was completed. The rubble and the gaps disappeared. The toothless smile of Budapest was gone. The memories and the spiritual lesions of the Rising and of the last war were still there in the minds of the people of Budapest and in the constraints of their lives because of the presence of an officially Communist government; but physically Budapest had become largely intact again.

And now millions—yes, millions—of tourists and visitors began to pour into Budapest every year, including tens of thousands who had fled it in 1956 and after, men and women who had once thought they would never return; and now they have been returning, year after year. They were coming to an Americanized Budapest: an imprecise and perhaps exaggerated adjective, yes, but not one without substance. By the 1980s many of the streets of Budapest have been choked by an Augean mass of colored steel. Over the city, even on clear days, hangs an enormous pall of diesel smoke. Most of the automobiles of the people of Budapest are not Western-made; yet Budapest is the only city in Eastern Europe with enormous daily traffic jams. That duality of the city, between West and East, America and the Soviet Union, is there, too, in the enormous hotels, made of concrete and glass and steel, lining the quays of the Danube again, especially between the Chain and Elizabeth bridges on the Pest side, built with American (and lately with Austrian) capital investment and with the consent and support of the Hungarian government. Who, in 1956 (or, indeed, many years later) would have believed that the leading hotels of Budapest (including some recently refurbished traditional ones) would bear the names of Hilton, Hyatt, Intercontinental, Ramada? Those names are surely symbolic of one aspect of Budapest now. But that other, more definite side is there, too, in the names of many of its streets and places. The Octagon Square—mentioned, among other places, in the very first pages of this book—is the Seventh of November Square, commemorating what had happened in 1917 in Petrograd. (That no one in Budapest calls it by that name remains true.)*

In another sense, too, there are two Budapests now. Those hotels and their famous restaurants are there for the tourists and visitors. They are beyond the reach of almost everyone else in Budapest, save for their staffs and managers and the young whores in their halls, together with other staple beneficiaries of a tourist-service economy; and for the Budapestian relatives of former Budapest people abroad, now here for a visit, entering those brightly lit halls with a little uneasy (though not unhappy) smile on their faces. There are no Soviet tourists in any of those hotels and restaurants.

---

*From 1938 to 1945 its name was Mussolini Square. It intersects that principal avenue of Budapest whose successive names from its beginning (1873) have been Avenue, Andrássy Avenue, Stalin Avenue and now Avenue of the Hungarian People's Republic.

Those who come from Moscow are driven across Budapest in large Russian buses and then herded to communal tables in third-class hotels along the outer boulevards. There are many Americans, among them many Hungarians with American passports, people who left in 1956 and are now coming back year after year: hardy (or not so hardy) perennials. But the large majority of the tourists are Germans and Austrians. There are signs that in Budapest, as elsewhere in Europe, the long and prosperous phase of Americanization may be fading; and in Budapest and Hungary the German presence and influence have risen again.

In any event, ninety years after its great flourishing and more than forty years after its destruction a new chapter in the history of Budapest has begun. New divisions among its people are opening. But continuity is as strong, if not stronger, than change. A kind of historical consciousness has seeped into the minds of the people of Budapest, something that is both less and more than tradition. In 1900 the people of Budapest were proud that their city was the newest metropolis in Europe. Now they have begun to cherish whatever is old.

References

INTRODUCTION (xv) "How many barren layers . . . " Hegedüs KAT, 229.

CHAPTER 1   *COLORS, WORDS, SOUNDS*

(3) ". . . the celebration of an immortal": *Richardson*, 283. (3–5) Munkácsy's funeral: *Perneczky*, 50 ff.; *Malonyay*, II, 120 ff.; *Budapesti Napló*, May 9, 1900. (5) The British Ambassador, Paris: *Richardson*, 287. (7) Munkácsy in America: manuscript by John Maass (Philadelphia, "Munkácsy in America," in my possession. (8) ". . . exaggerations of the Impressionists": *Malonyay*, II, 100; Dumas *fils* to Justh: *Lázár*, 124. (10) "This city": *Krúdy PBS*, 40. (17) American edition of Körmendi: *The Happy Generation* (New York, 1949); French: *Cette heureuse génération* (Paris, 1947). (18) "The generation": *Körmendi*, 40. (19) Krúdy: about his life see my article in *The New Yorker*, Dec. 1, 1986. (19) Krúdy about Franz Josef's visits to Budapest: *Krúdy MLVB* in *MVK*, 339; ". . . This *raffinée* courtesan": *ibid.*, 340–41. (20) ". . . saw that in the forest": *ibid.*, 249. (21) ". . . the blue-white towers and the endlessly rising roofs": *ibid.*, 251. (21) "They are reviling Budapest in the Parliament": *Krúdy PA*,

28–29. (22) "How much there is to say": *ibid.*, 231–32. (22) "The little squares": *Krúdy BUK,* 74. "Women smelled like oranges": *ibid.*, 76. (24) "They kept on building": *Krúdy SF* in *MT,* 40. (25) "I was telling myself: I am in love, I love": *Szép LA,* 32. "This was the age of love in Hungary": *Babits HF,* 51.

CHAPTER 2   *THE CITY*

(29–30) Blowitz: *The Nineteenth Century* (London, October 1894). (32) *Tharaud,* 17–18, 26. (45) Population: *BT* 455–58. (47) "the sheer quantity of eclectic buildings": Galántay-Preisich article in *Swissair,* June 1986; also *BT* 400 *passim;* 599 *passim;* Council of Public Works: *BT* 393. (49) Kálmán Tisza about the Parliament building: *Hegedüs KAT,* 201. (50) Parliament architecture: *Tharaud,* 143; *Leigh Fermor,* 39. (51) Monuments: *BT* 600; *Hanák,* 85. (52) Crowded conditions: *BT* 448; *Horváth,* 157; *Hanák,* 551 *passim.* (57) Tourism: *BT* 568. Railroad expansion: *Hanák,* 276 *passim,* 405; *BT* 325–26, 529. (58) Fluvial transportation: *BT* 532. (59) Electricity: *BT* 404; mail and telephones: *ibid.*, 533. (61) Comfort stations: *BT* 603. (62) Tisza: "Just contrast the picture": *Horváth,* 29. Vineyards: *BT* 591. Agricultural population: *BT* 577, 581. (64) "He certainly remembered": *Lees-Milne,* I, 3. (65) "four years of boredom": *Nicolson,* 78–80.

CHAPTER 3   *THE PEOPLE*

(71) The "Millennium": *BT* 515–20. (74) Death rate, diseases: *ibid.*, 578; infant mortality: *ibid.*, 382–83. Marriage statistics: *ibid.*, 381. (74) Sadoveanu (Bucharest, 1976). (81) Coffeehouses: see Chapter 5, pp. 137–81; *Bevilacqua, passim; BT* 350–51, 370–71. (82) Whorehouses: *Siklóssy RBE,* III, 200. (88) The gentry: *Concha,* 3–4. (93) Taxpayers' rolls: *BT* 219–20; *Vörös BA.* (97) ". . . No longer human beings": cited in *BT* 265; *Altisztek: Hanák,* 477. (99) Appellations: *Hanák,* 454; *Makkai UO, passim.* (99–100) Hunyady story: "Bakaruhában, *Hunyady AI-CSA,* 83. (100) Magyarization: *BT* 239, 452–56. (107) *Keresni: MNYTESZ,* 2.

CHAPTER 4   *POLITICS AND POWERS*

(109) "The parliament": *Babits HF,* 72; "The existence and the security of the nation": *Szerb,* 457; The Hungarian mind: *ibid.*, 451. (111) ". . . the optimistic national self-portrait": *ibid.*, 315. Rhetorical flamboyance: *Vermes,* 73. (112) "Whenever . . . Hungarians": *Apponyi EI,* I, 76; Herczeg citing Mikszáth: *Herczeg EM,* 413. (116) Origins of the term "dualism": *Szekfü,* 83. (120) "I have no other choice": cited by *Hanák,* 148. (123) "Since the Crown could count no longer": *Gratz,* II, 29. Tisza quoting Nelson, Pitt, etc.: *Hegedüs KAT,* 125. (126) "There can be only

one viable nation": *ibid.,* 187; ". . . eastern Switzerland": *Vermes,* 27; "being a unified national state": Bánffy cited by *Horváth,* 53. (128) ". . . total Hungarianness": *ibid.,* 38–39. Franz Josef on chauvinism: Staats-und Hofarchiv, Vienna, Aug. 24, 1878, cited by *Hegedüs KAT,* 213. "not capable of independent advancement": Grünwald quoted by *Hanák,* 165; also *Hóman-Szekfü,* V, 159; one rare example of Magyar self-criticism: *Borsszem Jankó,* cited by *Horváth,* 176. (134) Budapest elections 1905, Ninth District: *BT* 626, 654–56; *Hanák,* 553–606; *Hegedüs KAT,* 281 ff.

CHAPTER 5   *THE GENERATION OF 1900*

(137) The concept of generations: *Marías, passim.* (147) Hunyady-Molnár conversation: *Hunyady AI-CSA,* 180. (148) "Why don't you take time": *Hatvany GYP,* 21. (159) ". . . idyllic days of 1919": *Koestler BA,* 70. (162) "Apart from the artistic worth of his works": *Szerb,* 510. (163) Kosztolányi about "knife": *Kosztolányi GNY,* 36, 60–61. (165) "No one will ever be able": *Móricz V.,* 102. (166) Tisza and Ady: *Szerb,* 493. (174) "What are these ornaments for?": *Lechner,* 9. (178) Movies: *Erzsébetváros* 157 *passim;* 204. (180) "pallid" historians: *Szekfü,* 347.

CHAPTER 6   *SEEDS OF TROUBLES*

(183) "The liberal ideas": *Concha,* 10–13. (184) "the irresistible, and unhealthy, desire": *Hegedüs AB,* 67. "could not really find their place": *Concha,* 11. (188) Ady in 1905: *Nagyváradi Napló;* 1913: *Nyugat.* "we carried on with politics": Klebelsberg cited by *Vermes,* 183. (188) Andrássy cited by *Bartha,* 62. (189) "these two descendants": *Babits HF,* 456. (190) "often unbridgeable": *Szerb,* 466. (191) Ady about Goga: *Nyugat,* 1913. (192) A comedy by Ambrus: *Berzsenyi báró és családja* (1902). (193) Herczeg's unsuccessful novel: *Andor és András* (1904). (194) "a more general diffusion": *Concha,* 75; "The Danube flows along the edge": *A Hét,* April 9, 1900. (198) Ady: "A new humane": *Nagyváradi Napló,* 1905; "the pages": Jászi cited by *Gluck,* 90 (I revised her translation slightly). "We must create a new ethic": Jászi cited by *Horváth,* 132. (200) "It is not only the factories": Jászi in *Huszadik Század,* 1906. "Imre . . . now stood alone": *Babits HF,* 723. (201) "desperately sad allegory": Herczeg cited by *Horváth,* 205–6. Ignotus's answer: *ibid.,* 207–8; Réz comment: *ibid.,* 208. (203) The parable of the seeds: Mark 4:2–20. (205) The tornado in July 1914: *BT* 722. (207) Istóczy in 1899: *Verhovay-Napló* (Kecskemét, 1899). (207) *Párizs vagy Weimar:* Balázs, *Nyugat,* August 1914.

CHAPTER 7   *SINCE THEN*

(214) "This town": *Mencken,* 430, 431. (219) "I live with my memories": *Pilinszky,* 15.

Bibliography

The bibliography of this book is circumscribed by two limitations. One of these has been imposed by its author; the other by the subject itself.

The first limitation should be obvious. This is a book written for English-speaking readers. Consequently, anything resembling a complete bibliography of titles relating to its topic—nearly all of which are in Hungarian—would be senseless as well as purposeless. But because readers of this book should include historians and other people who may be further interested in its subject, this bibliographical introduction may serve as a guide.

Our subject—the historical description of a city in 1900, including its people and its civilization and culture and principal representatives of the latter—is so large that a *complete* bibliography, that is, a list of titles and materials encompassing Budapest in 1900, would have been impossible even decades ago. To this condition we must add the accumulation of the last twenty-five years, during which interest in this period (together with the weakening constraints of Marxist and other political restrictions on writing and publication in Hungary) has resulted in a propitious increase of books, articles and other studies relating to our subject. Even the carefully and often painstakingly compiled bibliographies of the history of the city of Budapest—**BTB** (see p. 233); also see **BSE, BSK, TBM**—could not and cannot list all of the extant materials, by which I mean not only many personal and family papers but also the rich variety of all kinds of literature dealing with the life of the city at the time.

However, we *are* blessed with a volume that is not only indispensable for our topic but that is (or, rather, should be) *a model* for every urban history in the modern world. This is Volume IV of the serial multivolume history of Budapest **BT,** encompassing the history of the city from 1848 to 1918. In this large volume the greater portion (1873 to 1918) is the work of the superb urban historian Károly Vörös. Within it approximately two hundred large-size, and fairly densely printed, pages deal with the years 1896 to 1914. Vörös's work is a masterpiece for many reasons—its economy, its style, Vörös's astonishingly encyclopedic knowledge and understanding of the period, very much including its literary, artistic and popular culture. Its introduction to the sources and to the problems of research, and its very extensive bibliographical reference notes are extraordinary, too.

Since a history of Budapest in 1900 is hardly separable from that of Hungary, a very considerable portion of a new history of Hungary 1890 to 1918—**Hanák**—deals with Budapest. Published forty years after the classic treatment by Szekfü in **Hóman-Szekfü, V,** it complements the latter by its detailed treatment of social and economic history (and by its bibliography). But I wish, too, to direct my readers' attention to the older works by **Gratz, Hegedüs KAT, Pethő** and **Szekfü,** which, because of their insights and interpretations, no matter how "old-fashioned," have stood the test of time very well.

Within the text of this book I made mention of those literary works that are both descriptive and relevant to our topic. Let me add that a large deposit of photographs of the city around 1900 exists, mostly in the so-called Klösz collection of pictures and plates (some of it lodged in the Museum of the History of the City of Budapest).

The following bibliography contains all books and sources read and consulted by this author. In it the reader will find the full titles of the works whose abbreviations figure in the Reference section and in the previous pages. I have refrained from listing the titles of articles, except when these are cited in the text.

WORKS CONSULTED
The place of publication is Budapest, unless otherwise noted.

JOURNALS, NEWSPAPERS AND OTHER PERIODICALS

A Hét
Az Élet

Borsszem Jankó
Budapesti Napló
BSK *Budapest Statisztikai Közleményei*
Fővárosi Lapok
Huszadik Század
Jelenkor
Magyar Kritika
Magyar Salon
Nineteenth Century (London)
Nyugat
Pester Lloyd
Pesti Napló
Századok
Tanulmányok Budapest multjából
Történelmi Szemle
Uj Idők
Uj Magyar Szemle
Vasárnapi Ujság

BOOKS (INCLUDING BIBLIOGRAPHIES, MEMOIRS, COLLECTED
EDITIONS, ETC.)

Ady OP Ady, Endre, *Összes prózai művei* (1–12). 1955–77.
Ambrus, Zoltán, *Berzsenyi báró és családja.* 1902.
Apponyi EI Apponyi, Albert, *Emlékirataim,* II. 1934.
Babits HF Babits, Mihály, *Halálfiai.* 1971 ed.
Babits, Mihály, *Kártyavár.* 1923.
Babits, Mihály, *Timár Virgil fia.* 1922.
Balla, Vilmos, *A kávéforrás—Régi pesti kávéházak legendái.* 1926.
Bartha Bartha, Miklós, *Kazárföldön.* 1939.
Beer-Csizmadia, *Történelmünk a jogalkotás tükrében.* 1966.
Berend-Ránki, *Közép-Kelet-Európa gazdasági fejlődése a 19.–20. században.*
    1976.
Bevilacqua Bevilacqua-Borsody-Mazsáry, *Pest-budai kávéházak,* I–II.
    1935.
Bródy Bródy, Sándor, *Erzsébet dajka.* 1901.
Budapest Anno (English edition). 1979.
BSK *Budapest statisztikai közleményei.* (especially No. 53: Thirring, G.,
    Budapest félévszázados fejlődése 1873–1923).
BSE *Budapest székesfőváros statisztikai évkönyve.* 1907–.
BT *Budapest Története,* IV. 1978. (See p. 231.)
BTB *Budapest történetének bibliográfiája.* 1974–.
Budapesti üdvözlet (Békéscsaba, 1983).
Concha Concha, Victor (Győző), *La Gentry* (French edition). 1912.

Bibliography

Csáky, Moritz, *Der Kulturkampf in Ungarn* (Graz, 1967).

Erzsébetváros *Erzsébetváros* (Timár Andor, ed.). 1970.

Farkas, Gyula, *Az asszimiláció kora a magyar irodalomban.* 1932.

Fényes, László, *A társadalom és a nemi kérdés.* 1906.

Ferenczy, Imre, *Lakáspolitika és lakásügyi intézmények.* 1910.

Fermor Fermor, Patrick Leigh, *Between the Woods and the Water* (New York, 1986).

Források Budapest multjából, II. 1873–1919 (Kohut Mária, ed.). 1971.

Fülep, Lajos, *Magyar művészet.* 1923.

Gedényi, Mihaly, *Krúdy Gyula bibliográfia.* 1978.

Genthon, István, *Az uj magyar festőművészet története.* 1935.

Glatz, Ferenc, *Történetirás és politika.* 1980.

Gluck Gluck, Mary, *Georg Lukács and his generation, 1900–1918* (Cambridge, Mass., 1985).

Gogolák, Lajos, *Mocsáry Lajos és a nemzetiségi kérdés.* n.d.

Granasztói, Pál, *Budapest egy épitész szemével.* 1971.

Gratz Gratz, Gusztáv, *A dualizmus kora,* I–II. 1934.

Halász, Gábor, *Magyar századvég.* 1940.

Halász, Lajos, *Az Országos Kaszinó 50 éves története.* 1923.

Hanák *Magyarország története 1890–1918,* I–II. (Hanák Péter, ed.). 1978.

Harrer, Ferenc, *Egy magyar polgár élete I.* 1968.

Hatvany, Lajos, *Emberek és korok,* II. 1964.

Hatvany GYP Hatvany Lajos, *Gyulai Pál estéje.* n.d.

Hegedüs AB Hegedüs, Lóránt, *Adórendszerünk betegségei.* 1906.

Hegedüs KAT Hegedüs, Lóránt, *Két Andrássy és két Tisza.* 1937.

Heltai, Jenő, *Tündérlaki lányok.* 1908.

Herczeg EM Herczeg, Ferenc, *Emlékezéseim.* 1939.

Herczeg, Ferenc, *A Gyurkovics-lányok.* 1893 (*A Gyurkovics-fiúk,* 1895).

Hóman-Szekfü Hóman-Szekfü, *Magyar történet V.* 1937.

Horváth Horváth, Zoltán, *Magyar századforduló. A második reformnemzedék története 1896–1914.* 1961.

Hunyady AI-CSA Hunyady, Sándor, *Családi album,* in *Aranyifjú.* 1983.

Istóczy, Győző, *Országgyülési beszédei.* 1904.

Jánszky, Béla, *A magyar formatörekvések történeti épitészetünkben.* 1929.

Jeszenszky Jeszenszky, Géza, *Az elveszett presztizs.* 1986.

Kann, Robert, *Das Nationalitätproblem der Habsburgmonarchie* I–II (Graz, 1964).

Kellér, Andor, *Iró a toronyban.* 1981.

Kemény, Gábor (ed.), *Iratok a nemzetiségi kérdés történetéhez Magyarországon a dualizmus korában,* I–V. 1952–71.

Klein, Ödön, *Tiszától Tiszáig.* 1922.

Kóbor Kóbor, Tamás, *Budapest.* 1901.

Koestler BA Koestler, Arthur, *Arrow in the Blue* (London, 1954).

Körmendi Körmendi, Ferenc, *A boldog emberöltő*. 1934.

Kosztolányi, Dezső, *Aranysárkány*. 1924.

Kosztolányi GNY Kosztolányi, Dezső, *Gondolatok a nyelvről* (Bucharest, 1977).

Kosztolányi, Dezső, *Pacsirta*. 1929.

Kovács, Alajos, *Magyarország népe és népesedésének kérdése*. 1941.

Kristóffy, József, *Magyarország kálváriája*. 1927.

Krúdy, Gyula, *A tegnapok ködlovagjai* I–II. 1925.

Krúdy, Gyula, *Budapest vőlegénye*. 1966.

Krúdy BUK Krúdy, Gyula, *Bukfenc*. 1958.

Krúdy MLVB in MVK Krúdy, Gyula, *Mit látott Vak Béla szerelemben és bánatban?* in *Mákvirágok kertje*. 1961.

Krúdy SF in MT Krúdy, Gyula, *Sneider Fáui* in *Magyar tükör*. 1984.

Krúdy PA Krúdy, Gyula, *Pesti album*. 1985.

Krúdy PBS Krúdy, Gyula, *Pest-Budai séták*. 1916.

Krúdy világa. 1964.

Kubinszky, Judit, *A politikai antiszemitizmus Magyarországon*. 1978.

Lázár, Béla, *A Munkácsy-kérdés*. 1936.

Lázár Lázár, Béla, *Munkácsy Mihály. Emlékek és emlékezések*. 1944.

Lechner *Lechner Ödön 1845–1914*. 1985.

Lees-Milne Lees-Milne, James, *Harold Nicolson: a biography* (London, 1981).

Lugossy-Paraszthy, *A kepviselőház a jelenben es a multban*. 1906.

Lyka, Károly, *Festészeti életünk a milleneumtól az első világháboruig*. 1951.

McCagg McCagg, William O., *Jewish Nobles and Geniuses in Modern Hungary* (Boulder, Colorado, 1973).

Makkai UO Makkai, János, *Urambátyám országa*. 1942.

Malonyay Malonyay, Dezső, *Munkácsy Mihály I–II*. 1906.

Marías Marías, Julián, *Generations: A Historical Method* (University of Alabama, 1971).

Mencken *Mencken and Sara: a Life in Letters: the Private Correspondence of H. L. Mencken and Sara Haardt* (New York, 1987).

Mérei, Gyula, *A magyar polgári pártok programjai*. 1971.

Mikszáth, Kálmán, *A Noszty-fiu esete a Tóth Marival*. 1908.

Mikszáth, Kálmán, *Különös házasság*. 1900.

Mikszáth, Kálmán, *Politikai karcolatok 1881–1908*. 1969.

Mikszáth, Kálmán, *Szent Péter esernyője*. 1895.

MNYTESZ *A magyar nyelv történeti-etimológiai szótára 2*. 1970.

Molnár, Ferenc, *A Pál-utcai fiúk*. 1908.

Móricz V. Móricz, Virág, *Apám regénye*. 1953.

Németh, G. Béla, *A magyar irodalomkritikai gondolkodás a pozitivizmus korában*. 1980.

Németh, G. Béla, *Századelőtől-szazadutóig*. 1982.

Németh, Lajos, *Magyar művészet 1890–1919* I. 1981.

Németh, Lajos, *Modern Art in Hungary.* 1969.

Nicolson Nicolson, Harold, *Lord Carnock—A Study in the Old Diplomacy* (London, 1930).

Pásztor, Árpád, *Vengerkák.* 1913.

Pásztor, Mihály, *A 150 éves Lipótváros.* 1940.

Pereházy, Károly, *A régi Belváros.* 1982.

Perneczky Perneczky, Géza, *Munkácsy* (German edition). 1970.

Pethő Pethő, Sándor, *Világostól Trianonig.* 1925.

Petrassevich, Géza, *Zsidó földbirtokosok és bérlők Magyarországon.* 1905.

Pilinszky *Beszélgetések Pilinszky Jánossal.* 1983.

Preisich Preisich, Gábor, *Budapest városépitésének története II.* 1964.

Prohászka, Ottokár, *Az ondovai vámos.* 1905.

Richardson Richardson, Joanna, *Victor Hugo: A Biography* (New York, 1976).

Sadoveanu Sadoveanu, Mihail, *Századvég Bukarestben* (Bucharest, 1976).

Siklóssy RBE Siklóssy, László, *A régi Budapest erkölcse III.* 1923.

Siklóssy, László, *Hogyan épült Budapest?* 1931.

Szabolcsi, Bence, *A magyar zene története rövid összefoglalásban.* 1964.

Szekfü Szekfü, Gyula, *Három nemzedék és ami utána következik.* 1934.

Szép LA Szép, Ernő, *Lila ákác.* 1967.

Szép, Ernő, *Patika.* n.d.

Szerb Szerb, Antal, *Magyar irodalomtörténet.* 1978 edition.

TBM *Tanulmányok Budapest multjából. A Budapesti Történeti Múzeum évkönyve.*

I–XX. 1932–74.

Tharaud Tharaud, Jérôme, *Quand Israël est roi* (Paris, 1921).

Thirring, Gusztáv, *Budapest székesfőváros a milleneumi évben.* 1898.

Tóth, Ede, *Mocsáry-Emlékkönyv.* n.d.

Verhovay-Napló (Kecskemét, 1899).

Vermes Vermes, Gábor, *István Tisza* (New York, 1985).

Vezér, Erzsébet, *Ady Endre élete és pályája.* 1977.

Vörös BA Vörös, Károly, *Budapest legnagyobb adófizetői 1873–1917.* 1979.

Zselenszky, Róbert, *Emlékeim.* 1940.

Acknowledgments

M y debts are numerous: unlike financial debts, they are pleasant
to record. I am grateful to the President of Chestnut Hill
College for a sabbatical semester; to the International Research and
Exchange Board and to the National Endowment for the Humani-
ties for small but useful travel grants; and to the Soros-MTA Foundation, which underwrote a substantial portion of the costs of my
stay in Budapest. Once there I had no obstacles to my reading and
research; indeed, my work was made easier by the generous assistance and interest of many people. They include Professors Géza
Jeszenszky, Mihály Szegedy-Maszák, Béla G. Németh, Lajos
Németh, László Péter; also Professor Tibor Frank and Dr. József
Bölöny; the staff of the national (Országos Széchenyi) library, in-
cluding Dr. Ilona Kovács; Dr. György Székely of the Museum of
the History of the City of Budapest; the staff of the American
Embassy and its Cultural Officer, Ken Moskovit; also Gabriella
Szvoboda (to whom I was directed by Professor Péter Hanák) and
Professor Katalin Keserü (to whom I was directed by Professor
Mihály Szegedy-Maszák), who were invaluable in helping me pro-

cure the photographic materials. My research assistant, András Bán (to whom I was directed by Professor Geza Jeszevnszky), was thoroughly knowledgeable, reliable (and charming). I am indebted to Jacques Barzun for a very careful reading of Chapter 5, and to George Feyer for a very thoughtful piece of advice about Chapter 7. Dr. Helen Hayes, librarian of Chestnut Hill College, was, as always, ready to provide answers to some of my strangest bibliographical queries, and very promptly indeed. A shortened version of Chapter 1 was published in the Spring 1988 number of *The American Scholar.*

Index

239

ABOUT THE AUTHOR

JOHN LUKACS, born in Hungary, came to America in 1946. A professor of history, he has authored thirteen books including *Philadelphia 1900–1950: Patricians and Philistines* and *Outgrowing Democracy: A History of the United States in the Twentieth Century,* and many articles. He lives with his wife and daughter in Chester County, Pennsylvania.